FILM, TELEVISION AND RADIO PRODUCTION

Elements, Dimensions and Trends

FILM, TELEVISION AND RADIO PRODUCTION

Elements, Dimensions and Trends

ANGELA WADIA

KANISHKA PUBLISHERS, DISTRIBUTORS
NEW DELHI-110 002

KANISHKA PUBLISHERS, DISTRIBUTORS
4697/5-21A, Ansari Road, Daryaganj
New Delhi -110 002
Phones : 2327 0497, 2328 8285
Fax : 011-2328 8285
E-mail : kanishka_publishing@yahoo.co.in

Film, Television and Radio Production:
Elements, Dimensions and Trends

First Edition 2008

Edition 2019

ISBN : 978-81-8457-079-3

PRINTED IN INDIA

Published by Madan Sachdeva for Kanishka Publishers, Distributors, 4697/5-21A, Ansari Road, Daryaganj, New Delhi-110 002, Typeset by Sunshine Graphics, Delhi, and Printed at Rajdhani Printers, Delhi.

Preface

This book titled "Film, Television and Radio Production: Elements, Dimensions and Trends" gives a detailed account of the subject matter under discussion. An Introductory overview of films is provided herein with a detailed historical account. Modern film industry is described at the global level with special focus on 'Indian Cinema' and 'Bollywood' film industry. The film making process in India has been outlined in brief. A retrospective of Indian film industry is provided herein with detailed account of regional language films, such as, Bengali, Tamil, Telgu, Malyalam, Assamese, Bojhpuri, Punjabi, Marathi, etc. The next chapter deals with the elements and dimensions of film making, including that of low-budget films, short films. An Overview of movie making manual and whole film making process is presented. Aspects related to pre-production, production and post-production are dealt in detail along with their meanings and implications. Stages related to preproduction of untitled films in studio, film production and post-production are discussed briefly. Other aspects of film making, such as blocking, lighting, music video, digital video, power sources, sound recording, shooting styles, still photography, character animation, etc. are also reflected upon. Crucial dimensions and aspects of cinematography and movie-making are described with focus on elements like slate, crew, director, actor, editor and screenplay writer. Various other elements, steps and stages of television production are outlined, so has been the whole production process. This book also focuses on issues related to TV broadcasting, production and scheduling of programmes. Special focus lies on Indian television industry. Select case studies and models are provided to highlight the themes further. Radio programming and programme production have also been covered in this book, with select global case studies. Important elements related to radio format, software, commercial, documentary and their production are described in details, supported by relevant case-studies and analytical studies. A detailed glossary of terms and bibliography are provided herein to make the book more user-friendly and research-oriented.

Angela Wadia

Contents

1

Film: An Introductory Overview with Historical Account

FILM

Film is a term that encompasses individual motion pictures, the field of film as an art form, and the motion picture industry. Films are produced by recording images from the world with cameras, or by creating images using animation techniques or special effects.

Films are cultural artifacts created by specific cultures, which reflect those cultures, and, in turn, affect them. Film is considered to be an important art form, a source of popular entertainment, and a powerful method for educating—or indoctrinating—citizens. The visual elements of cinema give motion pictures a universal power of communication; some movies have become popular worldwide attractions, by using dubbing or subtitles that translate the dialogue.

Traditional films are made up of a series of individual images called frames. When these images are shown rapidly in succession, a viewer has the illusion that motion is occurring. The viewer cannot see the flickering between frames due to an effect known as persistence of vision—whereby the eye retains a visual image for a fraction of a second after the source has been removed. Viewers perceive motion due to a psychological effect called beta movement.

The origin of the name "film" comes from the fact that photographic film (also called film stock) has historically been the primary medium for recording and displaying motion pictures. Many other terms exist for an individual motion picture, including *picture, picture show, photo-play, flick,* and most commonly, *movie.* Additional terms for the field in general include *the big screen, the silver screen, the cinema,* and *the movies.*

History

Mechanisms for producing artificially created, two-dimensional images in motion were demonstrated as early as the 1860s, with devices such as the zoetrope and the praxinoscope. These machines were outgrowths of simple optical devices (such as magic lanterns) and would display sequences of still pictures at sufficient speed for the images on the pictures to appear to be moving, a phenomenon called persistence of vision. Naturally, the images needed to be carefully designed to achieve the desired effect—and the underlying principle became the basis for the development of film animation.

With the development of celluloid film for still photography, it became possible to directly capture objects in motion in real time. Early versions of the technology sometimes required a person to look into a viewing machine to see the pictures which were separate paper prints attached to a drum turned by a handcrank. The pictures were shown at a variable speed of about 5 to 10 pictures per second depending on how rapidly the crank was turned. Some of these machines were coin operated. By the 1880s, the development of the motion picture camera allowed the individual component images to be captured and stored on a single reel, and led quickly to the development of a motion picture projector to shine light through the processed and printed film and magnify these "moving picture shows" onto a screen for an entire audience. These reels, so exhibited, came to be known as "motion pictures." Early motion pictures were static shots that showed an event or action with no editing or other cinematic techniques.

Ignoring Dickson's early sound experiments (1894), commercial motion pictures were purely visual art through the late nineteenth century, but these innovative silent films had gained a hold on the public imagination. Around the turn of the twentieth century, films began developing a narrative structure by stringing scenes together to tell narratives. The scenes were later broken up into multiple shots of varying sizes and angles. Other techniques such as camera movement were realized as effective ways to portray a story on film. Rather than leave the audience in silence, theater owners would hire a pianist or organist or a full orchestra to play music fitting the mood of the film at any given moment. By the early 1920s, most films came with a prepared list of sheet music for this purpose, with complete film scores being composed for major productions.

The rise of European cinema was interrupted by the breakout of World War I while the film industry in United States flourished with the rise of Hollywood. However in the 1920s, European film-makers such as Sergei Eisenstein, F.W. Murnau, and Fritz Lang, along with American innovator D.W. Griffith and the contributions of Charles Chaplin, Buster Keaton and others, continued to advance the medium. In the 1920s, new technology allowed film-makers to attach to each film a soundtrack of speech, music and sound effects synchronized with the action on the screen. These sound films were initially distinguished by calling them "talking pictures", or *talkies*.

The next major step in the development of cinema was the introduction of so-called "natural" colour. While the addition of sound quickly eclipsed silent film and theater musicians, colour was adopted more gradually as methods evolved making it more practical and cost effective to produce "natural colour" films. The public was relatively indifferent to colour photography as opposed to black-and-white, but as color processes improved and became as affordable as black-and-white film, more and more movies were filmed in colour after the end of World War II, as the industry in America came to view colour as essential to attracting audiences in its competition with television, which remained a black-and-white medium until the mid-1960s. By the end of the 1960s, colour had become the norm for film-makers.

Since the decline of the studio system in the 1960s, the succeeding decades saw changes in the production and style of film. New Hollywood, French New Wave and the rise of film school educated independent film-makers were all part of the changes the medium experienced in the latter half of the 20th century. Digital technology has been the driving force in change throughout the 1990s and into the 21st century.

Theory

Film theory seeks to develop concise, systematic concepts that apply to the study of film as art. It was started by Ricciotto Canudo's *The Birth of the Sixth Art*. Formalist film theory, led by Rudolf Arnheim, Béla Balázs, and Siegfried Kracauer, emphasized how film differed from reality, and thus could be considered a valid fine art. André Bazin reacted against this theory by arguing that film's artistic essence lay in its ability to mechanically reproduce reality not in its differences from reality, and this gave rise to realist theory. More recent analysis spurred by Lacan's psychoanalysis and Ferdinand de Saussure's among other things has given rise to psychoanalytical film theory, structuralist film theory, feminist film theory and others.

Criticism

Film criticism is the analysis and evaluation of films. In general, these works can be divided into two categories: academic criticism by film scholars, and journalistic film criticism that appears regularly in newspapers and other media.

Film critics working for newspapers, magazines, and broadcast media mainly review new releases. Normally they only see any given film once and have only a day or two to formulate opinions. Despite this, critics have an important impact on films, especially those of certain genres. Mass marketed action, horror, and comedy films tend not to be greatly affected by a critic's overall judgement of a film. The plot summary and description of a film that makes up the majority of any film review can still have an important impact on whether people decide to see a film. For prestige films such as most dramas, the influence of reviews is extremely important. Poor reviews will often doom a film to obscurity and financial loss.

The impact of a reviewer on a given film's box office performance is a matter of debate. Some claim that movie marketing is now so intense and well financed that reviewers cannot make an impact against it. However, the cataclysmic failure of some heavily-promoted movies which were harshly reviewed, as well as the unexpected success of critically praised independent movies indicates that extreme critical reactions can have considerable influence. Others note that positive film reviews have been shown to spark interest in little-known films. Conversely, there have been several films in which film companies have so little confidence that they refuse to give reviewers an advanced viewing to avoid widespread panning of the film. However, this usually backfires as reviewers are wise to the tactic and warn the public that the film may not be worth seeing and the films often do poorly as a result.

It is argued that journalist film critics should only be known as film reviewers, and true film critics are those who take a more academic approach to films. This line of work is more often known as film theory or film studies. These film critics attempt to come to understand how film and filming techniques work, and what effect they have on people. Rather than having their works published in newspapers or appear on television, their articles are published in scholarly journals, or sometimes in up-market magazines. They also tend to be affiliated with colleges or universities.

Industry

The making and showing of motion pictures became a source of profit almost as soon as the process was invented. Upon seeing how successful their new invention, and its product, was in their native France, the Lumières quickly set about touring the Continent to exhibit the first films privately to royalty and publicly to the masses. In each country, they would normally add new, local scenes to their catalogue and, quickly enough, found local entrepreneurs in the various countries of Europe to buy their equipment and photograph, export, import and screen additional product commercially. The Oberammergau Passion Play of 1898 was the first commercial motion picture ever produced. Other pictures soon followed, and motion pictures became a separate industry that overshadowed the vaudeville world. Dedicated theaters and companies formed specifically to produce and distribute films, while motion picture actors became major celebrities and commanded huge fees for their performances. Already by 1917, Charlie Chaplin had a contract that called for an annual salary of one million dollars.

In the United States today, much of the film industry is centered around Hollywood. Other regional centres exist in many parts of the world, such as Mumbai-centered Bollywood, the Indian film industry's Hindi cinema which produces the largest number of films in the world. Whether the ten thousand-plus feature length films a year produced by the Valley pornographic film industry should qualify for this title is the source of some debate. Though the expense involved in making movies has led cinema production to concentrate under the auspices of movie studios, recent advances in affordable film making equipment have allowed independent film productions to flourish.

Profit is a key force in the industry, due to the costly and risky nature of film-making; many films have large cost overruns, a notorious example being Kevin Costner's Waterworld. Yet many film-makers strive to create works of lasting social significance. The Academy Awards (also known as "the Oscars") are the most prominent film awards in the United States, providing recognition each year to films, ostensibly based on their artistic merits.

There is also a large industry for educational and instructional films made in lieu of or in addition to lectures and texts.

Production

The nature of the film determines the size and type of crew required during film-making. Many Hollywood adventure films need computer generated imagery (CGI), created by dozens of 3D modellers, animators, rotoscopers and compositors. However, a low-budget, independent film may be made with a skeleton crew, often paid very little. Also, an open source film may be produced through open, collaborative processes. Film-making takes place all over the world using different technologies, styles of acting and genre, and is produced in a variety of economic contexts that range from state-sponsored documentary in China to profit-oriented movie making within the American studio system.

A typical Hollywood-style film-making Production cycle is comprised of five main stages:

1. Development
2. Pre-production
3. Production
4. Post-production
5. Distribution

This production cycle typically takes three years. The first year is taken up with *development*. The second year comprises *preproduction* and *production*. The third year, *post-production* and *distribution*.

Crew

A film crew is a group of people hired by a film company, employed during the "production" or "photography" phase, for the purpose of producing a film or motion picture. *Crew* are distinguished from *cast*, the actors who appear in front of the camera or provide voices for characters in the film. The *crew* interacts with but is also distinct from the *production staff*, consisting of producers, managers, company representatives, their assistants, and those whose primary responsibility falls in pre-production or post-production phases, such as writers and editors. Communication between *production* and *crew* generally passes through the director and his/her staff of assistants. Medium-to-large crews are generally divided into departments with well defined hierarchies and standards for interaction and cooperation between the departments. Other than acting, the crew handles everything in the photography phase: props and costumes, shooting, sound, electrics (i.e., lights), sets, and production special effects. Caterers (known in the film industry as "craft services") are usually not considered part of the crew.

Independent

Independent film-making often takes place outside of Hollywood, or other major studio systems. An independent film (or indie film) is a film initially produced without financing or distribution from a major movie studio. Creative, business, and technological reasons have all contributed to the growth of the indie film scene in the late 20th and early 21st century.

On the business side, the costs of big-budget studio films also leads to conservative choices in cast and crew. There is a trend in Hollywood towards co-financing (over two-thirds of the films put out by Warner Bros. in 2000 were joint ventures, up from 10 per cent in 1987). A hopeful director is almost never given the opportunity to get a job on a big-budget studio film unless he or she has significant industry experience in film or television. Also, the studios rarely produce films with unknown actors, particularly in lead roles.

Before the advent of digital alternatives, the cost of professional film equipment and stock was also a hurdle to being able to produce, direct, or star in a traditional studio film. The cost of

35 mm film is outpacing inflation: in 2002 alone, film negative costs were 23 per cent, according to *Variety*.

But the advent of consumer camcorders in 1985, and more importantly, the arrival of high-resolution digital video in the early 1990s, have lowered the technology barrier to movie production significantly. Both production and post-production costs have been significantly lowered; today, the hardware and software for post-production can be installed in a commodity-based personal computer. Technologies such as DVDs, FireWire connections and non-linear editing system pro-level software like Adobe Premiere Pro, Sony Vegas and Apple's Final Cut Pro, and consumer level software such as Apple's Final Cut Express and iMovie make movie-making relatively inexpensive.

Since the introduction of DV technology, the means of production have become more democratized. Film-makers can conceivably shoot and edit a movie, create and edit the sound and music, and mix the final cut on a home computer. However, while the means of production may be democratized, financing, distribution, and marketing remain difficult to accomplish outside the traditional system. Most independent film-makers rely on film festivals to get their films noticed and sold for distribution. The arrival of internet-based video outlets such as YouTube and Veoh has further changed the film making landscape in ways that are still to be determined.

Open Content Film

An open content film is much like an independent film, but it is produced through open collaborations; its source material is available under a license which is permissive enough to allow other parties to create fan fiction or derivative works, than a traditional copyright. Like independent film-making, open source film-making takes place outside of Hollywood, or other major studio systems.

Fan Film

A fan film is a film or video inspired by a film, television programme, comic book or a similar source, created by fans rather than by the source's copyright holders or creators. Fan film-makers have traditionally been amateurs, but some of the more notable films have actually been produced by professional film-makers as film school class projects or as demonstration reels. Fan films vary tremendously in length, from short faux-teaser trailers for non-existent motion pictures to rarer full-length motion pictures.

Animation

Animation is the technique in which each frame of a film is produced individually, whether generated as a computer graphic, or by photographing a drawn image, or by repeatedly making small changes to a model unit (see claymation and stop motion), and then photographing the result with a special animation camera. When the frames are strung together and the resulting film is viewed at a speed of 16 or more frames per second, there is an illusion of continuous movement (due to the persistence of vision). Generating such a film is very labour intensive and tedious, though the development of computer animation has greatly sped up the process.

File formats like GIF, QuickTime, Shockwave and Flash allow animation to be viewed on a computer or over the Internet.

Because animation is very time-consuming and often very expensive to produce, the majority of animation for TV and movies comes from professional animation studios. However, the field of independent animation has existed at least since the 1950s, with animation being produced by independent studios (and sometimes by a single person). Several independent animation producers have gone on to enter the professional animation industry.

Limited animation is a way of increasing production and decreasing costs of animation by using "short cuts" in the animation process. This method was pioneered by UPA and popularized by Hanna-Barbera, and adapted by other studios as cartoons moved from movie theaters to television.

Although most animation studios are now using digital technologies in their productions, there is a specific style of animation that depends on film. Cameraless animation, made famous by moviemakers like Norman McLaren, Len Lye and Stan Brakhage, is painted and drawn directly onto pieces of film, and then run through a projector.

Venues

When it is initially produced, a feature film is often shown to audiences in a movie theater or cinema. The first theater designed exclusively for cinema opened in Pittsburgh, Pennsylvania in 1905. Thousands of such theaters were built or converted from existing facilities within a few years. In the United States, these theaters came to be known as nickelodeons, because admission typically cost a nickel (five cents).

Typically, one film is the featured presentation (or feature film). Before the 1970s, there were "double features"; typically, a high quality "A picture" rented by an independent theater for a lump sum, and a "B picture" of lower quality rented for a percentage of the gross receipts. Today, the bulk of the material shown before the feature film consists of previews for upcoming movies and paid advertisements (also known as trailers or "The Twenty").

Historically, all mass marketed feature films were made to be shown in movie theaters. The development of television has allowed films to be broadcast to larger audiences, usually after the film is no longer being shown in theaters. Recording technology has also enabled consumers to rent or buy copies of films on VHS or DVD (and the older formats of laserdisc, VCD and SelectaVision), and Internet downloads may be available and have started to become revenue sources for the film companies. Some films are now made specifically for these other venues, being released as made-for-TV movies or direct-to-video movies. The production values on these films are often considered to be of inferior quality compared to theatrical releases in similar genres, and indeed, some films that are rejected by their own studios upon completion are distributed through these markets.

The movie theater pays an average of about 50-55 per cent of its ticket sales to the movie studio, as film rental fees. The actual percentage starts with a number higher than that, and decreases as the duration of a film's showing continues, as an incentive to theaters to keep movies in the theater longer. However, today's barrage of highly marketed movies ensures that most movies are shown in first-run theaters for less than 8 weeks. There are a few movies every year that defy this rule, often limited-release movies that start in only a few theaters and actually grow their theater count through good word-of-mouth and reviews. According to a

2000 study by ABN AMRO, about 26 per cent of Hollywood movie studios' worldwide income came from box office ticket sales; 46 per cent came from VHS and DVD sales to consumers; and 28 per cent came from television (broadcast, cable, and pay-per-view).

Technology

Film stock consists of transparent celluloid, acetate, or polyester base coated with an emulsion containing light-sensitive chemicals. Cellulose nitrate was the first type of film base used to record motion pictures, but due to its flammability was eventually replaced by safer materials. Stock widths and the film format for images on the reel have had a rich history, though most large commercial films are still shot on (and distributed to theaters) as 35 mm prints.

Originally moving picture film was shot and projected at various speeds using hand-cranked cameras and projectors; though 1000 frames per minute (16⅔ per second) is generally cited as a standard silent speed, research indicates most films were shot between 16 and 23 fps and projected from 18 fps on up (often reels included instructions on how fast each scene should be shown). When sound film was introduced in the late 1920s, a constant speed was required for the sound head. 24 frames per second was chosen because it was the slowest (and thus cheapest) speed which allowed for sufficient sound quality. Improvements since the late 19th century include the mechanization of cameras—allowing them to record at a consistent speed, quiet camera design—allowing sound recorded on-set to be usable without requiring large "blimps" to encase the camera, the invention of more sophisticated filmstocks and lenses, allowing directors to film in increasingly dim conditions, and the development of synchronized sound, allowing sound to be recorded at exactly the same speed as its corresponding action. The soundtrack can be recorded separately from shooting the film, but for live-action pictures many parts of the soundtrack are usually recorded simultaneously.

As a medium, film is not limited to motion pictures, since the technology developed as the basis for photography. It can be used to present a progressive sequence of still images in the form of a slideshow. Film has also been incorporated into multimedia presentations, and often has importance as primary historical documentation. However, historic films have problems in terms of preservation and storage, and the motion picture industry is exploring many alternatives. Most movies on cellulose nitrate base have been copied onto modern safety films. Some studios save colour films through the use of separation masters—three B&W negatives each exposed through red, green, or blue filters (essentially a reverse of the Technicolour process). Digital methods have also been used to restore films, although their continued obsolescence cycle makes them (as of 2006) a poor choice for long-term preservation. Film preservation of decaying film stock is a matter of concern to both film historians and archivists, and to companies interested in preserving their existing products in order to make them available to future generations (and thereby increase revenue). Preservation is generally a higher-concern for nitrate and single-strip colour films, due to their high decay rates; black and white films on safety bases and colour films preserved on Technicolour imbibition prints tend to keep up much better, assuming proper handling and storage.

Some films in recent decades have been recorded using analog video technology similar to that used in television production. Modern digital video cameras and digital projectors are gaining ground as well. These approaches are extremely beneficial to moviemakers, especially because footage can be evaluated and edited without waiting for the film stock to be processed. Yet the migration is gradual, and as of 2005 most major motion pictures are still recorded on film.

Future State

While motion picture films have been around for more than a century, film is still a relative newcomer in the pantheon of fine arts. In the 1950s, when television became widely available, industry analysts predicted the demise of local movie theaters. Despite competition from television's increasing technological sophistication over the 1960s and 1970s, such as the development of colour television and large screens, motion picture cinemas continued. In the 1980s, when the widespread availability of inexpensive videocassette recorders enabled people to select films for home viewing, industry analysts again wrongly predicted the death of the local cinemas.

In the 1990s and 2000s, the development of digital DVD players, home theater amplification systems with surround sound and subwoofers, and large LCD or plasma screens enabled people to select and view films at home with greatly improved audio and visual reproduction. These new technologies provided audio and visual that in the past, only local cinemas had been able to provide: a large, clear widescreen presentation of a film with a full-range, high-quality multi-speaker sound system. Once again, industry analysts predicted the demise of the local cinema. Local cinemas will be changing in the 2000s and moving towards digital screens, a new approach which will allow for easier, quicker distribution of films (via satellite or hard disks), a development which may give local theaters a reprieve from their predicted demise.

HISTORY OF FILM

The **History of Film** spans over a hundred years, from the latter part of the 19th century to the beginning of the 21st. Motion pictures developed gradually from a carnival novelty to one of the most important tools of communication and entertainment, and mass media in the 20th century. Motion picture films have had a substantial impact on the arts, technology, and politics.

The Birth of Film

The two second experimental film, *Roundhay Garden Scene*, filmed by Louis Le Prince on October 1888 in Leeds, Yorkshire, is generally recognized as the earliest surviving motion picture.

William Kennedy Laurie Dickson, Chief Engineer with the Edison Laboratories, is credited with the invention of a practicable form of a celluloid strip containing a sequence of images, the basis of a method of photographing and projecting moving images. Celluloid blocks were thinly sliced, then removed with heated pressure plates. After this, they were coated with a photosensitive gelatin emulsion. In 1893 at the Chicago World's Fair, Thomas Edison introduced to the public two pioneering inventions based on this innovation; the Kinetograph, the first practical moving picture camera, and the Kinetoscope. The latter was a cabinet in which a continuous loop of Dickson's celluloid film (powered by an electric motor) was back lit by an incandescent lamp and seen through a magnifying lens. The spectator neared an eye piece. Kinetoscope parlours were supplied with fifty-foot film snippets photographed by Dickson, in Edison's "Black Maria" studio. These sequences recorded mundane events (such as *Fred Ott's Sneeze*, 1894) as well as entertainment acts like acrobats, music hall performers and boxing demonstrations.

Kinetoscope parlors soon spread successfully to Europe. Edison, however, never attempted to patent these instruments on the other side of the Atlantic, since they relied so greatly on previous experiments and innovations from Britain and Europe. This enabled the development of imitations, such as the camera devised by British electrician and scientific instrument maker Robert W. Paul and his partner Birt Acres.

Paul had the idea of displaying moving pictures for group audiences, rather than just to individual viewers, and invented a film projector, giving his first public showing in 1895. At about the same time, in France, Auguste and Louis Lumière invented the cinematograph, a portable, three-in-one device: camera, printer, and projector. In late 1895 in Paris, father Antoine Lumière began exhibitions of projected films before the paying public, beginning the general conversion of the medium to projection (Cook, 1990). They quickly became Europe's main producers with their *actualités* like *Workers Leaving the Lumière Factory* and comic vignettes like *The Sprinkler Sprinkled* (both 1895). Even Edison, initially dismissive of projection, joined the trend with the Vitascope within less than six months. The first public motion-picture film presentation in Europe, though, belongs to Max and Emil Skladanowsky of Berlin, who projected with their apparatus "Bioscop", a flickerfree duplex construction, November 1 through 31, 1895.

Still older, May, 1895, was Lauste in the U.S.A. with an Eidoloscope which he devised for the Latham family. The first public screening of film ever is due to Jean Aimé "Acme" Le Roy, a French photographer. On February 5, 1894, his 40th birthday, he presented his "Marvellous Cinematograph" to a group of around twenty show business men in New York City.

The movies of the time were seen mostly via temporary storefront spaces and travelling exhibitors or as acts in vaudeville programmes. A film could be under a minute long and would usually present a single scene, authentic or staged, of everyday life, a public event, a sporting event or slapstick. There was little to no cinematic technique: no editing and usually no camera movement, and flat, stagey compositions. But the novelty of realistically moving photographs was enough for a motion picture industry to mushroom before the end of the century, in countries around the world.

The Silent Era

Inventors and producers had tried from the very beginnings of moving pictures to marry the image with synchronous sound, but no practical method was devised until the late 1920s. Thus, for the first thirty years of their history, movies were more or less silent, although accompanied by live musicians and sometimes sound effects, and with dialogue and narration presented in intertitles.

Film History from 1895 to 1906

The first ten years of motion pictures show the cinema moving from a novelty to an established large-scale entertainment industry. The films themselves represent a movement from films consisting of one shot, completely made by one person with a few assistants, towards films several minutes long consisting of several shots, which were made by large companies in something like industrial conditions.

Film Business up to 1906

In 1896 it became clear that more money was to be made by showing motion picture films with a projector to a large audience than exhibiting them in Edison's Kinetoscope peep-show machines. The Edison company took up a projector developed by Armat and Jenkins, the "Phantoscope", which was renamed the Vitascope, and it joined various projecting machines made by other people to show the 35 mm width films being made by the Edison company and others in France and England.

However, the most successful motion picture company in the United States, with the largest production until 1900, was the American Mutoscope Company. This was initially set up to exploit peep-show type movies using designs made by W.K.L. Dickson after he left the Edison company in 1895. His equipment used 70 mm wide film, and each frame was printed separately onto paper sheets for insertion into their viewing machine, called the Mutoscope. The image sheets stood out from the periphery of a rotating drum, and flipped into view in succession. Besides the Mutoscope, they also made a projector called the Biograph, which could project a continuous positive film print made from the same negatives.

There were numerous other smaller producers in the United States, and some of them established a long-term presence in the new century. American Vitagraph, one of these minor producers, built studios in Brooklyn, and expanded its operations in 1905. From 1896 there was continuous litigation in the United States over the patents covering the basic mechanisms that made motion pictures possible.

In France, the Lumière company sent cameramen all round the world from 1896 onwards to shoot films, which were exhibited locally by the cameramen, and then sent back to the company factory in Lyons to make prints for sale to whoever wanted them. There were nearly a thousand of these films made up to 1901, nearly all of them actualities.

By 1898 Georges Méliès was the largest producer of fiction films in France, and from this point onwards his output was almost entirely films featuring trick effects, which were very successful in all markets. The special popularity of his longer films, which were several minutes long from 1899 onwards (while most other films were still only a minute long), led other makers to start producing longer films.

From 1900 Charles Pathé began film production under the Pathé-Frères brand, with Ferdinand Zecca hired to actually make the films. By 1905, Pathé was the largest film company in the world, a position it retained until World War I. Léon Gaumont began film production in 1900, with his production supervised by Alice Guy.

In England, Robert W. Paul, James Williamson and G.A. Smith and the other lesser producers were joined by Cecil Hepworth in 1899, and in a few years he was turning out 100 films a year, with his company becoming the largest on the British scene.

Film Exhibition

Initially films were mostly shown as a novelty in special venues, but the main methods of exhibition quickly became either as an item on the programmes of variety theatres, or by travelling showman in tent theatres, which they took around the fairs in country towns. It became the practice for the producing companies to sell prints outright to the exhibitors, at so much per foot, regardless of the subject. Typical prices initially were 15 cents a foot in the United States, and one shilling a foot in Britain. Hand-coloured films, which were being produced of the most popular subjects before 1900, cost 2 to 3 times as much per foot. There were a few producers, such as the American Mutoscope and Biograph Company, which did not sell their films, but exploited them solely with their own exhibition units. The first successful permanent theatre showing nothing but films was "The Nickelodeon", which was opened in Pittsburgh in 1905. By this date there were finally enough films several minutes long available to fill a programme running for at least half an hour, and which could be changed weekly when the local audience became bored with it. Other exhibitors in the United States quickly followed suit, and within a couple of years there were thousands of these nickelodeons in operation. The American situation led to a world-wide boom in the production and exhibition of films from 1906 onwards.

Film Technique

The first movie cameras were fastened directly to the head of their tripod or other support, with only the crudest kind of levelling devices provided, in the manner of the still-camera tripod heads of the period. The earliest movie cameras were thus effectively fixed during the course of the shot, and hence the first camera movements were the result of mounting a camera on a moving vehicle. The first known of these was a film shot by a Lumière cameraman from the back platform of a train leaving Jerusalem in 1896, and by 1898 there were a number of films shot from moving trains. Although listed under the general heading of "panoramas" in the sales catalogues of the time, those films shot straight forward from in front of a railway engine were usually specifically referred to as "phantom rides."

In 1897, Robert W. Paul had the first real rotating camera head made to put on a tripod, so that he could follow the passing processions of Queen Victoria's Diamond Jubilee in one uninterrupted shot. This device had the camera mounted on a vertical axis that could be rotated by a worm gear driven by turning a crank handle, and Paul put it on general sale the next year. Shots taken using such a "panning" head were also referred to as 'panoramas' in the film catalogues of the first decade of the cinema.

The standard pattern for early film studios was provided by the studio which Georges Méliès had built in May of 1897. This had a glass roof and three glass walls constructed after the model of large studios for still photography, and it was fitted with thin cotton cloths that could be stretched below the roof to diffuse the direct rays of the sun on sunny days. The soft overall light without real shadows that this arrangement produced, and which also exists naturally on lightly overcast days, was to become the basis for film lighting in film studios for the next decade.

Filmic Effects

Unique amongst all the one minute long films made by the Edison company, which recorded parts of the acts of variety performers for their Kinetoscope viewing machines, was *The Execution of Mary, Queen of Scots*. This showed a person dressed as the queen placing her head on the execution block in front of a small group of bystanders in Elizabethan dress. The executioner brings his axe down, and the queen's severed head drops onto the ground. This trick was worked by stopping the camera and replacing the actor with a dummy, then restarting the camera before the axe falls. The two pieces of film were then trimmed and cemented together so that the action appeared continuous when the film was shown.

This film was among those exported to Europe with the first Kinetoscope machines in 1895, and was seen by Georges Méliès, who was putting on magic shows in his Theatre Robert-Houdin in Paris at the time. He took up film-making in 1896, and after making imitations of other films from Edison, Lumière, and Robert Paul, he made *Escamotage d'un dame chez Robert-Houdin (The Vanishing Lady)*. This film shows a woman being made to vanish by using the same stop motion technique as the earlier Edison film. After this, Georges Méliès made many single shot films using this trick over the next couple of years.

The other basic set of techniques for trick cinematography involves double exposure of the film in the camera, which was first done by G.A. Smith in July 1898 in England. His *The Corsican Brothers* was described in the catalogue of the Warwick Trading Company, which took up the distribution of Smith's films in 1900, thus:

> "One of the twin brothers returns home from shooting in the Corsican mountains, and is visited by the ghost of the other twin. By extremely careful photography the ghost appears 'quite transparent'. After indicating that he has been killed by a sword-thrust, and appealing for vengeance, he disappears. A 'vision' then appears showing the fatal duel in the snow. To the Corsican's amazement, the duel and death of his brother are vividly depicted in the vision, and finally, overcome by his feelings, he falls to the floor just as his mother enters the room."

The ghost effect was simply done by draping the set in black velvet after the main action had been shot, and then re-exposing the negative with the actor playing the ghost going through the actions at the appropriate point. Likewise, the vision, which appeared within a circular vignette or matte, was similarly superimposed over a black area in the backdrop to the scene, rather than over a part of the set with detail in it, so that nothing appeared through the image, which seemed quite solid. Smith used this technique again a year later in *Santa Claus*.

Georges Méliès first used superimposition on a dark background in *la Caverne maudite (The Cave of the Demons)* made a couple of months later in 1898, and then elaborated it further with multiple superimpositions in the one shot in *l'Homme de têtes (The Troublesome Heads)*. He then did it with further variations in numerous subsequent films.

Other Special Techniques

The other special effect technique that G.A. Smith initiated was reverse motion. He did this by repeating the action a second time, while filming it with an inverted camera, and then joining the tail of the second negative to that of the first. The first films made using this device were *Tipsy, Topsy, Turvy* and *The Awkward Sign Painter*. *The Awkward Sign Painter* showed a sign painter lettering a sign, and in the reverse printing of the same footage appended to the standard print, the painting on the sign vanished under the painter's brush. The earliest surviving example of this technique is Smith's *The House That Jack Built*, made before September 1900. Here, a small boy is shown knocking down a castle just constructed by a little girl out of children's building blocks. Then a title appears, saying "Reversed", and the action is repeated in reverse, so that the castle re-erects itself under his blows.

Cecil Hepworth took this technique further, by printing the negative of the forwards motion backwards frame by frame, so producing a print in which the original action was exactly reversed. To do this he built a special printer in which the negative running through a projector was projected into the gate of a camera through a special lens giving a same-size image. This arrangement came to be called a "projection printer", and eventually an "optical printer." With it Hepworth made *The Bathers* in 1900, in which bathers who have undressed and jumped into the water appear to spring backwards out of it, and have their clothes magically fly back onto their bodies.

The use of different camera speeds also appeared around 1900. To make Robert Paul's *On a Runaway Motor Car through Piccadilly Circus* (1899), the camera was turned very slowly, so that when the film was projected at the usual 16 frames per second, the scenery appeared to be passing at great speed. Cecil Hepworth used the opposite effect in *The Indian Chief and the Seidlitz Powder* (1901), in which a naïve Red Indian eats a lot of the fizzy stomach medicine, causing his stomach to expand vastly. He leaps around in a way that is made balloon-like by cranking the camera much faster than 16 frames per second. This gives what we would call a "slow motion" effect.

Animation

The most important development in this area of special techniques did not happen until 1905, when Edwin Porter made *How Jones Lost His Roll*, and *The Whole Dam Family and the Dam Dog*. Both of these films had intertitles which were formed by the letters moving into place from a random scattering to form the words of the titles. This was done by exposing the film one frame at a time, and moving the letters a little bit towards their final position between each exposure. This is what has come to be called "single frame animation" or "object animation", and it needs a slightly adapted camera that exposes only one frame for each turn of the crank handle, rather than the usual eight frames per turn.

In 1906, Albert Edward Smith and James Stuart Blackton at Vitagraph took the next step, and in their *Humorous Phases of Funny Faces*, what appear to be cartoon drawings of people move from one pose to another. This is done for most of the length of this film by moving jointed cut-outs of the figures frame by frame between the exposures, just as Porter moved his letters. However, there is a very short section of the film where things are made to appear to move by altering the drawings themselves from frame to frame, which is how standard animated cartoons have since been made up to today.

Narrative Film Construction

The way forward to making films made up of more than one shot was led by films of the life of Jesus Christ. The first of these was made in France in 1897, and it was followed in the same year by a film of the Passion play staged yearly in the Czech town of Horitz. This was filmed by Americans for exhibition outside the German-speaking world, and was presented in special venues, not as a continuous film, but with the separate scenes interspersed with lantern slides, a lecture, and live choral numbers, to increase the running time of the spectacle to about 90 minutes.

Films of acted reproductions of scenes from the Greco-Turkish war were made by Georges Méliès in 1897, and although sold separately, these were no doubt shown in continuous sequence by exhibitors. In 1898 a few films of similar kind were made, but still none had continuous action moving from one shot into the next. The multi-shot films that Georges Méliès made in 1899 were much longer than those made by anybody else, but *l'Affaire Dreyfus (The Dreyfus Case)* and *Cendrillon (Cinderella)* still contained no action moving from one shot to the next one. Also, from *Cendrillon* onwards, Méliès made a dissolve between every shot in his films, which reduced any appearance of action continuity even further. To understand what is going on in both these films, the audience had to know their stories beforehand, or be told them by a presenter.

Film Continuity

Real film continuity, which means showing action moving from one shot into another joined to it, can be dated to Robert W. Paul's *Come Along, Do!*, made in 1898. In the first shot of this film, an old couple outside an art exhibition follow other people inside through the door. The second shot showed what they do inside.

The further development of action continuity in multi-shot films continued in 1899. In the latter part of that year, George Albert Smith, working in Brighton, England, made *The Kiss in the Tunnel*. This started with a shot from a "phantom ride" at the point at which the train goes into a tunnel, and continued with the action on a set representing the interior of a railway carriage, where a man steals a kiss from a woman, and then cuts back to the phantom ride shot when the train comes out of the tunnel. A month later, the Bamforth company in Yorkshire made a restaged version of this film under the same title, and in this case they filmed shots of a train entering and leaving a tunnel from beside the tracks, which they joined before and after their version of the kiss inside the train compartment.

In 1900, continuity of action across successive shots was definitively established by George Albert Smith and James Williamson, who also worked in Brighton. In that year Smith made *Seen Through the Telescope*, in which the main shot shows street scene with a young man tying the shoelace and then caressing the foot of his girlfriend, while an old man observes this through a telescope. There is then a cut to close shot of the hands on the girl's foot shown inside a black circular mask, and then a cut back to the continuation of the original scene.

Even more remarkable is James Williamson's *Attack on a China Mission Station*, made around the same time in 1900. The first shot shows the gate to the mission station from the outside being attacked and broken open by Chinese Boxer rebels, then there is a cut to the garden of the mission station where the missionary and his family are seated. The Boxers rush in and after exchanging fire with the missionary, kill him, and pursue his family into the house. His wife appears on the balcony waving for help, which immediately comes with an armed party of British sailors appearing through the gate to the mission station, this time seen from the inside. They fire at the Boxers, and advance out of the frame into the next shot, which is taken from the opposite direction looking towards the house. This constitutes the first "reverse angle" cut in film history. The scene continues with the sailors rescuing the remaining members of the missionary's family.

G.A. Smith further developed the ideas of breaking a scene shot in one place into a series of shots taken from different camera positions over the next couple of years, starting with *The Little Doctors* of 1901. In this film a little girl is administering pretend medicine to a kitten, and Smith cuts in to a big close up of the kitten as she does so, and then cuts back to the main shot. In this case the inserted close up is not shown as a point of view shot in a circular mask. He summed up his work in *Mary Jane's Mishap* of 1903, with repeated cuts in to a close shot of a housemaid fooling around, along with superimpositions and other devices, before abandoning film-making to invent the Kinemacolour system of colour cinematography.

James Williamson concentrated on making films taking action from one place shown in one shot to the next shown in another shot in films like *Stop Thief!* and *Fire!*, made in 1901, and many others.

Film Continuity Developed

Other film-makers then took up all these ideas, which form the basis of film construction, or "film language", or "film grammar", as we know it. The best known of these film-makers was Edwin S. Porter, who started making films for the Edison Company in 1901. When he began making longer films in 1902, he put a dissolve between every shot, just as Georges Méliès was already doing, and he frequently had the same action repeated across the dissolves. In other words, Edwin Porter did not develop the basics of film construction. The Pathé Company in France also made imitations and variations of Smith and Williamson's films from 1902 onwards using cuts between the shots, which helped to standardize the basics of film construction.

In 1903 there was a substantial increase in the number of film several minutes long, as a result of the great popularity of Georges Méliès' *le Voyage dans la lune (A Trip to the Moon)*, which came out in early 1902, though such films were still a very minor part of production. Most of them were what came to be called "chase films". These were inspired by James Williamson's *Stop Thief!* of 1901, which showed a tramp stealing a leg of mutton from a butcher's boy in the first shot, then being chased through the second shot by the butcher's boy and assorted dogs, and finally being caught by the dogs in the third shot.

Several English films made in the first half of 1903 extended the chase method of film construction. These included *An Elopement à la Mode* and *The Pickpocket: A Chase Through London*, made by Alf Collins for the British branch of the French Gaumont Company, *Daring Daylight Burglary*, made by the Sheffield Photographic Company, and *Desperate Poaching Affray*, made by the Haggar family, whose main business was exhibiting films made by others in their travelling tent theatre. All of these films, and indeed others of like nature were shown in the United States, and some of them were certainly seen by Edwin Porter, before he made *The Great Train Robbery* towards the end of the year. The time continuity in *The Great Train Robbery* is actually more confusing than that in the films it was modelled on, but nevertheless it was a greater success than them worldwide, because of its Wild West violence.

From 1900, the Pathé Company films also frequently copied and varied the ideas of the British film-makers, without making any major innovations in narrative film construction, but eventually the sheer volume of their production led to their film-makers giving a further precision and polish to the details of film continuity.

Film History from 1906 to 1914

The Film Business

By 1907 there were about 4,000 small "nickelodeon" cinemas in the United States. The films were shown with the accompaniment of music provided by a pianist, though there could be more musicians. There were also a very few larger cinemas in some of the biggest cities. Initially, the majority of films in the programmes were Pathé films, but this changed fairly quickly as the American companies cranked up production. The programme was made up of just a few films, and the show lasted around 30 minutes. The reel of film, of maximum length 1,000 feet (300 m), which usually contained one individual film, became the standard unit of film production and exhibition in this period. The programme was changed twice or more a week, but went up to five changes of programme a week after a couple of years. In general, cinemas were set up in the established entertainment districts of the cities. In other countries of the Western world the film exhibition situation was similar. With the change to "nickelodeon" exhibition there was also a change, led by Pathé in 1907, from selling films outright to renting them through film exchanges.

The litigation over patents between all the major American film-making companies had continued, and at the end of 1908 they decided to pool their patents and form a trust to use them to control the American film business. The companies concerned were Pathé, Edison, Biograph, Vitagraph, Lubin, Selig, Essanay, Kalem, and the Kleine Optical Company, a major importer of European films. The George Eastman company, the only manufacturer of film stock in the United States, was also part of the combine, which was called the Motion Picture Patents Company (MPPC), and Eastman Kodak agreed to only supply the members with film stock. License fees for distributing and projecting films were extracted from all distributors and exhibitors. The producing companies that were part of the trust were allocated production quotas (two reels, i.e. films, a week for the biggest ones, one reel a week for the smaller), which were supposed to be enough to fill the programmes of the licensed exhibitors. Vitagraph and Edison already had multiple production units, and so had no difficulty meeting their quota, but in 1908 Biograph lost their one working director. They offered the job of making their films to D.W. Griffith, an unimportant actor and playwright, who took up the job, and found he had a gift for it. Alone he made all the Biograph films from 1908 to 1910. This amounted to 30 minutes of screen time a week.

But the market was bigger than the Motion Picture Patents Company members could supply. Although 6,000 exhibitors signed with the MPPC, about 2,000 others did not. A minority of the exchanges (i.e. distributors) stayed outside the MPPC, and in 1909 these independent exchanges immediately began to fund new film producing companies. By 1911 there were enough independent and foreign films available to programme all the shows of the independent exhibitors, and in 1912 the independents had nearly half of the market. The MPPC had effectively been defeated in its plan to control the whole United States market, and the government anti-trust action, which only now started against the MPPC, was not really necessary to defeat it.

Multi-reel Films

It was around 1912 that the actors in American films, who up to this point had been anonymous, began to receive screen credit, and the way to the creation of film stars was opened. The appearance of films longer than one reel also helped this process. Such films were extremely rare, and almost entirely restricted to film versions of the life of Christ, which had reached three reels in length in the first few years of cinema. They were always shown as a special event in special venues, and supported by live commentary and music. A unique addition to this style of presentation was The Story of the Kelly Gang, made in Australia in 1906. This was a four-reel version of the career of this famous (in Australia) outlaw, and was incomprehensible without explanation. More multi-reel films were made in Europe than in the United States after 1906, because the MPPC insisted on working on the basis of one-reel films up until 1912. However, before this, some MPPC members got around this restriction by occasionally making longer stories in separate parts, and releasing them in successive weeks, starting with Vitagraph's *The Life of Moses* in five parts (and five reels) at the end 1909. In other countries this film was shown straight through as one picture, and it inspired the creation of other multi-reel films in Europe.

Pathé-Frères set up a new subsidiary company in the United States called Eclectic in 1913, and in 1914 this began production of features at the Pathé plant in New Jersey. The French Eclair company was already making films in the United States, and their production of features increased with the transfer of more film-makers when the French industry was shut down at the beginning of World War I.

Up to 1913, most American film production was still carried out around New York, but the move to filming in California had begun when Selig, one of the MPPC companies, sent a production unit there in 1909. Other companies, both independents and members of the MPPC, then sent units to work there in the summer to take advantage of the sunshine and scenery. The latter was important for the production of Westerns, which now formed a major American film genre. The first cowboy star was G.M. Anderson ("Broncho Billy"), directing his own Western dramas for Essanay, but in 1911 Tom Mix brought the kind of costumes and stunt action used in live Wild West shows to Selig film productions, and became the biggest cowboy star for the next two decades.

Most of the major companies made films in all the genres, but some had a special interest in certain kinds of films. Once Selig had taken up production in California, they used the (fairly) wild animals from the zoo that Colonel Selig had set up there in a series of exotic adventures, with the actors being menaced or saved by the animals. Essanay specialized in Westerns featuring "Broncho Billy" Anderson, and Kalem sent Sidney Olcott off with a film crew and a troupe of actors to various places in America and abroad to make film stories in the actual places they were supposed to have happened. Kalem also pioneered the female action heroine from 1912, with Ruth Roland playing starring roles in their Westerns.

Minor curiosities were some of the films of Solax directed by Herbert Blaché and his wife Alice Guy. They left American branch of the Gaumont company in 1912 to set up their own independent company. The distinguishing feature of some of their films was a deliberate attempt to use resolutely theatrical-type light comedy playing that was directed towards the audience. This went against the trend towards filmic restraint already visible in what were called "polite" comedies from other film companies.

In France, Pathé retained its dominant position, followed still by Gaumont, and then other new companies that appeared to cater to the film boom. A film company with a different approach was Film d'Art. This was set up at the beginning of 1908 to make films of a serious artistic nature. Their declared programme was to make films using only the best dramatists, artists and actors. The first of these was *l'Assassinat du Duc de Guise (The Assassination of the Duc de Guise)*, a historical subject set in the court of Henri III. This film used leading actors from the Comédie Francaise, and had a special accompanying score written by Camille Saint-Saens. The other French majors followed suit, and this wave gave rise to the English-language description of films with artistic pretensions aimed at a sophisticated audience as "art films." By 1910, the French film companies were starting to make films as long as two, or even three reels, though most were still one reel long. This trend was followed in Italy, Denmark, and Sweden.

Although the British industry continued to expand after its brilliant beginning, the new companies that replaced the first innovative film-makers proved unable to preserve their drive and originality.

New Film Producing Countries

With the world-wide film boom, yet more countries now joined Britain, France, and the United States in serious film production. In Italy, production was spread over several centres, with Turin being the first and biggest. There, Ambrosio was the first company in the field in 1905, and remained the largest in the country through this period. Its most substantial rival was Cines in Rome, which started producing in 1906. The great strength of the Italian industry was historical epics, with large casts and massive scenery. As early as 1911, Giovanni Pastrone's two-reel *la Caduta di Troia (The Fall of Troy)* made a big impression world-wide, and it was followed by even bigger spectacles like *Quo Vadis?* (1912), which ran for 90 minutes, and Pastrone's *Cabiria* of 1914, which ran for two and a half hours.

Italian companies also had a strong line in slapstick comedy, with actors like André Deed, known locally as "Cretinetti", and elsewhere as "Foolshead" and "Gribouille", achieving worldwide fame with his almost surrealistic gags.

The most important film-producing country in Northern Europe up until the First World War was Denmark. The Nordisk company was set up there in 1906 by Ole Olsen, a fairground showman, and after a brief period imitating the successes of French and British film-makers, in 1907 he produced 67 films, most directed by Viggo Larsen, with sensational subjects like *Den hvide Slavinde (The White Slave)*, *Isbjørnenjagt (Polar Bear Hunt)* and *Løvejagten (The Lion Hunt)*. By 1910 new smaller Danish companies began joining the business, and besides making more films about the white slave trade, they contributed other new subjects. The most important of these finds was Asta Nielsen in *Afgrunden (The Abyss)*, directed by Urban Gad for Kosmorama. This combined the circus, sex, jealousy and murder, all put over with great conviction, and pushed the other Danish film-makers further in this direction. By 1912 the Danish film companies were multiplying like rabbits.

The Swedish film industry was smaller and slower to get started than the Danish industry. Here, the important man was Charles Magnusson, a newsreel cameraman for the Svenskabiografteatern cinema chain. He started fiction film production for them in 1909, directing a number of the films himself. Production increased in 1912, when the company engaged Viktor Sjöström and Mauritz Stiller as directors. They started out by imitating the subjects favoured by the Danish film industry, but by 1913 they were producing their own strikingly original work, which sold very well.

Russia began its film industry in 1908 with Pathé shooting some fiction subjects there, and then the creation of real Russian film companies by Aleksandr Drankov and Aleksandr Khanzhonkov. The Khanzhonkov company quickly became much the largest Russian film company, and remained so until 1918.

In Germany, Oskar Messter had been involved in film-making from 1896, but did not make a significant number of films per year till 1910. When the world-wide film boom started, he, and the few other people in the German film business, continued to sell prints of their own films outright, which put them at a disadvantage. It was only when Paul Davidson, the owner of a chain of cinemas, brought Asta Nielsen and Urban Gad to Germany from Denmark in 1911, and set up a production company, Projektions-AG "Union" (PAGU), for them, that a change-over to renting prints began. Messter replied with a series of longer films starring Henny Porten, but although these did well in the German-speaking world, they were not particularly successful internationally, unlike the Asta Nielsen films. Another of the growing German film producers just before World War I was the German branch of the French Eclair company, Deutsche Eclair. This was expropriated by the German government, and turned into DECLA when the war started. But altogether, German producers only had a minor part of the German market in 1914.

Overall, from about 1910, American films had the largest share of the market in all European countries except France, and even in France, the American films had just pushed the local production out of first place on the eve of World War I. So even if the war had not happened, American films would have become dominant world-wide. Although the war made things worse for European producers, it was the technical qualities of American films that made them more attractive to audiences everywhere.

Film Technique

With the increased production required by the nickelodeon boom, extra artificial lighting was used more and more in the film studios to supplement diffuse sunlight, and so increase the hours that film could be shot during the day. The main sources used were modified arc lights made for street lighting. These were either hung on battens suspended forward of the actors from the roof, or mounted in groups on floorstands. The addition of a metal reflector round the arc source directed a very broad sweep of light in the desired direction. Large mercury vapour tube lights (Cooper-Hewitts) were also used in racks placed in the same way. Arc lights had been used to produce special lighting effects in films like the light from a lamp or firelight before 1906, but this now became more common.

A strong expressive use of a fire effect occurs in D.W. Griffith's *The Drunkard's Reformation* (1909). Here, the reformed drunkard is happily reunited with his family before the fire in the hearth, in a set-up reproducing that at the beginning of the film in which the fire is out, and the hearth is cold, and the family is destitute.

Low-key lighting (i.e. lighting in which most of the frame is dark) slowly began to be used for sinister scenes, but not in D.W. Griffith films. Vitagraph's thriller, *The Mystery of Temple Court* (1910) has low-key lighting for a scene of murder, and their *Conscience* (1912) shows low-key lighting done solely with artificial light for a scene of terror.

This sort of lighting was appearing occasionally in European films by 1911, and in some cases was pushed much further. Lighting from a low angle was used more strongly in the Italian epic film *Quo Vadis?* in 1912, and then in the famous *Cabiria* (1914) to reinforce the weird atmosphere in one scene.

Silhouette effects in location scenes began to appear in 1909 in both the United States and Italy; though as things developed, European film-makers made more use of this than the Americans did.

The most important aspect of this was that such shots involved having the sun light the scene from behind, and this approach was extended by using the reflected sunlight from a white surface below the camera to light up the shadow on the actors faces from the front. This is the one novel technique that D.W. Griffith and his cameraman Billy Bitzer may really have invented. The next step was to transfer this kind of back-lighting onto the lighting of actors on studio sets. Up to this point artificial lighting in studio scenes had always been put on from the front or side-front, but in 1912 there began to be a few cases where light was put onto the actors from arc floodlights out of shot behind them and to one side, to give a kind of backlighting. It was not until 1915 that the effect of backlighting of the actors by the sun was fully mimicked in studio lighting, by using a powerful arc spotlight shining from above and behind the set down onto the actors. This slowly became a standard component of the studio lighting of figures in American films, but it took much longer to catch on with European cameramen.

Animation Develops

The technique of single frame animation was further developed in 1907 by Edwin S. Porter in *The Teddy Bears* and by J. Stuart Blackton with *Work Made Easy*. In the first of these the toy bears were made to move, apparently on their own, and in the latter film building tools were made to perform construction tasks without human intervention, by using frame-by-frame animation. The technique got to Europe almost immediately, and Segundo de Chomon and others at Pathé took it further, adding clay animation, in which sculptures were deformed from one thing into another thing frame by frame in *Sculpture moderne* (1908), and then Pathé made the next step to the animation of silhouette shapes. Also in France, Emile Cohl fully developed drawn animation in a series of films starting with *Fantasmagorie* (1908), in which humans and objects drawn as outline figures went though a series of remarkable interactions and transformations. In the United States the response was from the famous strip cartoon artist Winsor McCay, who drew much more realistic animated figures going through smoother, more naturalistic motion in a series of films starting with the film *Winsor McCay*, made for Vitagraph in 1911. In the next few years various others took part in this development of animated cartoons in the United States and elsewhere.

Cross-cutting between Parallel Actions

As the film boom got under way, the Pathé film-makers continued to refine the continuity of action from shot to shot in their films. In films like Pathé's *le Cheval emballé (The Runaway Horse)* (1907), there appeared a new feature, which can be called cross-cutting between parallel actions. In this film, a delivery man is going about his business inside an apartment house while his horse steals a big meal from a bag of oats outside a feed store. The film cuts back and forwards between the two chains of action four times before the delivery man comes out, and the horse runs away with him. More importantly, early next year the Pathé production unit down in the south of France in Nice made *le Médecin du chateau (The Physician of the Castle)*, in which there are cuts back and forth between criminals threatening a doctor's wife and child, while the doctor himself drives home to rescue them after being warned by telephone. This film also contains a cut in to a closer shot of the doctor as he hears the dreadful news on the telephone, which uses the new idea of getting in closer to the actor to accentuate the emotion.

In the United States, Vitagraph was also trying cross-cutting for suspense in 1907 and 1908 with *The Mill Girl* and *Get Me a Stepladder*. Before D.W. Griffith started directing at Biograph in May 1908, he had seen the two Pathé films just mentioned, and a number of Vitagraph films as well. But Griffith's first use of cross-cutting in *The Fatal Hour*, made in July of 1908, has a much stronger suspense story served by this construction than those in the earlier Pathé examples. From this point onwards Griffith certainly developed the device much further, gradually increasing the number of alternations between two, and later three, sets of parallel scenes, and also their speed. This intensified usage was only slowly taken up by other American film-makers. So although he did not invent the technique of cross-cutting, he did consciously develop it into a powerful method of film construction. It is also important to note that Griffith described cross-cutting indiscriminately as the 'switch-back' or 'cut-back' or 'flash-back' technique, and that by the last of these terms he did not mean what we now understand by a 'flash-back'. The true 'flash-back' was also developed in this period, but not at all by D.W. Griffith.

Although D.W. Griffith did not invent any new film techniques, he was the best film director working up to 1913, and this was because he made better dramatic and artistic use of the medium than other directors. One aspect of this was the structure he gave his films, with the final scene mirroring the opening scene, as in the example of *A Drunkard's Reformation* already mentioned above. Many other examples of this like *The Country Doctor* (1908) can easily be found in his work. But the most important thing Griffith did was work out significant and expressive natural gestures in intensive rehearsal periods with his actors, before the film was shot, such as the enraged and jealous husband in *The Voice of the Child* (1911) walking around his office chomping on a cigar and puffing clouds of smoke out of it through clenched teeth. Griffith's increased use of cross-cutting between parallel actions helped him to get more shots into his films than other directors, but he also had another method for doing this. This was to split a scene that could have been played in room (or other place), into two or more sections that moved backwards and forwards between adjoining rooms or spaces. The result of this was that D.W. Griffith's films had at least twice as many shots in them as did those of other American directors. Over this period, the other directors speeded up, but so did Griffith. At first, the technique of cutting in to a closer shot of an actor in a scene made no contribution to the increase in cutting rate, because it was still very rarely done, despite having been established as a possibility in the previous period. The exception to this was a close shot of an object, which was sometimes used to make clear exactly what a person was doing. It was only towards 1913 that film-makers began to cut into closer shots with any regularity.

However, American film-makers did get closer to the actors *on the average* by shooting the whole scene with the camera closer than previously. The Vitagraph company led the way here, by using what they called "the nine-foot line" from 1910 onwards. This meant that the actors played a scene up to a line marked on the ground nine feet from the camera lens, which meant that they were shown cut off at the waist in the image. Some, but not all, American film-makers followed their example, calling it the "American foreground", while European film-makers stayed with the "French foreground" established by the Pathé about 1907, which only cut the actors off at the shins. This corresponded to the actors playing up to a line put down 4 metres in front of the camera lens.

Point of View Shots

An even more important development was the in the use of the Point of View shot. Previously, these had only been used to convey the idea of what someone in the film was seeing through a telescope (or other aperture), and this was indicated by having a black circular mask or vignette within the film frame. The true Point of View (POV) shot, in which a shot of someone looking at something is followed by a cut to a shot taken from their position without any mask, took longer to appear. In 1910, in Vitagraph's *Back to Nature* we see a Long Shot of people looking down over the rail of a ship taken from below, followed by a shot of the lifeboat they are looking at taken from their position.

However, the Vitagraph film-makers continued to be a little uneasy with the device, as a true POV shot is introduced by an explanatory intertitle, "What they saw in the house across the court" in Larry Trimble's *Jean and the Waif,* made at the end of 1910. But a few months later, Trimble made *Jean Rescues*, another of the popular series starring the fictional exploits of his Border Collie, which has POV shots introduced at an appropriate point without explanation. After this, un-vignetted POV shots began to appear fairly frequently in Vitagraph films, and also occasionally in films from other American companies. However, D.W. Griffith only used them in a theatrical situation, to show what the audience in a theatre were looking at, as did European film-makers.

Reverse-angle Cutting

Another important development was in the use of reverse angle shots; that is, continuing a scene with a cut to a shot of the action taken from the opposite direction. There were isolated examples of this very early, and the first of these, Williamson's *Attack on a China Mission* (1900) has already been mentioned. But in 1908, starting with *l'Assassinat du duc de Guise (The Assassination of the Duc de Guise)*, there began to be other films in which a scene was shown from another direction by cutting to the opposite side. This was effect imitated occasionally in Europe and the United States over the next couple of years, and came to be called a "reverse scene".

The next step, in which two actors facing each other are shown in successive close shots from opposite directions towards each of them, is first to be seen at the end of 1911 in *The Loafer*, made by Arthur Mackley for Essanay. This is what is called "reverse-angle cutting", and it is used constantly in present day film-making. However, it took some years to catch on with other American film-makers, but by 1913, it was starting to occur with greater frequency in the work of a few directors. A leading example is *His Last Fight* (1913), directed by Ralph Ince for Vitagraph, in which one-third of the cuts are between a shot and the reverse angle. However, this sort of thing never happened in D.W. Griffith's films, or in European films.

Flash-Back Construction

Another important device for the construction of film narratives is the use of "flash-backs", in the sense that the term is understood nowadays. That is, having a scene in the present followed by a scene in the past, and eventually returning to scenes in the present of the story. In the earliest days of film-making, this was only done as a representation of a character dreaming about the past, as in the 1901 Pathé film *Histoire d'un crime (The Story of a Crime)*. The first film in which a character remembers the past while awake was Vitagraph's *Napoleon—Man of Destiny* of 1909. In this film, Napoleon is in his palace after the battle of Waterloo remembering notable scenes of his past life. A superimposed title appears identifying the event he is thinking about, and the film then cuts straight to this scene, and afterwards back to Napoleon thinking about it. The idea slowly spread over the next few years, and in these usually the framing action shows a character narrating the story of the past events to people listening to them. This happens in Luigi Maggi's *Nozze d'oro (Golden Wedding)* of 1911, and amongst other films in the Edison company's *The Passer-by* of 1912. This film introduces what was to become a standard way of getting into a flash-back. As the person telling the story of their past starts talking, the camera tracks in to his face, then there is a dissolve to his younger face and the camera tracks back to reveal the scene in the past. There are many examples of single shot memory flashbacks by 1913, while a memory shown in an extended series of shots is much rarer. There is even an example of a flash-back inside a flashback in *Just a Shabby Doll*, made by the Thanhouser company in 1913.

Representing drug hallucinations in films was one way that subjective effects were developed. Victorin Jasset's master criminal thriller *Zigomar contre Nick Carter (Zigomar versus Nick Carter)* (1912) contains a sequence in an opium den, and the drugged vision of one of the clients is represented as a series of superimpositions overlaid onto the main scene, which eventually build up into a set of multiple images within the one frame. There is a development of this idea the next year in the Itala company's *Tigris* (1913). As the effect of the drug takes hold, this is represented by tilting the frame sideways, then superimposing a series of disjointed images fading and dissolving in and out on a patterned background.

Symbolism and Insert Shots

In this period the word "Art" was mentioned more and more in connection with motion pictures, and as a result of the increasing artistic ambitions of film-makers, poems began to be transposed directly into films. D.W. Griffith went further than this, by creating the visual equivalent of the poetic or musical refrain in *The Way of the World* (1910), by cutting in shots of church bells at intervals down the length of the film. However, this was an exceptional case, and it is not until 1912 that there were the first signs of the special expressive use of Insert Shots; that is, shots of objects rather than people. In the Italian Ambrosio companies film *La mala planta (The Evil Plant)*, directed by Mario Caserini, which involves a case of poisoning, there is an Insert shot of a snake slithering over the 'Evil Plant'. Another of the still very rare examples at this date is in Griffith's *The Massacre*, which was made at the end of 1912. This includes an Insert Shot of a candle at a sick man's bedside guttering out to indicate his death. Yet another is in the Ambrosio company version of *Gli ultimi giorni di Pompei (The Last Days of Pompeii)* (1913). This film includes a scene, preceded by the title "The thorns of jealousy", in which a rejected woman overhears the man she loves with another woman, and this is followed by a fade to a shot of a pair of doves, which then dissolves into a shot of a bird of prey.

It was in 1914 that D.W. Griffith began to bend the use of the Insert towards truly dramatically expressive ends, but he had not done this often, and it is really only with his *The Avenging Conscience* of 1914 that a new phase in the use of the Insert Shot starts. In this film the intertitle "The birth of the evil thought" precedes a series of three shots of the protagonist looking at a spider, and ants eating an insect, though at a later point in the film, when he prepares to kill someone, these shots are cut straight in without explanation. As well as the symbolic inserts already mentioned, *The Avenging Conscience* also made extensive use of large numbers of Big Close Up shots of clutching hands and tapping feet as a means of emphasizing those parts of the body as indicators of psychological tension. Griffith never went so far in this direction again, but his use of the Insert shot made its real impression on other American film-makers during the years 1915-1919.

Film Art

The vast increase in film production after 1906 inevitably brought specialist writers into film-making as part of the increasing sub-division of labour, but even so the film companies still had to buy stories from outsiders to get enough material for their productions. This introduced a greater variety into the types of story used in films. The use of more complex stories derived from literary and stage works of the recent past also contributed to developments in script film construction. The general American tendency was to simplify the plots borrowed from novels and plays so that they could be dealt with in one reel and with the minimum of titling and the maximum of straightforward narrative continuity, but there were exceptions to this. In these cases the information that was difficult to film and lacking in strong dramatic interest was put into narrative titles before each scene, and this was also mostly the custom in European films of the more seriously intended kind. Motion pictures were classified into genres by the film industry following the divisions already established in other media, particularly the stage. The main division was into comedy and drama, but these categories were further subdivided. Comedy could be either slapstick (usually referred to as "burlesque farce"), or alternatively "polite comedy", which later came to be referred to as "domestic comedy" or "sophisticated comedy." D.W. Griffith made a small number of the latter type of film in his first two years at Biograph, but had little interest or aptitude for the genre. From 1910 he let Frank Powell, and then Mack Sennett direct the Biograph comedies. Sennett left in 1912 to set up the Keystone company, where he could give his enthusiasm for the slapstick comedy style derived from the earlier Pathé comedies like *le Cheval emballé (The Runaway Horse)* full reign. In Europe the more restrained type of comedy was developed in substantial quantities in France, with the films of Max Linder for Pathé representing the summit of the genre from 1910 onwards. Linder's comedy was set in an upper middle-class milieu, and relied on clever and inventive ways of getting around the embarrassments and obstacles arising in his single-minded pursuit of a goal. Quite often a goal of a sexual nature.

D.W. Griffith had a major influence on the simplification of film stories. After he had been at Biograph for a year, Griffith started to make some films that had much less story content than any previous one-reel films. In *The Country Doctor*, the action is no more than various people, including the doctor, hurrying backwards and forwards between the doctor's house, where his child is sick, and a neighbouring cottage, where another child is also sick. By 1912 and 1913, there are beginning to be many films from many American companies that rely on applying novel decoration to the story, rather than supplying any twists to the drama itself to sustain interest.

Intertitles

Intertitles containing lines of dialogue began to be used consistently from 1908 onwards. In that year, Vitagraph's *An Auto Heroine;* or, *The Race for the Vitagraph Cup and How It Was Won*, contains a couple of dialogue titles, and the same firm's *Julius Caesar* includes three lines of dialogue from Shakespeare's play quoted in intertitles before the actors speak them, finishing with "This was the noblest Roman of them all." From 1909 a small number of American films, and even one or two European ones, came to include a few dialogue titles, or "spoken titles" as they were called at the time. Film-makers slowly progressed from putting these dialogue titles before the scene in which they were spoken, to cutting them into the middle of the shot at the point at which they were understood to be actually spoken by the characters. This transition began in 1912. Once underway, the trend was aided by the move towards the increasing use of cuts within scenes in American films. In 1913 a substantial proportion of the dialogue titles that were used in American films were cut in at the point when they were spoken. Hardly any of the films where this happened were D.W. Griffith films, and indeed many of his 1913 films still contain no dialogue titles at all. Although a some European film-makers picked up the trend towards using dialogue titles, they did not pick up on the move towards cutting them into the scene at the point at which they were actually spoken until a few years later. The introduction of dialogue titles was far from being a trivial matter, for they entirely transformed the nature of film narrative. When dialogue titles came to be always cut into a scene just after a character starts speaking, and then left with a cut to the character just before they finish speaking, then one had something that was effectively the equivalent of a present-day sound film.

Film History from 1914 to 1919

The Film Business from 1914 to 1919

The years of the First World War were a complex transitional period for the film industry. It was the period when the exhibition of films changed from short programmes of one-reel films to longer shows consisting of a feature film of four reels or longer, though still supported by short films. The exhibition venues also changed from small nickelodeon cinemas to larger cinemas charging higher prices. These higher prices were partly justified by the new film stars who were now being created. In the United States, nearly all the original film companies which formed the Motion Picture Patents Company went out of business in this period because of their resistance to the changeover to long feature films. The one exception to this was the Vitagraph company, which was already moving over to long films by 1914. The move towards shooting more films on the West coast around Los Angeles continued during World War I, until the bulk of American production was carried out there.

The Universal Film Manufacturing Company had been formed in 1912 as an umbrella company for many of the independent producing companies, and continued to grow during the war. Other independent companies were grouped under the Mutual banner in 1912, and there were also important new entrants, particularly the Jesse Lasky Feature Play Company, and Famous Players, which were both formed in 1913 to take advantage of the fact that films could reproduce the real substance of a stage play (plus embellishments), and so the best plays and actors from the legitimate stage could be enticed into films. In fact, the film industry adopted the term "photoplay" for motion pictures at this time. In 1914 the Lasky company and Famous Players were amalgamated into Famous Players-Lasky, with distribution of their films handled by the new Paramount Pictures Corporation.

Another new major producing company formed during the war years was Triangle, with Mack Sennett, D.W. Griffith and Thomas Ince heading its production units. Despite the talents involved, it only lasted from 1915 to 1917, after which its separate producers took their films to Paramount for distribution. Equally short-lived, but still very important, was the World Film Company, which recruited most of the French directors, cameramen, and designers who had previously been working at the Fort Lee, New Jersey studios for Pathé and Eclair.

The biggest success of these years was D.W. Griffith's *Birth of a Nation* (1915), made for Triangle. Griffith applied all the ideas for film staging that he had worked out in his Biograph films to a bigoted white southerner's epic view of the Civil War and its aftermath. Despite protests in the northern cities of the United States organized by the National Association for the Advancement of Coloured People and others, it took many millions at the box office. Stung by the criticism of his film, Griffith made a new film he had just finished, *The Mother and the Law*, into one of the strands of an even bigger film with an even bigger theme, *Intolerance* (1916).

European Film Production

In France, film production and exhibition closed down as its personnel became part of the general military mobilization of the country at the beginning of the war. Although film production began again in 1915, it was on a reduced scale, and the biggest companies gradually retired from production, to concentrate on film distribution and exhibition. Hence the cinemas were given over to imported films, particularly American ones. New small companies entered the business, and new young directors arrived to replace those drafted or working in the United States. The most notable of these was Abel Gance.

Italian film production held up during the war, with long features already established as the main form. However, there was a disastrous move in subject matter to what were called "diva films." These romantic dramas had the female star (the "diva") suffering from unhappy love, and striking endless anguished Art Nouveau poses, while surrounded by male admirers and luxury. They were a commercial failure outside Italy.

In Denmark the Nordisk company increased its production so much in 1915 and 1916 that it could not sell all its films, which led to a very sharp decline in Danish production, and the end of Denmark's importance on the world film scene. The Nordisk distribution and cinema chain in Germany was effectively expropriated by the German government in 1917. The Swedish industry did not have this problem, as its production was more in balance with the market, and more importantly, the quality of its films was now superior to those from Denmark.

The German film industry was seriously weakened by the war, though with the major companies continuing as before. The distribution organization Projektions-AG "Union" (PAGU) acted as an umbrella company backing production by individual producers, and the Messter company also made many films. The most important of the new film producers at the time was Joe May, who made a series of thrillers and adventure films through the war years, but Ernst Lubitsch also came into prominence with a series of very successful comedies and dramas.

Because of the large local market for films in Russia, the industry there was not harmed by the war at first, although the isolation of the country led many Russian films to develop peculiarly distinctive features. The Khanzhonkov company retained its dominance, but the Ermoliev company, which had been formed in 1914, became its principal competitor, propelled by the work of its star, Ivan Mosjoukin, and principal director, Yakov Protazanov. The Bolshevik revolution in October 1917 did not eliminate the privately owned film companies at first, though production was reduced through 1918. It was only in 1919 that the exodus of talent from the country took place, and fiction film production was reduced to practically nothing.

Film Studios

The major change in film production methods in the United States during this period was the change to shooting in "dark" studios. The existing glass-roofed studios were blacked out, and the many new ones being built around Los Angeles were constructed with solid walls and ceilings. This meant that shooting could continue all day and night, without being limited by the changing sunlight. The general diffuse daylighting in the old studios was completely replaced with floodlights, and the actors were individually lit with floodlights on floorstands. The use of a spotlight from high at the back onto the actors to rimlight them became more frequent, and around 1918 some American cameramen started to use spotlights to light the actors from the front. All this meant that the figures of the actors were modelled more by the lighting, and more separated from the background by the lower light levels now used on the sets. This was a major step towards the standard studio lighting methods of the sound period. At the same time there was the beginning of a move towards using artificial light to light the actors on location, and some of the biggest studios bought electric generator trucks for this purpose. All these developments took years to reach Europe.

Irising and Soft Focus

A very noticeable technical development was the wide-spread adoption of irising-in and out to begin and end scenes. This is the revelation of a film shot by its appearance inside a small circular vignette mask which gradually gets larger till it expands beyond the frame, and the whole image is in the clear. D.W. Griffith, who used it relentlessly, was responsible for the popularization of this device. By 1918 the use of the iris to begin and end sequences was starting to decrease in the United States, though in Europe it was just starting to become fashionable. At that date it is quite easy to find American films such as *Stella Maris* in which only fades are used. There were other variants of the simple iris as well and in these the mask opening or closing in front of the lens had shapes other than circular. One of the more frequent of these shapes was the opening slit; a vertical central split appears in the totally black frame, and widens till the whole frame is clear, revealing the scene that is about to start. Eventually the diagonally opening slit appeared as well, and then there was the diamond-shaped opening iris, as in *Poor Little Peppina* and *Alsace* (1916), rather than the usual circle. Again, all of these variant forms were very infrequently used, and when they did occur in American films it was usually in the introductory stages. By 1918 the edges of ordinary circular irises were becoming very fuzzy when they were used in American films.

Enclosing the image inside static vignettes or masks of shapes other than circular also began to appear in films during the years 1914-1919, including symbolic shapes such as a cruciform cut-out in the Mary Pickford film *Stella Maris* (Marshall Neilan, 1918), and Maurice Elvey in Britain put romantic scenes inside a heart-shaped mask in *Nelson; The Story of England's Immortal Naval Hero* (1918) and *The Rocks of Valpré* (1919). The most elegant variants occur in some films Ernst Lubitsch made in 1919. In *Die Austernprinzessin (The Oyster Princess)* a triple layer of horizontal rectangles with rounded ends enclose sets of dancing feet at the frenzied peak of a foxtrot, and in *Die Puppe (The Doll)* a dozen gossiping mouths are each enclosed in individual small circular vignettes arranged in a matrix.

A new idea taken over from still photography was "soft focus." This began in 1915, with some shots being intentionally thrown out of focus for expressive effect, as in Mary Pickford's *Fanchon the Cricket*. The idea developed slowly through the war years, until in D.W. Griffith's *Broken Blossoms* (1918) all the Close Ups of Lillian Gish are heavily diffused by the use of layers of fine black cotton mesh placed in front of the lens. Heavy lens diffusion was also used on all the other shots carrying forward the romantic and sentimental parts of the story of this film.

Subjective Effects

It was during this period that camera effects intended to convey the subjective feelings of characters in a film really began to be established. These could now be done as Point of View (POV) shots, as in Sidney Drew's *The Story of the Glove* (1915), where a wobbly hand-held shot of a door and its keyhole represents the POV of a drunken man. In *Poor Little Rich Girl* (1917) a camera shot tilting sideways is intended to convey delirium, and by 1918 the idea had got to Russia, in *Baryshnya i khuligan (The Lady and the Hooligan)*, where the Hooligan's infatuation with the Lady is conveyed by his Point of View of her splitting into a multiply superimposed image. The use of anamorphic (in the general sense of distorted shape) images first appears in these years with Abel Gance's *la Folie du Docteur Tube (The Madness of Dr. Tube)*. In this film the effect of a drug administered to a group of people was suggested by shooting the scenes reflected in a distorting mirror of the fairground type. Later we have *Till the Clouds Roll By* (Victor Fleming, 1919), where anamorphosis is used to depict the nightmare effects of indigestion in a comic manner. In fact, like so many film effects that distort the representation of reality, anamorphosis was first used exclusively in comic contexts.

"Poetic Cinema" and Symbolism

Symbolic effects taken over from conventional literary and artistic tradition continued to make some appearances in films during these years. In D.W. Griffith's *The Avenging Conscience* (1914), the title "The birth of the evil thought" precedes a series of three shots of the protagonist looking at a spider, and ants eating an insect, though at a later point in the film when he prepares to kill someone these shots are cut straight in without explanation. Possibly as a result of Griffith's influence, 1915 was a big year for symbolism, allegories, and parables in the American cinema. Films following this route invariably included female figures in light, skimpy draperies, and indeed sometimes wearing nothing at all, doing "expressive" dances or striking plastic poses in sylvan settings. Titles include Lois Weber's *Hypocrites*, Vitagraph's *Youth*, someone else's *Purity*, and so on. *The Primrose Path* starts with a large painting illustrating the concept, which dissolves into a replica of the same scene with actors posed, and then they come to life. This is then amplified by closer detailed live action representations of stations on "The Primrose Path." An interesting German example from a few years later is Robert Reinert's *Opium* (1919), which has some notable innovations in the use of Insert shots to help convey the sensation of the drug reveries. These are travelling landscape shots taken from a boat going down a river, and they are intentionally shot out of focus, or underexposed, or cut into the film upside down.

Symbolist art and literature from the turn of the century also had a more general effect on a small number of films made in Italy and Russia. The supine acceptance of death resulting trom passion and forbidden longings was a major feature of this art, and states of delirium dwelt on at length were important as well. The first Russian examples were all made by Yevgeni Bauer for Khanzhonkov during the First World War, and include *Grezy, Schastye vechnoi nochi*, and *Posle smerti*, all from 1915. These to some extent live up to the promise of the 'decadent' aesthetic suggested by their titles; *Daydreams, Happiness of Eternal Night*, and *After Death. Schastye vechnoi nochi* includes a visually very striking vision of a medusa-like monster superimposed on a night-time snow scene, and 'Posle smerti' has a somewhat subtler dream vision of a dead girl, picked out by extra arc lighting, walking through a wind-blown cornfield in the dusk. In Italy, another country somewhat isolated filmically by the war, the same kind of realization of the fin-de-siecle decadent symbolist aesthetic can be found, mostly in films associated with the "diva" phenomenon. The most complete example, which also has decor to match, is Charles Kraus' *Il gatto nero (The Black Cat)*. This last is one of the few films of this kind to use atmospheric insert shots to heighten the mood. The first film explicitly intended by its maker to be a visual analogue of poetry, Marcel L'Herbier's *Rose-France* (1919), continues further along these same paths.

Insert Shots

The use of Insert Shots, i.e. Close Ups of objects other than faces, was established very early, but apart from the special case of Inserts of a letter that was being read by one of the characters, they were infrequently used before 1914. It is really only with his 'The Avenging Conscience' of 1914 that a new phase in the use of the Insert Shot starts. As well as the symbolic inserts already mentioned, *The Avenging Conscience* also made extensive use of large numbers of Big Close Up shots of clutching hands and tapping feet as a means of emphasizing those parts of the body as indicators of psychological tension. Griffith never went so far in this direction again, but his use of the Insert made its real impression on other American film-makers during the years 1914-1919. Cecil B. DeMille was a leading figure in the increased use of the Insert, and by 1918 he had reached the point of including about 9 Inserts in every 100 shots in *The Whispering Chorus*. He also pushed the insert into areas of visual sensuality inaccessible to D.W. Griffith, with such images as a Close Up of a silver-plated revolver nestling in a pile of silken sexy ribbons in a drawer in *Old Wives for New* (1918).

The Atmospheric Insert

Like many other devices that were more fully developed in Europe during the next decade, what could be called the "Atmospheric Insert Shot" made its first appearance in American films during the years before 1919. This kind of shot is one in a scene which neither contains any of the characters in the story, nor is a Point of View shot seen by one of them. An early example is in Maurice Tourneur's *The Pride of the Clan* (1917), in which there is a series of shots of waves beating on a rocky shore which are shown when the locale of the story, which is about the harsh lives of fisher folk, is being introduced. Simpler and cruder examples from the same year occurs in William S. Hart's *The Narrow Trail*, in which a single shot of the mouth of San Francisco Bay taken against the light (the Golden Gate) is preceded by a narrative title explaining its symbolic function in the story. This film also contains a shot of wild hills and valleys cut in as one character comments that the country far from the city is so clean and pure. By 1918 we can find a shot of the sky being used to reflect the mood of one of the characters without specific explanation in *The Gun Woman* (Frank Borzage), but it must be emphasized that these examples are very rare, and did not either then, or within the next several years, constitute regular practice in the American cinema. The Tourneur example just mentioned also could stand as part of the beginning of the "montage sequence." Maurice Elvey's *Nelson—England's Immortal Naval Hero* (1919) has a symbolic sequence dissolving from a picture of Kaiser Wilhelm II to a peacock, and then to a battleship. The atmospheric Insert began its notable career in European art cinema in Marcel L'Herbier's *Rose-France*. Here amongst the intentionally "poetic" uses of vignettes and filters and literary intertitles, a shot of the empty path once trod by the lovers is used to evoke the past.

Continuity Cinema

The years 1914-1919 in America also saw the consolidation of the forms of what was to become the dominant mode of commercial cinema: "continuity cinema", or "classical cinema." During this period there were other styles that were still important, and these can be considered to lie along a spectrum between the best examples of "continuity cinema" at one extreme, and at the other extreme the "Dis-continuity cinema" of D.W. Griffith. There are a number of factors involved in the strong and apparent visual discontinuities between successive shots in Griffith's films, and the use of cross-cutting between parallel actions is only the most obvious of these. In 1915, cuts within the duration of a scene were still relatively infrequent in his films, and when they do occur they were frequently from Long Shot or Medium Long Shot (which were the shots he most used) to a Big Close Up of an insert detail, which only occupied a small part of the frame in the previous shot. This in itself introduces a fairly strong visual discontinuity across the cut, but as well as that, the cut-in shot might often have a circular vignette mask if it were a Close Up of a person, so reinforcing the effect. And sometimes the now-standard Griffith iris-out and iris-in might also be left on the inserted shot, even though it had action continuity with the shots on either side of it. As well as all this there was Griffith's habit of moving the action into another shot in an adjoining space, and then back again if it was at all possible, which produced a marked change in background, which also made its small contribution to the discontinuity between shots.

One of the advanced continuity techniques involves the exact way the movement of actors from a shot in one location to another in a neighbouring location is handled. At best this kind of transition had previously been dealt with by having the directions of travel of the actor in the two shots correspond on the screen, but in a film such as *The Bank Burglar's Fate* (Jack Adolfi, 1914), one can see shot transitions in which a cut is made from an actor just leaving the frame, to a shot of him well inside the frame in an adjoining location, which have the positions and directions so well chosen that to the casual eye his movement appears quite continuous, and the real space and time ellipsis between the shots is concealed. Other good examples of this technique for eliminating several yards of waste space and a few seconds of waste time can be seen in Ralph Ince's films, particularly *The Right Girl* (1915), and by 1919 it was widely diffused in American films, but not in those made in Europe. All this connects with the rise of the use of cutting to different angles within a scene during the years 1914-1919, and in particular to the development of reverse-angle cutting.

Reverse-angle Cutting

Cutting to different angles within a scene now became well-established as a technique for dissecting a scene into shots in American films. This approach had appeared a few times in earlier years, but in general cuts to or from a closer shot within a scene were still being made more or less down the lens axis as established in the Long Shot of the scene in question. The particular form of cutting to different angles within a scene in which the direction changes by more than ninety degrees is called reverse-angle cutting by film-makers. The leading figure in the full development of reverse-angle cutting was Ralph Ince. Films that he made at Vitagraph in 1915 such as *The Right Girl and His Phantom Sweetheart* have a large number of reverse-angle cuts in interior, as well as exterior, scenes. Other directors were also just starting to take up this style in 1915, for instance William S. Hart in *Bad Buck of Santa Ynez*.

As for Griffith, in *Birth of a Nation* there are just eight cuts to reverse-angle shots in the scene in Ford's Theatre, while elsewhere throughout the two-and-a-half hour length of this film there are only four more true reverse-angle cuts. Nevertheless, the Griffith style of film-making was still followed in its full idiosyncrasy, with extensive use of side by side spaces and a definite "front" for the camera, in most slapstick comedy. Directors of dramatic films who had worked Griffith also followed his style fairly closely, and it the standard for films made by his Fine Arts section of the Triangle company.

By 1916 there are a number of films in which there are around 15 to 20 true reverse-angle cuts per hundred shot transitions, such as *The Deserter* (Scott Sidney) and *Going Straight*. By the end of the war such films formed an appreciable but minor part of production: e.g. *The Gun Woman* (F. Borzage, 1918) and *Jubilo* (Clarence Badger, 1919). All this hardly concerned European cinema, where those few reverse-angle cuts used were mostly between a watcher and what he sees from his Point of View, both being filmed in a fairly distant shot. However, after the end of the war some of the brighter young directors such as Lubitsch started using a few reverse-angle cuts, mostly in association with Point of View cutting.

The Flash-back

The use of flash-back structures continued to develop in this period, and the usual way of entering and leaving a flash-back was through a dissolve, and this was in fact the principal use at this time for this device. The Vitagraph company's *The Man That Might Have Been* (William Humphrey, 1914), is even more complex, with a series of reveries and flash-backs that contrast the protagonist's real passage through life with what might have been, if his son had not died. In this film dissolves are used both to enter and leave the flash-backs, and also the wish-dreams, and also for a time-lapse inside a reverie at one point. But fades are also used for these purposes in this and other films of the period, and flash-back transitions are also done with irising in other films, and even straight cuts. During World War I the use of flash-backs occurred in films from all the major European film-making countries as well, from Italy (*Tigre reale*) to Denmark (*Evangeliemandens Liv*) to Russia (*Grezy* and *Posle smerti*), where it arrived in 1915.

As the years moved on a sudden decline in the use of long flash-back sequences set in around 1917, but on the other hand the use of a transition to and from a brief single shot memory scene remained quite common in American films. However, there could still be an even more complex flash-back construction in American films in the case of W.S. Van Dyke's, *The Lady of the Dugout* (1918). This film has a story that happened long before which is narrated by one character in the framing scene, and initially accompanied by his narrating dialogue in intertitles, though after a while this stops, and the intertitles then convey the dialogue occurring within the flash-back. Inside this main flash-back there develops cross-cutting to another story, happening at the same time, and at first apparently unconnected with it, though the connection eventually appears. Next, inside this first flash-back, the Lady of the title narrates another story, presented in flash-back form, but with cutaways inside it back to events occurring in the time frame in which she is doing her narrating. Actually, all this is fairly easy to follow while watching the film, in part because what happens in all these strings of action is relatively simple.

Cross-Cutting between Parallel Actions

After 1914 cross-cutting between parallel actions came to be used whenever appropriate in American films, though this was not the case in European films. It should be noted that a good deal of the American use of cross-cutting was not the rapid alternation between parallel chains of action developed by D.W. Griffith, but a limited number of alternations to make it possible to leave out uninteresting bits of action with no real plot function. In Europe, some of the most enterprising directors did use cross-cutting sometimes, but they never attained the speed of the many American examples of this technique.

Cross-cutting was also used to get new effects of contrast, such as the cross-cut sequence in Cecil B. DeMille's *The Whispering Chorus*, in which a supposedly dead husband is having a liaison with a Chinese prostitute in an opium den, while simultaneously his unknowing wife is being remarried in church. All this was simple compared to D.W. Griffith's *Intolerance* (1916), in which four parallel stories are intercut throughout the whole length of the film, though in this case the stories are more similar than contrasting in their nature. The use of cross-cutting within these parallel stories as well as between them produced a complexity that was beyond the comprehension of the average audience of the time. The influence of *Intolerance* produced a few other films that combined a number of similar stories having similar themes, such as Maurice Tourneur's *Woman* (1918), but the box-office failure of *Intolerance* ensured that these later films had simpler structures.

The Development of Film Art

The general trend in the development of cinema, led from the United States, was towards using the newly developed specifically filmic devices for expression of the narrative content of film stories, and combining this with the standard dramatic structures already in use in commercial theatre. D.W. Griffith had the highest standing amongst American directors in the industry, basically because of the dramatic excitement he got into his films. But there were others who were also considered as major figures at the time. The first of these was , whose films, such as *The Cheat* (1915), brought out the moral dilemmas facing their characters in a more subtle way than Griffith. DeMille was also in closer touch with the reality of contemporary American life. Maurice Tourneur was also highly ranked for the pictorial beauties of his films, together with the subtlety of his handling of fantasy, while at the same time he was capable of getting greater naturalism from his actors at appropriate moments, as in *A Girl's Folly* (1917). Sidney Draw was the leader in developing "polite comedy", while slapstick was refined by Fatty Arbuckle and Charles Chaplin, who both started with Mack Sennet's Keystone company. They reduced the usual frenetic pace of Sennett's films to give the audience a chance to appreciate the subtlety and finesse of their movement, and the cleverness of their gags. By 1917 Chaplin was also introducing more dramatic plot into his films, and mixing the comedy with sentiment.

In Russia, Evgeni Bauer put a slow intensity of acting combined with Symbolist overtones onto film in a unique way.

In Sweden, Victor Sjöström made a series of films that combined the realities of people's lives with their surroundings in a striking manner, while Mauritz Stiller developed sophisticated comedy to a new level.

In Germany, Ernst Lubitsch got his inspiration from the stage work of Max Reinhardt, both in bourgeois comedy and in spectacle, and applied this to his films, culminating in his *die Puppe (The Doll), die Austernprinzessin (The Oyster Princess)* and *Madame Dubarry*.

Hollywood Triumphant

Until this point, the cinemas of France and Italy had been the most globally popular and powerful. But the United States was already gaining quickly when World War I (1914-1918) caused a devastating interruption in the European film industries. The American industry, or "Hollywood," as it was becoming known after its new geographical centre in California, gained the position it has held, more or less, ever since: movie factory for the world, exporting its product to most countries on earth and controlling the market in many of them.

By the 1920s, the U.S. reached what is still its era of greatest-ever output, producing an average of 800 feature films annually, or 82 per cent of the global total (Eyman, 1997). The comedies of Charlie Chaplin and Buster Keaton, the swashbuckling adventures of Douglas Fairbanks and the romances of Clara Bow, to cite just a few examples, made these performers' faces well-known on every continent. The Western visual norm that would become classical continuity editing was developed and exported—although its adoption was slower in some non-Western countries without strong realist traditions in art and drama, such as Japan.

This development was contemporary with the growth of the studio system and its greatest publicity method, the star system, which characterized American film for decades to come and provided models for other movie industries. The studios' efficient, top-down control over all stages of their product enabled a new and ever-growing level of lavish production and technical sophistication. At the same time, the system's commercial regimentation and focus on glamorous escapism discouraged daring and ambition beyond a certain degree, a prime example being the brief but still legendary directing career of the iconoclastic Erich von Stroheim in the late teens and the '20s.

World Film at the Peak of the Silents

But even now, the dominance of mainstream Hollywood entertainment was not as strong as it would be, and alternatives were still widely seen and influential.

In 1915, after a ban was ended on foreign imports in France the early Hollywood fare inspired the birth of the cinematic avant-garde. A group of film-makers began experimenting with optical and pictorial effects as well as rhythmic editing. The trend became known as French Impressionist Cinema.

Germany was America's strongest competitor. Its most distinctive contribution was the dark, hallucinatory worlds of German Expressionism, which advanced the power of anti-realistic presentation to put internal states of mind onscreen, as well as strongly influenced the emerging horror genre.

The newborn Soviet cinema was the most radically innovative. There, the craft of editing, especially, surged forward, going beyond its previous role in advancing a story. Sergei Eisenstein perfected the technique of so-called dialectical or intellectual montage, which strove to make non-linear, often violently clashing, images express ideas and provoke emotional and intellectual reactions in the viewer.

Meanwhile, the first feature-length silent film was made in India by Dadasaheb Phalke, considered to be the father of Indian cinema. The film was the period piece *Raja Harishchandra* (1913), and it laid the foundation for a series of period films. By the next decade the output of Indian cinema was an average of 27 films per year.

The cultural avant gardes of a number of countries worked with experimental films, mostly shorts, that completely abandoned linear narrative and embraced abstraction, pure aestheticism and the irrational subconscious, most famously in the early work of Spanish surrealist Luis Buñuel. In some ways, in fact, this decade marked the first serious split between mainstream, "popular" film and "art" film.

But even within the mainstream, refinement was rapid, bringing silent film to what would turn out to be its aesthetic summit. The possibilities of cinematography kept increasing as cameras became more mobile (thanks to new booms and dollies) and film stocks more sensitive and versatile. Screen acting became more of a craft, without its earlier theatrical exaggeration and achieving greater subtlety and psychological realism. As visual eloquence increased, reliance on intertitles decreased; the occasional film, such as F.W. Murnau's *The Last Laugh* (Germany, 1926) even eschewed them altogether. Paradoxically, at about this time, the silent cinema period ended.

The Sound Era

Experimentation with sound film technology, both for recording and playback, was virtually constant throughout the silent era, but the twin problems of accurate synchronization and sufficient amplification had been difficult to overcome (Eyman, 1997). In 1926, Hollywood studio Warner Brothers introduced the "Vitaphone" system, producing short films of live entertainment acts and public figures and adding recorded sound effects and orchestral scores to some of its major features. During late 1927, Warners released *The Jazz Singer*, which was mostly silent but contained the first synchronized dialogue (and singing) in a feature film. It was a great success, as were follow-ups like Warners' *The*

Lights of New York (1928), the first all-synchronized-sound feature. The early sound-on-disc processes such as Vitaphone were soon superseded by sound-on-film methods like Fox Movietone, DeForest Phonofilm, and RCA Photophone. The trend convinced the largely reluctant industrialists that "talking pictures", or "talkies," were the future.

Industry Impact of Sound

The change was remarkably swift. By the end of 1929, Hollywood was almost all-talkie, with several competing sound systems (soon to be standardized). Total changeover was slightly slower in the rest of the world, principally for economic reasons. Cultural reasons were also a factor in countries like China and Japan, where silents co-existed successfully with sound well into the 1930s, indeed producing what would be some of the most revered classics in those countries, like Wu Yonggang's *The Goddess* (China, 1934) and Yasujiro Ozu's *I Was Born, But...* (Japan, 1932). But even in Japan, a figure such as the *benshi*, the live narrator who was a major part of Japanese silent cinema, found his acting career was ending.

Sound further tightened the grip of major studios in numerous countries: the vast expense of the transition overwhelmed smaller competitors, while the novelty of sound lured vastly larger audiences for those producers that remained. In the case of the U.S., some historians credit sound with saving the Hollywood studio system in the face of the Great Depression (Parkinson, 1995). Thus began what is now often called "The Golden Age of Hollywood," which refers roughly to the period beginning with the introduction of sound until the late 1940s. The American cinema reached its peak of efficiently manufactured glamour and global appeal during this period. The top actors of the era are now thought of as the classic movie stars, such as Clark Gable, Katharine Hepburn, Humphrey Bogart and the greatest box office draw of the 1930s, child performer Shirley Temple.

Creative Impact of Sound

Creatively, however, the rapid transition was a difficult one, and in some ways, film briefly reverted to the conditions of its earliest days. The late '20s were full of static, stagey talkies as artists in front of and behind the camera struggled with the stringent limitations of the early sound equipment and their own uncertainty as to how to utilize the new medium. Many stage performers, directors and writers were introduced to cinema as producers sought personnel experienced in dialogue-based storytelling. Many major silent film-makers and actors were unable to adjust and found their careers severely curtailed or even ended.

This awkward period was fairly short-lived. 1929 was a watershed year: William Wellman with *Chinatown Nights* and *The Man I Love*, Rouben Mamoulian with *Applause*, Alfred Hitchcock with *Blackmail* (Britain's first sound feature), were among the directors to bring greater fluidity to talkies and experiment with the expressive use of sound (Eyman, 1997). In this, they both benefited from, and pushed further, technical advances in microphones and cameras, and capabilities for editing and post-synchronizing sound (rather than recording all sound directly at the time of filming).

Sound films emphasized and benefited different genres more so than silents did. Most obviously, the musical film was born; the first classic-style Hollywood musical was *The Broadway Melody* (1929) and the form would find its first major creator in choreographer/director Busby Berkeley (*42nd Street*, 1933, *Dames*, 1934). In France, avant-garde director René Clair made surreal use of song and dance in comedies like *Under the Roofs of Paris* (1930) and *Le Million* (1931). The trend thrived best in India, where the influence of the country's traditional song-and-dance drama made the musical the basic form of most sound movies (Cook, 1990); virtually unnoticed by the Western world for decades, this Indian popular cinema would nevertheless become the world's most prolific.

At this time, American gangster films like *Little Caesar* and Wellman's *The Public Enemy* (both 1931) became popular. Dialogue now took precedence over "slapstick" in Hollywood comedies: the fast-paced, witty banter of *The Front Page* (1931) or *It Happened One Night* (1934), the sexual double entrendres of Mae West (*She Done Him Wrong*, 1933) or the often subversively anarchic nonsense talk of the Marx Brothers (*Duck Soup*, 1933). 1939, a major year for American cinema, brought such films as *The Wizard of Oz* and *Gone with The Wind*.

The 1940s: The War and Post-War Years

The desire for wartime propaganda created a renaissance in the film industry in Britain, with realistic war dramas like *Forty-Ninth Parallel* (1941), *Went the Day Well?* (1942), *The Way Ahead* (1944) and Noel Coward and David Lean's celebrated naval film *In Which We Serve* in 1942, which won a special Academy Award. These existed alongside more flamboyant films like Michael Powell and Emeric Pressburger's *The Life and Death of Colonel Blimp* (1943), *A Canterbury Tale* (1944) and *A Matter of Life and Death* (1946), as well as Laurence Olivier's 1944 film *Henry V*, based on the Shakespearean history *Henry V*.

The onset of US involvement in WWII also brought a proliferation of movies as both patriotism and propaganda. American propaganda movies included *Desperate Journey*, *Mrs. Miniver*, *Forever and a Day* and *Objective Burma*. Notable American films from the war years include the anti-Nazi *Watch on the Rhine* (1943), scripted by Dashiell Hammett; *Shadow of a Doubt* (1943), Hitchcock's direction of a script by Thornton Wilder; the George M. Cohan biopic, *Yankee Doodle Dandy* (1942), starring James Cagney, and the immensely popular *Casablanca*, with Humphrey Bogart. Bogart would star in 36 films between 1934 and 1942 including John Huston's *The Maltese Falcon* (1941), one of the first movies now considered a classic film noir.

The strictures of wartime also brought an interest in more fantastical subjects. These included Britain's Gainsborough melodramas (including *The Man in Grey* and *The Wicked Lady*), and films like *Here Comes Mr. Jordan*, *Heaven Can Wait*, *I Married a Witch* and *Blithe Spirit*. Val Lewton also produced a series of atmospheric and influential small-budget horror films, some of the more famous examples being *Cat People*, *Isle of the Dead* and *The Body Snatcher*. The decade probably also saw the so-called "women's pictures," such as *Now, Voyager*, *Random Harvest* and *Mildred Pierce* at the peak of their popularity.

In 1941, RKO Pictures released Citizen Kane made by Orson Welles. It is often consided the greatest film of all time. It would set the stage for the modern motion picture, as it revolutionized film story telling.

1946 saw RKO Radio releasing *It's a Wonderful Life* directed by Frank Capra. Soldiers returning from the war would provide the inspiration for films like *The Best Years of Our Lives*, and many of those in the film industry had served in some capacity during the war. Samuel Fuller's experiences in WWII would influence his largely autobiographical films of later decades such as *The Big Red One*. The Actor's Studio was founded in October 1947 by Elia Kazan, Robert Lewis, and Cheryl Crawford, and the same year Oskar Fischinger filmed *Motion Painting No. 1*.

In 1943, *Ossessione* was screened in Italy, marking the beginning of Italian neorealism. Major films of this type during the 1940s included *Bicycle Thieves, Rome, Open City*, and *La Terra Trema*. In 1952 *Umberto D* was released, usually considered the last film of this type.

In the late 1940s, in Britain, Ealing Studios embarked on their series of celebrated comedies, including *Whisky Galore!, Passport to Pimlico, Kind Hearts and Coronets* and *The Man in the White Suit*, and Carol Reed directed his influential thrillers *Odd Man Out, The Fallen Idol* and *The Third Man*. David Lean was also rapidly becoming a force in world cinema with *Brief Encounter* and his Dickens adaptations *Great Expectations* and *Oliver Twist*, and Michael Powell and Emeric Pressburger would experience the best of their creative partnership with films like *Black Narcissus* and *The Red Shoes*.

The 1950s

The House Un-American Activities Committee investigated Hollywood in the early 1950s. Protested by the Hollywood Ten before the committee, the hearings resulted in the blacklisting of many actors, writers and directors, including Chayefsky, Charlie Chaplin, and Dalton Trumbo, and many of these fled to Europe, especially the United Kingdom.

The Cold War era zeitgeist translated into a type of near-paranoia manifested in themes such as invading armies of evil aliens (*Invasion of the Body Snatchers, The War of the Worlds*); and communist fifth columnists (*The Manchurian Candidate*).

During the immediate post-war years the cinematic industry was also threatened by television, and the increasing popularity of the medium meant that some movie theatres would bankrupt and close. The demise of the "studio system" spurred the self-commentary of films like *Sunset Boulevard* (1950) and *The Bad and the Beautiful* (1952).

In 1950, the Lettrists avante-gardists caused riots at the Cannes Film Festival, when Isidore Isou's Treatise on Slime and Eternity was screened. After their criticism of Charlie Chaplin and split with the movement, the Ultra-Lettrists continued to cause disruptions when they showed their new hypergraphical techniques. The most notorious film is Guy Debord's Bombs in Favour of DeSade of 1952.

Distressed by the increasing number of closed theatres, studios and companies would find new and innovative ways to bring audiences back. These included attempts to literally widen their appeal with new screen formats. Cinemascope, which would remain a 20th century Fox distinction until 1967, was announced with 1953's *The Robe*. VistaVision, Cinerama, boasted a "bigger is better" approach to marketing movies to a dwindling US audience. This resulted in the revival of epic films to take advantage of the new big screen formats. Some of the most successful examples of these Biblical and historical spectaculars include *The Ten Commandments* (1956), *The Vikings* (1958), *Ben-Hur* (1959), *Spartacus* (1960) and *El Cid* (1961).

Gimmicks also proliferated to lure in audiences. The fad for 3-D film would last for only two years, 1952-1954, and helped sell *House of Wax* and *Creature from the Black Lagoon*. Producer William Castle would tout films featuring "Emergo", "Percepto", the first of a series of gimmicks that would remain popular marketing tools for Castle and others throughout the 1960s.

In the U.S., a post-WW2 tendency toward questioning the establishment and societal norms and the early activism of the Civil Rights Movement was reflected in Hollywood films such as *Blackboard Jungle* (1955), *On the Waterfront* (1954), Paddy Chayefsky's *Marty* and Reginald Rose's *12 Angry Men* (1957).

Disney's *Sleeping Beauty* was released on January 29, 1959 by The Walt Disney Company after nearly a decade in production.

Across the globe, the 1950s marked a very productive period for Indian cinema, with more than 200 films being made. Indian films also gained greater recognition through films like Pather Panchali (1955), from critically acclaimed Academy Award winning director Satyajit Ray. Television began competing seriously with films projected in theatres, but surprisingly it promoted more moviegoing rather than curtailing it.

1960s

During the 1960s the studio system in Hollywood declined, because many films were now being made on location in other countries, or using studio facilities abroad, such as Pinewood in England and Cinecittà in Rome. "Hollywood" movies were still largely aimed at family audiences, and it was often the more old-fashioned films that produced the studios' biggest successes. Productions like *Mary Poppins* (1964), *My Fair Lady* (1964) and *The Sound of Music* (1965) were among the biggest money-makers of the decade. The growth in independent producers and production companies, and the increase in the power of individual actors also contributed to the decline of traditional Hollywood studio production.

There was also an increasing awareness of foreign language cinema during this period. During the late 1950s and 1960s the French New Wave directors such as François Truffaut and Jean-Luc Godard produced films such as *Les quatre cents coups* and *Jules et Jim* which broke the rules of Hollywood cinema's narrative structure. As well, audiences were becoming aware of Italian films like Federico Fellini's *La dolce vita* and the stark dramas of Sweden's Ingmar Bergman.

In Britain, the "Free Cinema" of Lindsay Anderson, Tony Richardson and others lead to a group of realistic and innovative dramas including *Saturday Night and Sunday Morning, A Kind of Loving* and *This Sporting Life*. Other British films such as *Repulsion, Darling, Alfie, Blowup* and *Georgy Girl* (all in 1965-1966) helped to reduce prohibitions sex and nudity on screen, while the casual sex and violence of the James Bond films, beginning with *Dr. No* in 1962 would render the series popular worldwide.

During the 1960s, Ousmane Sembène produced several French- and Wolof-language films and became the 'father' of African cinema. In Latin America the dominance of the "Hollywood" model was challenged by many film-makers. Fernando Solanas and Octavio Gettino called for a politically engaged Third Cinema in contrast to Hollywood and the European auteur cinema.

Further, the nuclear paranoia of the age, and the threat of an apocalyptic nuclear exchange (like the 1963 close-call with the USSR during the Cuban missile crisis) prompted a reaction within the film community as well. Films like Stanley Kubrick's Dr. Strangelove and Fail Safe with Henry Fonda were produced in a Hollywood that was once known for its overt patriotism and wartime propaganda.

In documentary film the sixties saw the blossoming of Direct Cinema, an observational style of film-making as well as the advent of more overtly partisan films like *In the Year of the Pig* about the Vietnam War by Emile de Antonio. By the late 1960s however, Hollywood film-makers were beginning to create more innovative and groundbreaking films that reflected the social revolution taken over much of the western world such as *Bonnie and Clyde* (1967), *The Good, The Bad, The Ugly* (1967), *The Graduate* (1967), *2001: A Space Odyssey* (1968), *Rosemary's Baby* (1968), *Midnight Cowboy* (1969), *Easy Rider* (1969) and *The Wild Bunch* (1969). *Bonnie and Clyde* is often considered the beginning of the so-called New Hollywood.

1970s: The 'New Hollywood' or Post-classical Cinema

'The New Hollywood' and 'post-classical cinema' are terms used to describe the period following the decline of the studio system during the 1950s and 1960s and the end of the production code. During the 1970s, film-makers increasingly depicted explicit sexual content and showed gunfight and battle scenes that included graphic images of bloody deaths.

'Post-classical cinema' is a term used to describe the changing methods of storytelling of the "New Hollywood" producers. The new methods of drama and characterization played upon audience expectations acquired during the classical/Golden Age period: story chronology may be scrambled, storylines may feature unsettling "twist endings", main characters may behave in a morally ambiguous fashion, and the lines between the antagonist and protagonist may be blurred. The beginnings of post-classical storytelling may be seen in 1940s and 1950s film noir movies, in films such as *Rebel Without a Cause* (1955), and in Hitchcock's *Psycho*.

During the 1970s, a new group of American film-makers emerged, such as Francis Ford Coppola, Steven Spielberg, George

Lucas and Brian de Palma. This coincided with the increasing popularity of the auteur theory in film literature and the media, which posited that a film director's films express their personal vision and creative insights. The development of the auteur style of film-making helped to give these directors far greater control over their projects than would have been possible in earlier eras. This led to some great critical and commercial successes, like Coppola's *The Godfather* films, Spielberg's *Jaws* and *Close Encounters of the Third Kind* and George Lucas's *Star Wars*. It also, however, resulted in some failures, including Peter Bogdanovich's *At Long Last Love* and Michael Cimino's hugely expensive Western epic *Heaven's Gate*, which helped to bring about the demise of its backer, United Artists.

The financial disaster of *Heaven's Gate* marking the end of the visionary "auteur" directors of the "New Hollywood", who had unrestrained creative and financial freedom to develop films. The phenomenal success in the 1970s of *Jaws* and *Star Wars* in particular, led to the rise of the modern "blockbuster." Hollywood studios increasingly focused on producing a smaller number of very large budget films with massive marketing and promotional campaigns. This trend had already been foreshadowed by the commercial success of disaster films such as *The Poseidon Adventure* and *The Towering Inferno*.

During the mid-1970s, more pornographic theatres, euphemistically called "adult cinemas", were established, and the legal production of hardcore pornographic films began. Porn films such as *Deep Throat* and its star Linda Lovelace became something of a popular culture phenomenon and resulted in a spate of similar sex films. The porn cinemas finally died out during the 1980s, when the popularization of the home VCR and pornography videotapes allowed audiences to watch sex films at home. In the early 1970s, English language audiences became more aware of the new West German cinema, with Werner Herzog, Rainer Werner Fassbinder and Wim Wenders among its leading exponents.

The end of the decade saw the first major international marketing of Australian cinema, as Peter Weir's films *Picnic at Hanging Rock* and *The Last Wave*, and Fred Schepisi's *The Chant of Jimmie Blacksmith* gained critical acclaim. In 1979, Australian film-maker George Miller also garnered international attention for his violent, low-budget action film *Mad Max*.

1980s: Sequels, Blockbusters and Videotape

During the 1980s, audiences began increasingly watching movies on their home VCRs. In the early part of that decade, the movie studios tried legal action to ban home ownership of VCRs as a violation of copyright, which proved unsuccessful. Eventually, the sale and rental of movies on home video became a significant "second venue" for exhibition of films, and an additional source of revenue for the movie companies.

The Lucas-Spielberg combine would dominate "Hollywood" cinema for much of the 1980s, and lead to much imitation. Two follow-ups to *Star Wars*, three to *Jaws*, and three Indiana Jones films helped to make sequels of successful films more of an expectation than ever before. Lucas also launched THX Ltd, a division of Lucasfilm in 1982, while Spielberg enjoyed one of the decade's greatest successes in *E.T.* the same year. American independent cinema struggled more during the decade, although Martin Scorsese's *Raging Bull* (1980), *After Hours* (1985), and *The King of Comedy* (1983) helped to establish him as one of the most critically acclaimed American film-makers of the era. Also during 1983 *Scarface* was released, was very profitable and resulted in even greater fame for its leading actor Al Pacino. Probably the most successful film commercially was vended during 1989: Tim Burton's version of Bob Kane's creation, Batman, exceeded box-office records. Jack Nicholson's portrayal of the demented Joker earned him $60,000,000 (the most money an actor has ever made from one film) and it brought Tim Burton and Michael Keaton great fame.

British cinema was given a boost during the early 1980s by the arrival of David Puttnam's company Goldcrest Films. The films *Chariots of Fire*, *Gandhi*, *The Killing Fields* and *A Room with a View* appealed to a "middlebrow" audience which was increasingly being ignored by the major Hollywood studios. While the films of the 1970s had helped to define modern blockbuster motion pictures, the way "Hollywood" released its films would now change. Films, for the most part, would premiere in a wider number of theatres, although, to this day, some movies still premiere using the route of the limited/roadshow release system. Against some expectations, the rise of the multiplex cinema did not allow less mainstream films to be shown, but simply allowed the major blockbusters to be given an even greater number of screenings. However, films that had been overlooked in cinemas were increasingly being given a second chance on home video and later DVD.

1990s: New Special Effects, Independent Films and DVDs

The early 1990s saw the development of a commercially successful independent cinema in the United States. Although cinema was increasingly dominated by special-effects films such as *Terminator 2: Judgement Day* (1991) and *Titanic* (1997), independent films like Steven Soderbergh's *sex, lies, and videotape* (1989) and Quentin Tarantino's *Reservoir Dogs* (1992) had significant commercial success both at the cinema and on home video.

The major studios began to create their own "independent" production companies to finance and produce non-mainstream fare. One of the most successful independents of the 1990s, Miramax Films, was bought by Disney the year before the release of Tarantino's runaway hit *Pulp Fiction* in 1994. The same year marked the beginning of film and video distribution online. Animated films aimed at family audiences also regained their popularity, with Disney's *Beauty and the Beast*, *Aladdin* and *The Lion King*. During 1995 the first feature length computer-animated feature, *Toy Story*, was produced by Pixar Animation Studios and released by Disney. After the success of Toy Story, Disney returned to traditional animation and made three more popular films: *The Hunchback of Notre Dame* in 1996, *Hercules* in 1997, and *Mulan* in 1998. In 1999, Disney released *Tarzan*, which employed the use of a CGI rendering technique called Deep Canvas. During the late 1990s, another cinematic transition began, from physical film stock to digital cinema technology. Meanwhile DVDs became the new standard for consumer video, replacing VHS tapes.

2000s

The documentary film also rose as a commercial genre for perhaps the first time, with the success of films such as *March of the Penguins* and Michael Moore's *Bowling for Columbine* and *Fahrenheit 9/11*. A new genre was created with Martin Kunert and Eric Manes' *Voices of Iraq*, when 150 inexpensive DV cameras were distributed across Iraq, transforming ordinary people into collaborative film-makers. The success of *Gladiator* lead to a revival of interest in epic cinema, and *Moulin Rouge!* renewed interest in musical cinema. Home theatre systems became increasingly sophisticated, as did some of the special edition DVDs designed to be shown on them. *The Lord of the Rings Trilogy* was released on DVD in both the theatrical version and in a special extended version intended only for home cinema audiences.

The Long Tail

One major new development in the early 21st century is the development of systems that make it much easier for regular people to write, shoot, edit and distribute their own movies without the large apparatus of the film industry. This phenomenon and its repercussions are outlined in Chris Anderson's theory, *The Long Tail*.

The Underground

Alongside the Hollywood tradition, there has also been an "underground film" tradition of small-budget, often self-produced works created outside of the studio system and without the involvement of labour unions.

2

Modern Film Industry: Special Focus on Bollywood

FILM INDUSTRY

The film industry consists of the technological and commercial institutions of film-making: i.e. film production companies, film studios, cinematography, film production, screen-writing, pre-production, post-production, film festivals, distribution; and actors, film directors and other film personnel.

Though the expense involved in making movies almost immediately led film production to concentrate under the auspices of standing production companies, advances in affordable film-making equipment, and expansion of opportunities to acquire investment capital from outside the film industry itself, have allowed independent film production to evolve.

Modern Film Industry

The film industry as it stands today spans the globe. The major business centres of film-making are concentrated in the United States, Eastern Europe, India and China.

Distinct from the business centres are the locations where movies are filmed. Because of labour and infrastructure costs, many films are produced in countries other than the one in which the company which pays for the film is located. For example, many U.S. movies are filmed in Canada, the United Kingdom, Australia, New Zealand or in Eastern European countries.

United States

Hollywood, California is the primary nexus of the U.S. film industry. However, five of the major film studios are owned by

East Coast companies. Only The Walt Disney Company (owner of Walt Disney Pictures, Touchstone Pictures, Hollywood Pictures, Miramax Films, and the Pixar Animation Studios) is actually headquartered in Southern California.

Networking

Networking and establishing strong relationships are a vital part of Hollywood. The town is scattered with talented artists who do not possess the means to pitch their ideas or acquire representation. Reading the trades, Hollywood jargon for reading Daily Variety or The Hollywood Reporter, and joining a networking group or tracking board are ways to stay on top of the job market as well as the project market.

India

The Indian film industry is multi-lingual and the largest in the world (1200 movies released in the year 2002). The industry is supported mainly by a vast film-going Indian public (the largest in the world in terms of annual ticket sales), and Indian films have been gaining increasing popularity in the rest of the world—notably in countries with large numbers of expatriate Indians. One-third of the India's film industry is mostly concentrated in Mumbai and is commonly referred to as "Bollywood" as an amalgamation of Mumbai and Hollywood. The remaining majority portion is spread across South India (in Telugu and Tamil speaking areas). However, there are several smaller centres of Indian film industries in regional languages (Apart from Hindi, Telugu and Tamil) centred in the states those languages are spoken.

China

Hong Kong, China is a film-making hub for the Chinese-speaking world (including the worldwide diaspora) and East Asia in general. For decades it was the third largest motion picture industry in the world (after Indian and Hollywood) and the second largest exporter. Despite an industry crisis starting in the mid-'90s and Hong Kong's return to Chinese sovereignty in July 1997, Hong

Kong film has retained much of its distinctive identity and continues to play a prominent part on the world cinema stage.

Unlike many film industries, Hong Kong has enjoyed little to no direct government support, through either subsidies or import quotas. It has always been a thoroughly commercial cinema, concentrating on crowd-pleasing, like comedy and action, and heavily reliant on formulas, sequels and remakes. Typically of commercial cinemas, its heart is a highly developed star system, which in this case also features substantial overlap with the pop music industry.

Nigeria

Also known as "Nollywood." Nigeria was ushered into modern film-making by a film known as "Living in Bondage", which featured Kenneth Okonwo, Kanayo O. Kanayo, Bob Manuel Udokwu, Francis Agu, Ngozi Nwosu, Nnena Nwabueze, etc. This movie, which hit the market in 1992, marked a turning point in the Nigerian Movie Industry and heralded the trend in modern day movie making in Nigeria.

The movie capital of the country was in Lagos. However, over the years, there has been a shift from Lagos to Enugu, in the eastern part of the country. This shift is said to be chanpioned by Pete Edochie — a veteran in the communications industry who turned an actor and has become one of the most successful in Nigeria.

Now, with the Launching of TINAPA Studios in Cross River State of Nigeria, we expect yet another shift in the regular base of the movie industry in Nigeria, considering the attractive ultra modern facilities, and beautiful scenery and location of Calabar, the capital of Cross Rivers.

The movie industry in Nigeria would not be complete without a mention of those behind the movies. Not the actors this time, but the sponsors or producers who are mostly based in Onitsha, the commercial capital of Anambra State of Nigeria.

History

The first feature film ever made was that of *The Story of the Kelly Gang*, an Australian film based on the infamous Kelly Gang. In 1906 Dan Barry and Charles Tait of Melbourne produced and directed 'The Story of the Kelly Gang', a silent film that ran continuously for a breathtaking 80 minutes. It was not until 1911 that countries other than Australia began to make feature films. By this time Australia had made 16 full length feature films.

In the early 1900s, in the earliest years of the industry, motion picture production companies from New York and New Jersey started moving to California because of the good weather and longer days. Although electric lights existed at that time, none were powerful enough to adequately expose film; the best source of illumination for movie production was natural sunlight. Besides the moderate, dry climate, they were also drawn to the state because of its open spaces and wide variety of natural scenery.

Another reason was the distance of Southern California from New Jersey, which made it more difficult for Thomas Edison to enforce his motion picture patents. At the time, Edison owned almost all the patents relevant to motion picture production and, in the East, movie producers acting independently of Edison's Motion Picture Patents Company were often sued or enjoined by Edison and his agents. Thus, movie makers working on the West Coast could work independent of Edison's control. If he sent agents to California, word would usually reach Los Angeles before the agents did and the movie makers could escape to nearby Mexico.

Hollywood

The first movie studio in the Hollywood area, Nestor Studios, was founded in 1911 by Al Christie for David Horsley in an old building on the southeast corner of Sunset Boulevard and Gower Street. In the same year, another fifteen independents settled in Hollywood. Hollywood came to be so strongly associated with the film industry that the word "Hollywood" came to be used colloquially to refer to the entire industry.

In 1913, Cecil B. DeMille, in association with Jesse Lasky, leased a barn with studio facilities on the southeast corner of Selma and Vine Streets from the Burns and Revier Studio and Laboratory, which had been established there. DeMille then began production of *The Squaw Man* (1914). It became known as the Lasky-DeMille Barn and is currently the location of the Hollywood Heritage Museum.

The Charlie Chaplin Studios, on the northeast corner of La Brea and De Longpre Avenues just south of Sunset Boulevard, was built in 1917. It has had many owners after 1953, including Kling Studios, who produced the Superman TV series with George Reeves; Red Skelton, who used the sound stages for his CBS TV variety show; and CBS, who filmed the TV series *Perry Mason* with Raymond Burr there. It has also been owned by Herb Alpert's A&M Records and Tijuana Brass Enterprises. It is currently The Jim Henson Company, home of the Muppets. In 1969, The Los Angeles Cultural Heritage Board named the studio a historical cultural monument.

The famous Hollywood sign originally read "Hollywoodland." It was erected in 1923 to advertise a new housing development in the hills above Hollywood. For several years the sign was left to deteriorate. In 1949, the Hollywood Chamber of Commerce stepped in and offered to remove the last four letters and repair the rest.

The sign, located at the top of Mount Lee, is now a registered trademark and cannot be used without the permission of the Hollywood Chamber of Commerce, which also manages the venerable Walk of Fame.

The first Academy Awards presentation ceremony took place on May 16, 1929 during a banquet held in the Blossom Room of the Hollywood Roosevelt Hotel on Hollywood Boulevard. Tickets were USD $10.00 and there were 250 people in attendance.

From about 1930, five major Hollywood movie studios from all over the Los Angeles area, Paramount, RKO, 20th Century Fox, Metro-Goldwyn-Mayer and Warner Bros., owned large, grand theaters throughout the country for the exhibition of their movies. The period between the years 1927 (the effective end of the silent era) to 1948 is considered the age of the "Hollywood studio system", or, in a more common term, the *Golden Age of Hollywood*. In a landmark 1948 court decision, the Supreme Court ruled that movie studios could not own theaters and play only the movies of their studio and movie stars, thus an era of Hollywood history had unofficially ended. By the mid-1950s, when television proved a profitable enterprise that was here to stay, movie studios started also being used for the production of programming in that medium, which is still the norm today.

BOLLYWOOD: INDIAN FILM INDUSTRY AND MOVIE-MAKING

Indian movie-making industry that began in Bombay (now Mumbai) in the 1930s and developed into an enormous film empire. Bombay Talkies, launched in 1934 by Himansu Rai, spearheaded the growth of Indian cinema. Throughout the years, several classic genres emerged from Bollywood: the historical epic, notably *Mughal-e-azam* (1960; "The Great Mughal"); the curry western, such as *Sholay* (1975; "The Embers"); the courtesan film, such as *Pakeezah* (1972; "Pure Heart"), which highlights stunning cinematography and sensual dance choreography; and the mythological movie, represented by *Jai Santoshi Maa* (1975; "Hail Santoshi Maa"). Star actors, rather than the films themselves, have accounted for most box-office success. Standard features of Bollywood films include formulaic story lines, expertly choreographed fight scenes, spectacular song-and-dance routines, emotion-charged melodrama, and larger-than-life heroes. At the beginning of the 21st century, Bollywood produced as many as 1,000 feature films annually, and international audiences began to develop among Asians in the U.K. and the U.S.

The Indian Film Industry

The Beginnings

Films arrived in India less than a year after the Lumieres first exhibited their cinematographie in Paris. On July 7, 1896, an agent who had brought equipment and films from France first showed his moving pictures in Bombay. That was an important day in the social and cultural history of the Indian people.

The first Indian-made feature film (3700 feet long) was released in 1913. It was made by Dadasaheb Phalke and was called *Raja Harishchandra*. Based on a story from the *Mahabharata* it was a stirring film concerned with honour, sacrifice and mighty deeds. From then on many "mythologicals" were made and took India by storm. Phalke's company alone produced about a hundred films.

What little remains of Indian silent cinema up to 1931 barely fills six video-cassettes in the National Film Archives of India, but it is remarkable for the way traditional "theatrical" framing (static characters, faced front on by the camera) is animated by a considerable investment in location shooting, both in natural surroundings and in the city. This is evident not only in *Raja Harishchandra*, but also in historical—stunt films such as *Diler Jigar/ Gallant Hearts* (S.S. Agarwal; 1931) and *Gulaminu Patan/The Fall of Slavery* (S.S. Agarwal; 1931), and in the international co-productions directed by Himansu Rai and the German Franz Osten. Among these, *Light of Asia* (1925), about the Buddha, and *Shiraz* (1928), about the origins of the Taj Mahal, referred to as 'Romances from India' by their producers, render "India" as a startling, exotic assemblage: scenes of ancient and medieval court life, attended by the ritual of courtly gesture, and by spectacular processions of elephants and camels, are juxtaposed with a glittering naturalism.

Advent of Sound

By the time of the First World War, and the phenomenal expansion of Hollywood, 85 per cent of feature films shown in India were American. But the introduction of sound made an immediate difference. In 1931, India's first talkie, *Alam Ara*, was released, dubbed into Hindi and Urdu. As the talkies emerged over the next decade, so too did a new series of issues. The most prominent of these, of course, was language, and language markets; alongside, there are considerations of regional identity, of the different places that separately and together make up India. Many films of the time were produced both in the regional language (Bengali, Marathi), and in Hindi, so that they could be oriented to the larger Hindi-speaking market. The Indian public quite naturally preferred to see films made in their own language and the more songs they had the better. In those days, the films made had upto 40 songs. This song tradition still persists in Indian commercial cinema.

The 1930s and 1940s

While addressing social differences of caste, class and the relations between the sexes, the "social" films of the 1930s adopted a modernist outlook in an essentially converging of society. Many directors of the time showed great innovation. The Marathi director, V. Shantaram, for example, was alert to world trends in film-making, deploying expressionist effects intelligently in such works as *Amrit Manthan* (Prabhat Talkies; 1934).

In what was probably the most important film of the period, *Devdas* (1935), the director Pramathesh Barua created a startlingly edited climax to a tale of love frustrated by social distinction and masculine ineffectuality. Released in Bengali, Hindi and Tamil, *Devdas* created an oddly ambivalent hero for this period (and again, through a Hindi remake directed by Bimal Roy in 1955), predicated on indecision, frustration and a focus on failure and longing rather than on achievement.

By the 1940s the social film further delimited its focus by excluding particularly fraught issues, especially of caste division. A representative example, prefiguring the kind of entertainment extravaganza that has become the hallmark of the Bombay film, was *Kismet/Fate* (Gyan Mukerji; Bombay Talkies, 1943), which broke all box-office records and ran for more than two years. Family and class become the key issues in the representation of society, and the story's location is an indeterminate urban one.

Although this became the model for popular cinema, especially after the decline of regional industries in Maharashtra and Bengal by the end of the 1940s, different strains are observable in the Tamil films of the same period. In the 1930s, the Tamil cinema gained national recognition with the costume extravaganza, *Chandralekha*, directed by S.S. Vasan for Gemini studios, and called by its director a "pageant for our peasants" (a large section of the audience would have been illiterate). Its story, of the conflict for the inheritance of an empire, is laden with overblown set-pieces and crowds of extras. Even more significant than this investment in the spectacular was its "Tamil-ness", the recognition of a national existence different to that portrayed in the Bombay output.

The 1950s

By the start of the 1950s, Calcutta (now Kolkata) became the vanguard of the art cinema, with the emergence of the film society movement at the end of the 1940s and Satyajit Ray's *Pather Panchali/Song of the Road*, produced with West Bengal state government support in 1955. Post-independence, despite a relatively sympathetic government enquiry in 1951, the industry became the object of considerable moral scrutiny and criticism, and was subject to severe taxation. A covert consensus emerged between proponents of art cinema and the state, all focussing on the imperative to create a "better" cinema. The Film and Television Institute of India was established at Pune in 1959 to develop technical skills for an industry seen to be lacking in this field. However, active support for parallel cinema, as it came to be called, only really took off at the end of the 1960s, under the aegis of the government's Film Finance Corporation, set up in 1961 to support new film-makers.

Ironically, this pressure and vocal criticism occurred at a time when arguably some of the most interesting work in popular cinema was being produced. Radical cultural organizations, loosely associated with the Indian Communist Party, had organized themselves as the All India Progressive Writers Association and the Indian People's Theatre Association (IPTA). The latter had produced *Dharti ke Lal/Sons of the Soil* (KA Abbas; 1943), and its impact on the industry can be seen in the work of radical writers such as Abbas, lyricists such as Sahir Ludhianvi, and directors such as Bimal Roy and Zia Sarhady.

In addition, directors such as Raj Kapoor, Guru Dutt and Mehboob Khan, while not directly involved with IPTA, created films that reflected a passionate concern for questions of social justice. Largely studio-based, the films of this era nevertheless incorporated vivid stylistic experimentation, influenced by international currents in film-making. Such effects are evident in *Awara/The Vagabond* (Raj Kapoor, 1951, script by K.A. Abbas), *Awaaz/The Call* (Zia Sarhady; 1956) and *Pyaasa/Craving* (Guru Dutt; 1957).

The First International Film Festival, held in Mumbai in 1951, showed Italian works for the first time in India. The influence of Neorealism can be seen in films such as *Do Bigha Zamin/Two Measures of Land* (Bimal Roy, 1953), a portrait of father and son eking out a living in Kolkata that strongly echoes the narrative of Vittorio de Sica's *Bicycle Thief* (1948). Mehboob Khan's *Andaz/Style* (1949), an upperclass love triangle founded on a tragic misunderstanding, draws on codes of psychological representation—hallucinations and dreams that feature strongly in 1940s Hollywood melodrama. Mehboob's tendency to make a visual spectacle of his material, and his involvement with populist themes and issues make him a good example of popular cinema of the time.

The Art Cinema

India's emergent art cinema, led by the Bengali directors Satyajit Ray, Mrinal Sen and Ritwik Ghatak reacted against such spectacle. Satyajit Ray's world-famous debut, *Pather Panchali* (1955), is based on many of the themes that engaged contemporary popular film-makers of the time, such as loss of social status, economic injustice, uprootment, but sets them within a naturalistic, realist frame which put a special value on the Bengali countryside, locating it as a place of nostalgia, to which the urban and individualist sensibility of its protagonist, Apu, looked with longing.

In Ray's later work on urban middle-class existence, *Mahanagar/Big City* (1963), *Charulata* (1964), *Seemabadha/Company Limited* (1971), *Pratidwandi/The Protagonist* (1970), and *Jana Aranya/The Middleman* (1975), his rational, humanist vision is at the same time at home in the city, and repulsed by it; overarching estrangement is relayed through images of futile job interviews, cynical corporate schemes, murky deals in respectable cafes. Wedded to the traditions of the nineteenth-century intelligentsia, he finds society wanting, vilifies it for its ignorance and corruption, and oversees the malignant terrain below with a lofty disdain. Ray's women, such as the mother, Sarbojaya of Pather Panchali, the tomboy Aparna Sen of *Samapti/The End* (1961), Madhabi Mukherjee in *Charulata* and *Mahanagar*, and Kaberi Bose in *Aranyer din Ratri*, are splendidly drawn portraits in the realist tradition.

In contrast to Ray, his contemporaries Mrinal Sen and Ritwik Ghatak set out to expose the dark underside of India's lower middle-class and unemployed. Sen, after a phase of uneven, didactic political cinema at the height of the Maoist-inspired Naxalite movement of the early 1970s—marked by the trilogy *Interview* (1971), *Calcutta 71* (1972) and *Padatik/The Guerrilla Fighter* (1973)—made two films, *Akaler Sandhane/Search of Famine* (1980) and *Khandar/Ruins* (1983), about film-making itself, exploring its inherent distance and disengagement, and the problems entailed in trying to record "reality."

Perhaps the most outstanding figure of this generation, fulfilling the potential of the radical cultural initiatives of the IPTA, was the great Ritwik Ghatak. Disruption, the problems of locating oneself in a new environment, and the indignities and oppression of common people are the recurrent themes of this poet of Partition, who lamented the division of Bengal in 1947. Disharmony and discontinuity could be said to be the hallmark of *Nagarik/Citizen* (1952) and *Meghe Dhaka Tara/Cloud-capped Star* (1960), where studio sets of street corners mingle uneasily with live-action shots of Kolkata. There is something deliberately jarring about the rhythms of editing, the use of sound, and the compositions, as if the director refuses to allow us to settle into a comfortable, familiar frame of viewing. In *Aajantrik/Man and Machine* (1958) and *Subarnarekha* (1952, released 1965) he juxtaposes the displaced and transient urban figure with tribal peoples; placing the human figure at the edge of the frame, dwarfed by majestic nature.

The Indian Popular Cinema and the Superstars

During the 1960s, popular cinema had shifted its social concerns towards more romantic genres, showcasing such new stars as Shammi Kapoor—a kind of Indian Elvis—and later, Rajesh Khanna, a soft, romantic hero. The period is also notable for a more assertive Indian nationalism. Following the Indo-Pakistan wars of 1962 and 1965, the Indian officer came to be a rallying point for the national imagination in films such as *Sangam/Meeting of Hearts* (Raj Kapoor, 1964) and *Aradhana/Adoration* (Shakti Samanta; 1969).

However, the political and economic upheaval of the following decade saw a return to social questions across the board, in both the art and popular cinemas. The accepted turning point in the popular film was the angry, violent *Zanjeer/The Chain* (Prakash Mehra; 1973), which fed into the anxieties and frustrations generated by the quickening but lopsided pace of industrialization and urbanization. Establishing Amitabh Bachchan as the biggest star of the next decade, its policeman hero is ousted from service through a conspiracy, and takes the law into his own hands to render justice and to avenge his deceased parents.

The considerable political turmoil of the next few years, including the railway strike of 1974 and the *Nav Nirman* movement led by J.P. Narayan in Bihar and Gujarat, ultimately led to the declaration of Indira Gandhi's Emergency in 1975. It was as if the state and the people had split apart. As the cities grew, so did the audiences. The popular cinema generated an ambiguous figure to express this alienation. At the level of images, there was a greater investment in the stresses of everyday life and, unlike the 1950s, in location shooting. In *Zanjeer*, the casual killing of a witness on Bombay's commuter trains conjures up the perils of life in the metropolis. This is echoed in images of the dockyard, taxi-rank, railtrack and construction site in *Deewar/The Wall* (Yash Chopra; 1975), also starring Amitabh Bachchan.

The recurrent narrative of these films, of protagonists uprooted from small town and rural families to the perils of the city, is shared by the street children researched by professional sociologists in Mira Nair's *Salaam Bombay* (1988). The Bombay films very excesses, their grand gestures, and the priority given to emotion and excitement may more truly reflect the dominant rhythms of urban life in India. At the level of plot and character, however, the Bombay films simultaneously simplify and collapse our sense of India, reducing the enormous variety of identity—social, regional, ethnic and religious—that makes up Indian society. Where these identities appear, they do so as caricatures and objects of fun.

The Art Cinema of the 1980s

To counter this, the art cinema of the 1980s diversified from its Bengali moorings of the earlier period under the aegis of the Film Finance Corporation. Works by Shyam Benegal, Gautam Ghose, Saeed Mirza, B.V. Karanth, Girish Kasaravalli, Mrinal Sen, M.S. Sathyu, Satyajit Ray, and Kundan Shah, among others, actively addressed questions of social injustice: problems of landlord exploitation, bonded labour, untouchability, urban power, corruption and criminal extortion, the oppression of women, and political manipulation. Ghatak in particular had addressed many of these issues earlier, but never had there been such an outpouring of the social conscience, nor such a flowing of new images—of regional landscapes, cultures, and social structures. Many of the films may seem didactic and uncomplex, undercutting the attention to form that had marked the earlier period—but not all. Benegal's first two films indicate an unusual concern with the psychology of domination and subordination. *Ankur/The Seedling* (1974), starring Shabana Azmi, is particularly striking not only for this but also for the open, fluid way it captures the countryside.

Among Kannada directors, working in south India, Kasaravalli in *Ghattashradha* (1981) effected an intimate vision of the oppression of widows through the view of a child. And special mention must be made of Kundan Shah's *Jaane Bhi Do Yaaron/Let Sleeping Dogs Lie* (1984), a wonderful exercise in farce and slapstick that is also a brilliant portrait of Mumbai.

The South

The most notable of the directors who speak specifically about their own cultures, and about the possibilities of change, are Adoor Gopalakrishnan and Aravindan from Kerala. A key to their productivity was the overall development of film culture in Kerala, India's most literate state. In his films Gopalakrishnan transformed the lush countryside, busy towns and animated culture of Kerala into a strange, dissociated place, fraught with communicative gaps, menacing, inexplicable characters, and an overall sense of the impenetrable. Subjects range from the mounting tragedies that beset a young couple in the city (*Swayamvaram/One's Own Choice*; 1972), and the effete authoritarianism of a declining feudal landlord (*Elippathayam/The Rat-Trap*; 1984), to the mysterious spiritual decline of a popular communist activist (*Mukha Mukham/Face to Face*; 1987).

The late Aravindan, sometime cartoonist and employee of the Kerala Rubber Board, had something of the mystic in him, but went through a range of styles, including a *cinemaverite* approach, as in *Thampu/The Circus Tent* (1978), in which circus performers speak direct to the camera. His episode from the Ramayana, *Kanchana Sita/Golden Sita*, places the action against the grain of the high Hindu tradition by situating it among tribes in the verdant landscape of the Kerala forests. At his best, his narrative style refuses a didactic approach, generating a whimsical sense of how destinies are shaped.

Contemporary Indian Cinema

In the 1990s, video, national and satellite/cable television have resulted in the development of a prolonged crisis in India's movie industry, where commercial and art films are equally at risk of failing at the box office. The problems of the latter are mainly due to a persistent failure to find distribution outlets. Now, more and more film-makers of both streams look to television. The state film finance unit (now named the National Film Development Corporation) has a major stake in the expansion of the national network.

There have been two responses to this crisis. The first, at the economic level, has been to try and curb film piracy, and to systematize the relationship of film to video. The second is an investment in new technology, and in new forms of story-telling. The Telugu and Tamil industries, and directors such as Ram Gopal Varma and Mani Ratnam, are at the forefront of such moves, showing a lively interest in new techniques in American cinema. Varma's *Shiva* (1990) and *Raat/Night* (1991) showcase the use of steadicam—in the latter, to the exclusion of any serious narrative. The technical virtuosity of Mani Ratnam's works as well as their elegant story-telling and restrained performances have attracted a following among film buffs across the country, who identify with his style and, implicitly, with the image of a dynamic, modern identity. In 1993, Ratnam made an important breakthrough with *Roja*, a love story about a young Tamil peasant woman and her husband, a cryptographer who decodes messages for military intelligence. The couple are transported to Kashmir, which is subject to sustained separatist extremism. Embroiling the Tamil couple in a national issue that might have seemed remote to an earlier generation, the film identified a new pan-Indian field of interest. Dubbed into Hindi, it was a national success, giving rise to the dubbing of a number of southern films.

A Brief History of Bollywood: An Industry Viewpoint

At the turn of this century, when the country was poised for major social and political reforms, a new entertainment form dawned in India—the Cinema. The first exposure to motion pictures which India received was in 1896, when the Lumiere Brothers' Cinematography unveiled six soundless short films at Watson Hotel, Esplanade Mansion, Bombay on July 7. And the first exposing of celluloid in camera by an Indian and its consequent screening took place in 1899, when Harishchandra Bhatvadekar (Save Dada) shot two short films and exhibited them under

Edison's projecting kinetoscope. Hiralal Sen and F.B. Thanawalla were two other Indian pioneers engaged in the production of short films in Calcutta and Bombay in 1900. Around 1902, J.F. Madan and Abdullah Esoofally launched their career with Bioscope shows of imported short films. In 1912, N.G. Chitre and R.G. Torney made a silent feature film Pundalik which was released on May 18, and it was half British in its make. Dhundiraj Govind Phalke, more generally known as Dada Saheb Phalke was responsible for the production of India's first fully indigenous silent feature film Raja Harishchandra which heralded the birth of the Indian film industry. The film had titles in Hindi and English and was released on May 3, 1913 at the Coronation Cinema, Bombay. In 1917, Bengal saw the birth of its first feature film-Satyabadi Raja Harishchandra made by Madan's Elphinstone Bioscope Company. In Madras, the first feature film of South India Keechaka Vadham was made by Nataraja Mudaliar in 1919. After stepping into 1920, the Indian cinema gradually assumed the shape of a regular industry. The industry also came within the purview of the law. The new decade saw the arrival of many new companies and film makers. Dhiren Ganguly (England Returned), Baburao Painter (Savkari Pash), Suchet Singh (Sakuntala), Chandulal Shah (Guna Sundari), Ardershir Israni, and V. Santharam were the prominent film makers of the twenties.

The most remarkable things about the birth of the sound film in India is that it came with a bang and quickly displaced the silent movies. The first Indian talkie Alam Ara produced by the Imperial film company and directed by Ardershir Irani was released on March 14, 1931 at the Majestic Cinema in Bombay; The talkie had brought revolutionary changes in the whole set up of the industry. The year 1931 marked the beginning of the talking ear in Bengal and South India. The first talkie films in Bengali (Jumai Shasthi), Telugu (Bhakta Prahlad) and Tamil (Kalidass) were released in the same year. The thirties is recognised as the decade of social protests in the history of Indian Cinema. Three big banners—Prabhat, Bombay Talkies and New Theatres gave the lead in making serious but gripping sand entertaining films for all classes of the wide audience. A number of films making a strong plea against social injustice were also made in this period like V. Santharam's Duniya Na Mane, Aadmi and Padosi, Franz Osten's Achut Kanya, Damle and Fatehlal's Sant Thukaram, Mehboob's

Watan, Ek hi Raasta and Aurat. For the first time Ardeshir Irani attempted a colour picture in 1937 with Kisan Kanya. The decade also witnessed the release of the first talkie films in Marathi (Ayodhiyecha Raja 1932), Gujarathi (Narasinh Mehta-32), Kannada (Dhurvkumar-34); Oriya (Sita Bibaha-34); Assamese (Joymati-35); Punjabi (Sheila-35) and Malayalam (Balan-38). The decade during which the second world was fought and Indian independence won, was a momentous one for cinematography all over India. Some memorable films were produced during the forties such as Shantharam's Dr. Kotnis Ki Amar Kahani, Mehboob's Roti, Chetan Anand's Neecha Nagar, Uday Shanker's Kalpana, Abbas's Dharti Ke Lal, Sohrab Modi's Sikander, Pukar and Prithvi Vallabh, J.B.H. Wadia's Court Dancer, S.S. Vasan's Chandralekha, Vijay Bhatt's Bharat Milap and Ram Rajya, Rajkapoor's Barsaat and Aag.

The first International Film Festival of India held in early 1952 at Bombay had great impact of Indian Cinema. The big turning point camp in 1955 with the arrival of Satyajit Ray and his classic Pather Panchali which opened up a new path leading the Indian film to the World Film Scene. International recognition came to it with the Cannes award for best human document followed by an unprecedented crop of foreign and national awards. In Hindi Cinema too, the impact of neorealism was evident in some distinguished films like Bimal Roy's Do Bigha Zamin, Devadas and Madhumati, Rajkapoor's Boot Polish, Shri-420 and Jagte Raho, V. Shantharam's Do Aankhen Barah Haath and Jhanak Jhanak Payal Baaje, Mehbood's Mother India. Gurudutt's Pyaasa, and Kagaz Ke Phool and B.R. Chopra's Kanoon; The first Indo-Soviet co-production Pardesi by K.A. Abbas was also made during the fifties. The transition to colour and the consequent preference for escapist entertainment and greater reliance on stars brought about a complete change in the film industry. The sixties was a decade of mediocre films made mostly to please the distributors and to some extent, meet the demands of the box office. The sixties began with a bang with the release of K. Asif's Mughal-E-Azam which set a record at the box-office. It was followed by notable productions which include romantic musical and melodramas of a better quality. Rajkapoor's Jis Desh Mein Ganga Behti Hai, Sangam, Dilip Kumar's Gunga Jamna, Gurudutt's Sahib Bibi Aur Gulam, Dev Anand's Guide; Bimal Roy's Bandini, S. Mukherji's Junglee, Sunil Dutt's Mujhe Jeene Do and the experimental

Yaadein, Basu Bhatacharya's Teesri Kasam, Pramod Chakravorthy's Love in Tokyo, Ramanand Sagar's Arzoo, Sakhti Samantha's Aradhana, Hrishikesh Mukherji's Aashirwad and Anand, B.R. Chopra's Waqt, Manoj Kumar's Upkar, and Prasad Productions Milan were the significant Hindi films of the decade. Among the regional languages, Malayalam cinema derived much of its strength from literature during the sixties. Malayalam cinema hit the head lines for the first time when Ramu Kariat's Chemmeen (1965) won the President's Gold Medal. Towards the end of the decade, Mrinal Sen's Bhuvan Shome, signalled the beginnings of the new wave in Indian Cinema.

The New Indian Cinema emerged as a reaction to the popular cinema's Other Worldliness. It is a cinema of social significance and artistic sincerity, presenting a modern, humanist perspective more durable than the fantasy world of the popular cinema. Satyajit Ray, Ritwik Ghatak and Mrinal Sen were the founding fathers of the new cinema in India. Acclaimed as India's foremost director Satyajit Ray has made 30 feature films and five documentaries, tacking a wide range of rural, urban historical themes. His cinematography places him away form the inheritors of the neorealist school, and yet his films are infused with an unusual humaneness. Pather Panchali, Apur Sansar, Charulata, Jalsaghar, Goopy Gyne Bagha Byne, Seemabadha, Jana Aranya, Ashani Sanket and Agantuk are some of his outstanding films. He was fortunate enough to present his films in almost all the leading films festivals of the world. The national and international awards won by Ray are numerous. Ritwik Ghatak swooped on the Indian scene with new dynamism. His films constitute a record of the traumas of change form the desperation of the rootless and deprived refugees from East Bengal.(Meghe Dhaka Tara, Ajantrik, Komal Ghandhar, Subarnarekha). Mrinal Sen is the ebullient one-experimenting with neorealism as well as new wave and fantasy. His notable films are Bhuvan Shome, Chorus, Mrigaya, Ek Din Pratidin, Akaler Sandhane, Kharij and Khandahar. He has also won several national an international awards. In Bombay, a new group of film makers emerged on the Hindi cinema. Notable amongst them are Basu Chatterji (Sara Akash), Rajinder Singh Bedi (Dastak), Mani Kaul (Uski Roti, Duvidha), Kumar Shahani (Maya Darpan), Avtar Kaul (27-Down), Basu Bhattacharya (Anubhav), M.S. Sathyu (Garam Hawa), Shyam Benegal (Ankur), and

Kanthilal Rathod (Kanku). In Calcutta, following the trend set by Ray, Ghatak and Sen, Tapan Sinha and Tarun Majumdar also made some note worthy films. (Kabuliwala, Hatey Bazarey, Harmonium, Safed Haathi; Balika Bodhu, Nimantran, Ganadevta, Dadar Kirti).

The seventies has further-widened the gap between multistar big budgeted off beat films. The popular Hindi hits of the decade include Kamal Amrohis Pakeeza, Rajkapoor's Bobby, Devar's Haathi Mere Saathi, Ramesh Sippy's Sholay, Zanjeer, Deewar, Khoon Pasina, Yaadon Ki Baarat, Kabhi Kabhi, Dharamveer, Amar Akbar Anthony, Hum Kisise Kum Nahin, and Muqaddar ka Sikandar. Of these majority of the films were action oriented with revenge as the dominating theme. Down in the South, the new wave cinema originated in Karnataka and Kerala. Pattabhi Rama Reddy's Damskara (70) and Adoor Gopalakrishnan's Swayamvaram (72) were the trend setters in Kannada and Malayalam respectively. This continued with a series of socially conspicuous films like M.T. Vasidevan Nair's Nirmalyam, B.V. Karanth's Chomana Dudi, Girish Karnad's Kaadu, Girish Kasara Valli's Ghatasradha, G. Aravindan's Uttarayanam and Thamp, K. Balachander's Arangetram, Avargal and Apoorva Ragangal, Adoor's Kodyettam, K.G. George's Swapnadanam and P.A. Backer's Chuvanna Vithukal and G.V. Iyer's Hamsageethe. The Hindi avante garde or new wave seems to have reached its bloom period towards the end of the seventies with the coming of film makers like Govind Nihalani (Aakrosh), Saeed Mirza (Albert Pinto Ko Gussa Kyon Aata Hai, Aravind Desai ki Ajeeb Daastan), Rabindra Dharmaraj (Chakra), Sai Paranjpe (Sparsh), Muzafar Ali (Gaman) and Biplab Roy Chowdhari (Shodh). The movement spread to the other regional cinemas such as Marathi, Gujarathi, Assamese, Oriya and Telugu. Directors like Jabbar Patel (Samna, Simhasan), Ramdas Phuttane (Sarvasakshi), Ketan Mehta (Bhavni Bhavai). Babendranath Saikia (Sandhya Rag), Jahanu Barua (Aparoopa, Papori), Manmohan Mohapatra (Klanta Aparanha, Majhi Pahacha), Nirad Mohapatra (Maya Miriga) and Gautam Ghose (Ma Bhoomi) came to the scene with their films. Also from the South came film makers such as Jayakantan, John Abraham, Bharathan, Padmarajan, Balu Mahendra, Bharathi Raja, T.S. Ranga, T.S. Nagabharana, K.R. Mohanan, G.S. Panicker, Chandrasekhar Kambar, P. Lankesh, C. Radhakrishnan and Bhagyaraj who presented significant films like Unnai Pol Oruvan, Agraharathil

Kazhuthai, Prayanam, Peruvazhiambalam and Oridathsoru Phayalvan, Kokila, 16 Vayathinile and Kizhakke Pokum Rail, Geejegand Goodu, Grahana, Aswathama, Ekakini, Kaadu Kudre, Pallavi, Agni, Suvar Illatha Chithrangal and Mundani Mudichu.

The new cinema movement continued with full spirit in. the next decade (eighties) also. Shyam Benegal presented some good movies like Manthan, Bhumika, Nishant, Janoon, and Trikal. Nihlani's Aaghat and Tamas were remarkable works. Other important films with new style of treatment include Damul (Prakash Jha), 36-Chowringhee Lane (Aparna Sen), New Delhi Times (Ramesh Sharma), Mirch Masala (Ketan Mehta), Rao Saheb (Vijaya Mehta), Debshishu (Utpalendu Chakraborthy), Massey Saheb (Pradeep Kishna), Trishagni (Nabayendu Ghosh), Ijaazat (Gulzar), Umrao Jaan (Muzafar Ali), Dakhal, Paar (Gautam Ghose), Dooratwa, Neem Annapurana, Andhi Gali (Buddhadeb Dasgupta), Aajka Robin Hood (Tapan Sinha), Tabarana Kathe, Bannada Vesha (Girish Kasara Valli), Accident and Swamy (Shanker Naag), Daasi (B. Narasinga Rao) and Phaniyamma (Prema Karanth). The new wave masters of Kerala, Adoor and Arvindan, consolidated their position in the eighties with their films Elippathayam, Mukha Mukham, Anantharam, Esthappan, Pokkuveyil, Chidambaram, and Oridath, Elippathayam has won the prestigious British film Institute award for 1982. Shaji N. Karun's maiden film Piravi (1988) bagged several national and international awards and was shown in nearly forty film festivals. Meera Nair, the young woman director, won the Golden Camera award at Cannes for her first film Salaam Bombay in 1989. In 1990, Adoor Gopalakrishnan's Mathilukal won the FIPRESCI and UNICEF awards. The late eighties and early nineties saw the revival of the musical love stories in Hindi cinema. Mr. India, Tezaab, Qayamat se Qayamat Tak, Main Pyar Kiya, Chandni, Tridev, Hum, Ghayal, Saudagar, Rakhwala, Jo Jeeta Wohi Sikander, Hum Hain Rahi Pyarke, Baazigar, Aaina, Yeh Dillagi, Hum Apake Hai Kaun, Krantiveer, Raja and Rangeela were some of the popular Hindi films of the last decade. The first half of nineties witnessed the release of some better films in Hindi as well as in other regional languages. Drishti and Drohkal (Nihalani), Lekin (Gulzar), Disha (Sai Paranjpe), Prahar (Nana Patekar), Parinda (Vinod Chopra), Diskha (Arun Kaul), Kasba (Kumar Shahani), Rudaali (Kalpana Lajmi), Maya Memsaab (Ketan Mehta), Mujhse Dosti Karoge (Gopi

Desai), Suraj Ka Satwan Ghoda and Mammo (Benegal), Who Chokri (Subhankar Ghosh) and Ek Doctor Ki Maut (Tapan Sinha), were some of the notable Hindi films from Bengal, Orissa, Assam and Manipur came films like Tahader Katha, Bagh Bahadur, Charachar (Buddhadeb Dasgupta), Uttoran (Sandip Ray), Wheel Chair (Tapan Sinha), Unishe April (Rituparno Ghosh), Adi Mimansa, Lalvanya Preethi (A.K. Bir), Nirbachana (Biplab Roy Chowdhari), Halodhia Choraya Baodhan Khai, Firingoti (Jahau Barua), Haladhar (Sanjeev Hazarika), and Ishanou (Aribam Shayam Sharma). In the South Malayalam Cinema presented some notable films. They include Vasthuhara (Aravindan), Vidheyan (Adoor) Kireedom, Bharatham (Siby Mmalayil), Amaram (Bharathan) Innale (Padmarajan), Oru Vadakkan Veeragatha, Sargam, Parinayam (Hariharan), Devasuram (I.V. Sasi). Kilukkam, Thenmavin Kombath (Priyadarsan), Perumthachan (Ajayan), Daivathinte Vikurthikal (Lenin Rajendran), (Sivan), Manichithrathazu (Fazil), Ponthanmada (T.V. Chandran) and Swaham (Shaji), From Tamil and Telugu cinema, there came few films like Anjali, Roja and Bombay (Mani Ratnam), Marupakkam and Nammavar (Sethsumadhavan), Karuthamma (Bharathi Raja), Surigadu (Dasari Narayana Rao), Swathi Kiranam (K. Viswanath), Mogha Mul (G. Rajasekharan) etc. English film like Miss Beatty's Children (Pamela Rooks), and English August (Dev Benegal) were also produced during this period. All in all, it has been a long story of nearly nine decades, with the early shaky screen images turning into a multi pronged and multi winged empire of its own, that has yielded about 27,000 feature films and thousands of documented short films. Cinema has raised India's flag high in the world as the consistently largest film producer. But when it comes to quality the flag has to fly half mast. All the above information is courtesy of: All India.

A RETROSPECTIVE OF INDIAN FILM INDUSTRY

At this stage it is worth mentioning yet another incredible Indian institution: the Indian film industry. Rumi's stereotypical image of western women had come mainly from American movies, which seem all the more lewd and free-lovin' because Indian most movies do not even show kissing, let alone nudity. But what Indian flicks lose in censorship, they more than make up for in sheer exuberance.

Mumbai is the official centre of Indian film, so much so that the films are known as 'Bollywood' movies (which is unlikely to change to 'Mollywood' with Bombay's name change to Mumbai). Bollywood churns out twice as many films every year as Hollywood, and where the average Hollywood blockbuster clocks in at about 90 minutes, Bollywood epics run to an exhausting average of two-and-a-half hours. Each movie has at least five sing-along dance routines, and every type of film genre—action, romance, thriller, crime and musical—is packed into the celluloid equivalent of bubble and squeak.

To a westerner the films can appear a little amateurish, but the figures point to an industry that is far from unsuccessful. Bollywood blockbusters, of which there are more than 800 produced every year, have million-dollar budgets, produce over 100 million ticket sales every week, have huge advertising campaigns (the posters mount up on walls and telegraph poles, only to be nibbled off by passing goats and cows) and have made a lot of Mumbai residents very rich indeed.

The actors, once in the big time, are made for life. The men are mostachioed podges who all look identical, and the women are rotund and coyly flirtatious: this excess of weight denotes prosperity in much the same way it does in Polynesia. Once an actor or actress makes it, he or she will end up acting in loads of films, all at the same time: stories of actors working on over 100 films simultaneously are not uncommon, because it is actors that sell films. Directors also spread their talents thinly: one successful director was so overbooked he directed his movies by phone. And if an actor or actress becomes well known for a certain 'device', they tend to use that device in every film they star in; thus, if Ursula Andress was an Indian film star, they would find an opportunity for her to slink out of the sea in a black bikini and knife belt in every one of her movies.

The plots can also feel rather unsophisticated, at least as far as the western film critic goes. To the untrained eye (and ear) Bollywood films are formulaic, to say the least. There is a handsome hero and a beautiful heroine, normally from different classes, as well as an evil seductress and a villain. The hero has a friend, who falls in love with the seductress and manages to change her ways, and in the end good always conquers evil. Mixed into this less-than-thrilling piece of screenwriting are the sing-along pieces, which spring up with a spontaneity and inappropriateness that even *Fame* has trouble beating. The action scenes are never far away—fights break out so quickly you are left wondering what sparked them off—and involve plenty of martial manoeuvres and overdubbed grunts and groans. The romantic scenes are renowned for their lack of content rather than their promiscuity: one film I heard about had two lovers embracing, about to go for a kiss, and just as the dirty deed was to be shown the scene cut to romantic orchestral overtures and a picture of the Eiffel Tower thrusting manfully into the sky. With Bollywood, you sometimes just have to use your imagination.

But it is easy to understand the reason for such repetitiveness in theme and presentation. The audience in India must be one of the most varied and diverse cross-sections of mankind ever to go to the movies, so to get big ticket sales, you have to appeal to everyone. So there is no sex, which would offend the more pious pundits; no heavy historical or mythological themes, which would annoy the revisionists; no specifically regional films, which would restrict the audience on geographical terms (films about the Mughals would not be popular in the deep south, since the Mughals never reached there); films about the western world would only appeal to educated people, and they do not make up the masses; yes, the common denominator is sing-along action romance, and it is everywhere. There are some arty films that are successful abroad, but as they normally concentrate on poverty and real life, Indians do not want to watch them: they want escapism at the flicks, just like the rest of us.

And, truth be told, Bollywood reflects the country itself. Colourful, noisy, brash, romantic, coy but seductive, festive and larger than life, watching an Indian movie is the next best thing to being here. It is *poor* second, though...

R.K. FILMS AND MEDIA ACADEMY (RKFMA): A CASE STUDY

R.K. Films and Media Academy, after its launch with a bang, has trained a number of enthusiastic and creative youngsters dedicated to their goals of making their career in the field of acting, modelling, mime, singing, dancing and film technologies, for e.g., film editing, photography, character dubbing, sound recording, film make-up, compering, mass communication, media journalism, etc.

RKFMA has on its roll, number of such mind blowing performers who are being enlisted in our Star Search Section their art with photograph.

RKFMA also posses its own in-house studios which are also available for commercial use and on hiring basis. To list few, the facilities available includes:

- Photography Studios with latest gadgets and canvas
- Video Editing Lab with advanced Editing Suites and Beta Machines
- Sound and Audio Recording Studio with Dubbing facilities
- Make-up Studio
- In-House Shooting Floor

RKFMA has also tied-up with renowned film production houses of Mumbai and New Delhi who have to their credit the production of number of feature films, T.V. shows, Documentaries and Ad-Films, etc.

RKFMA is a better option and choice amongst the Film Producers, Ad Films Makers, Event Management Companies, Corporate Fashion Shows Organizers, Hotel and Hospitality Stage Managers and many others who are associated with the show business as they are able to locate many facilities under one brand:

1. *Artists*: A good collection of talented faces with profile for modelling, acting, singing, dancing, choreography, compering, photographers, editors, etc.

2. *Training* in film acting, modelling, non-linear video editing with Vfx, professional photography, mass communication and journalism, sound recording and with Sfx, TV and Stage shows anchoring.

3. *Film & T.V. Serial Production Facilities*: Production management relating to films, documentaries, advertisements, event promotion, etc. by providing artists, video editing and sound recording with dubbing facilities, animations, make-up artists, camera and lighting technicians, etc.

4. *Event Management*: Managing and arranging star nights, musical shows, fashion shows, theme parties, talent competitions, theatre and dramas and other events.

5. *Production of Ad-Films*: Corporate movies, music albums, jingles, audios, videos, film advertisements, etc.

6. *Film Studios and Equpiment on-Hire*: The professionally designed and developed film studios with all modern equipment and softwares are made available at very competitve charges which can be done either on hourly or on project-wise studios includes Sound Recording, Video Editing, Photography, Make-up/Green Room and In-campus Shooting floor.

SHOOT RAJASTHAN: A CASE STUDY

Shoot Rajasthan welcomes you. We are one of the leading teams of professionals excelling in executing and handling Film Shooting and Film Crews, for the last Ten Years, in India and South Asia. We are handling the shoot of Feature Films, Commercials, Promos, Documentaries, Still Shoot, Serial, Songs, Event Management in Rajasthan, India.

Complete film shooting solutions, that is we offer. Shoot Rajasthan have complete infrastructure for smooth production. It is a production service company having team of professionals, which organize everything from selecting of the best locations including completion of all kind of formalities like taking necessary permission from Government bodies so as to complete the task smoothly.

Shoot Rajasthan is well known name in Film and Ad world. We have built our reputation for reliability, quality services and the fact that we have never gone over budget and time limit in the projects we have completed.

Company Profile

We have been associated with various prestigious International and Indian organizations. We have been facilitating them in the entire shooting process. Our core competency is working in different parts of India. We are based in Jaipur and have been shooting in various other Indian states like Punjab, Haryana, Uttar Pradesh, Uttaranchal, Rajasthan, Gujarat, Madhya Pradesh, Maharashtra and West Bengal.

The location scouting, location permissions and fixing, logistics, assigning crew, coordination on shoot and other logistic activities are our forte. We can handle Features Films/ Commercials/Documentaries Films/Still Shoots/Promos/Serials/

Songs Picturization/Events Management in Rajasthan and other parts of India.

We could look for a location depending on your script and story board. We can e-mail you some of the photographs to give you a right idea of the location. Depending on mountain, forts, Palaces, or deserts any requirement of yours, could be taken care of.

As per ones requirement we can arrange permissions from the Ministry of Information and Broadcasting, Ministry of External Affairs, Ministry of Home and any other government authority wherever required for shooting (Railways, Civil Aviation, Archeological Survey of India etc.). All private permission could also be obtained.

We can negotiate with hotels, transporters, arrange for custom clearance for equipment to get the shoot planed and arrange on a daily basis. And thereafter do the post production as per your requirement.

Work Profile

- Location scouting and location racy.
- Heading the production and Technical department.
- Preparing of budget for the all in-house programme.
- Planning of the technical configuration of the broadcast equipment for the studio set-up.
- Roistering of the technical crew and assigning there duties.
- Managing the logistic of the shooting equipment.
- Preparing MIS for the utilization of the equipment and technical manpower.
- Co-ordination of the vehicles.
- Facilitating the shooting crew.
- Arranging for the freelancer technical crew if required.
- Finalization of the rate and the payment terms.
- Arranging for the technical crew and equipment.
- Controlling of production during the shoot.
- Arranging for the broadcast equipment.
- Arranging for the technical crew and assigning there duties.

Our Services

We provide complete infrastructural support for foreign and Indian film producers along with the following services:

Location Scouting

- Location best suited to your script and storyboard.
- E-mail you the photographs of the location that give you a right idea.

Permission/Visa

- From the ministry of information and broadcasting.
- From the ministry of external affairs, ministry of home and other local government authority.
- From railways, civil aviation, and archeological survey of India etc.
- All private permission is also arranged.
- And also visa clearance.
- Customs clearance of equipment (import and re-export)
- Work visas clearance for the entire crew.

Budget

- The costing of total project professional.
- We are proud of our reliability and the fact that we have never gone over budget in the past.

Hiring of Crew and Technical People

- We can provide experienced crew.
- Technical people who have been worked with foreign crew earlier.

Casting

- Proper casting for your project.
- Only experienced casting Directors.

Hotel and Transportation

- Air ticketing domestic and international
- Negotiate with hotels
- Transporter

Catering

- All kind of Multi-cuisine A, B, C catering in budget

Security/Police Protection/Insurance

- We mainly concern about crew safety.
- We can provide security and insurance for equipments, main talent-cast, crew set.
- Insurance of cast and crew and set.

Setting up Production Office

- Stock
- Art, property (prop) and set
- Legal assistance
- Information about weather department
- Processing and editing facilities
- Translators
- Post-production service
- Any thing, which meet your project's requirement.

CINEMA IN REGIONAL LANGUAGES IN INDIA

Marathi Cinema

Marathi cinema is one of the oldest in regional Indian films industry. The first Marathi talkie film "Ayodhyecha Raja" (produced by Prabhat Films) was released in 1932, just one year after "Alam Ara" the first Indian (Hindi) talkie film. Marathi cinema has grown in recent years—the industry is based in Mumbai, India.

Marathi Cinema is as old as Cinema in India. In fact the pioneer of cinema in India was Dadasaheb Phalke—a Marathi man, who brought the revolution of moving images to India with his first indigenously made film Raja Harishchandra. It was of course a silent film. However it can be called the first Marathi film as it was conceived by a Marathi speaking person. As cinema grew in India, big production houses came on the stage and one of them was again a company owned wholly by Maharashtrians. It was indeed the mighty Prabhat film company. Some of India's landmark films were made by the Prabhat Film Company, which, apart from being good cinema, had social responsibility and human values. Prabhat's Sant Tukaram was the first Indian film to win the Best Film Award at the Venice film festival way back in 1937. In 1954, at the very first edition of the National Awards, the winner of the President's Gold Medal was *Shyamchi Aai*, Acharya P.K. Atre's film version of the eponymous novel by Sane Guruji. Marathi Cinema was in its full bloom by this time with the advent of greats like V. Shantaram, Master Vinayak, Bhalji Pendharkar, Acharya Atre, followed by Raja Paranjpe, G.D. Madgulkar, Sudhir Phadke. Later years—that is the 60s—saw the emergence of directors like Anant Mane who made Marathi films based on the folk art form Tamasha. Then came directors like Datta Dharmadhikari and Raj Dutt who made traditional family dramas. The early 70s saw the advent of Dada Kondke who captured the audiences with his sense of humour. He however went on to make films with double meaning dialogues and created an audience of his own. By this time Marathi Cinema was caught in either the Tamasha genre or sob stories revolving around traditional family dramas on one side and the double meaning comedies of Dada Kondke. Then came the 80s. This decade saw two comedy heroes catapult to superstardom Ashok Saraf and Laxmikant Berde. Around the mid 80s two young actors donned the director's mantle. Mahesh Kothare and Sachin Pilgaonkar. Sachin made a film—*Navri Mile Navryala* and around the same time Mahesh Kothare made a film—*Dhumdhadaka*. Sachin's film became a big box-office hit while Mahesh Kothare's film not only became a mega hit at the box-office but it also became a trend setter and brought the young audiences to Marathi Cinema. Mahesh Kothare then went on to make comedy films which became big hits. He made the first Marathi film shot on the anamorphic format (Cinemascope)—*Dhadakebaaz*. He brought a great deal of innovations in the technical quality of Marathi films and was also the first to bring Dolby Digital sound to Marathi Cinema with the film *Chimni Pakhara*. He made the first Marathi film with Digital Special Effects—*Pachadlela* in 2004.

While the theatre of Maharashtra earned recognition at the national level, the cinema of the state, struggled as an alsoran, unable to make a mark. The proximity to the production centre of Hindi cinema (Bollywood) which encroached on the identity of Marathi cinema, the shortage of cinema halls for exhibition, a vibrant theatre, television, then infamous state government subsidy scheme whereby a producer gets some Rs. 16 lakh to make a film, tries hard to save a couple of lakhs even from that meagre amount and ends up with a tacky final product, lack of marketing etc. It also lacked the powerful lobby at the national level unlike Bengal or South Indian cinema. In past few years, Marathi cinema industry has produced many movies that are not only critically acclaimed but commercially successful also. This has given Marathi viewers as well as producers confidence that was very much needed. Although budgets of Marathi movies is not high the quality of subjects and presentations have been in fact better than peer industries. Marathi Cinema also got the highest critical acclaim in the year 2004 with the film *Shwaas* bagging the Golden Lotus National Award. It was also India's official entry to the 77th Academy Awards and it also won the President medal for the best film. Shwaas, after *Shyaamchi aai* (1950) is only Marathi film to won president's medal and only regional film to enter Academy awards as India's official entry. The Maharashtra state government has started the grant given to Marathi film (from 15-30 lakh rupees) and since post-Shwaas, media players like Shringar Films and Zee Telefilms are now showing a keen interest in Marathi cinema. The growing popularity of Marathi television (notably Zee Marathi and ETV Marathi) has also helped Marathi cinema a lot. In fact, Zee Talkies, a 24 hour channel dedicated to Marathi movies has been introduced. Movies like *Aga bai areccha, Khabardar, Dombivali fast, Sarivar sari, Yanda kartavya aahe, Uttarayan, Tingya, Valu, Kadachit* have received commercial and/or critical success. This decade has seen the emergence of stars like Sunil Barve, Sadashiv Amrapurkar, Sonali Kulkarni, Amruta Subhash, Ashwini Bhave, Sanjay Narvekar, Atul Kulkarni, Bharat Jadhav. Film-makers like Kedar Shinde, Gautam Joglekar, Gajendra Ahire, Bipin Nadkarni, Mahesh Manjrekar, Chandrakant Kulkarni, Umesh Kulkarni, Mangesh Hadawale are new entrants with veterans like Mahesh Kothare, Smita Talwalkar, Amol Palekar.

Filmfare Awards

Production Year	Film	Director	Actor	Actress	Music
1963	Maza Hoshil Ka	L.B. Thakur			
1964	Sant Nivrutti Gyandeo	Vinayak Sarasvate and Bal Chavan			
1965	Lakshmi Aali Ghara	Madhav Shinde			
1966	Gurukilli	Raja Paranjpe			
1967	Pawnakanthcha Dhondi	Vinayak Thakur			
1968	Ekti	G. Chaugule			
1969	Jiwhala	Atmaram			
1970	Apradh	Sharad Pilgaonkar			
1971	Shantata! Court Chaloo Ahe	Satyadev Dubey and Govind Nihalani			
1972	Kunku Mazhe Bhagyache	Shamrao Mane			
1973	Andhala Marto Dola	Dada Kondke			
1974	Sugandhi Katta	Not Awarded	Shreeram Lagoo (Sugandhi Katta)	Sarla Yevlekar (Sugandhi Katta)	
1975	Samna	Jabbar Patel (Samna)	Shreeram Lagoo (Samna)	Sandhya (Chandanachi Choli Ang Ang Jali)	
1976	Aaram Haram Aahe	Vasant Joglekar (Ha Khel Saavlyancha)	Ravindra Mahajani (Zunj)	Asha Kale (Ha Khel Saavlyancha)	
1977	Naon Mothan Lakshan Khotan	Murlidhar Kapdi (Naon Mothan Lakshan Khotan)	Shreeram Lagoo (Bhingree)	Usha Chavan (Naon Mothan Lakshan Khotan)	
1978	Devki Nandan Gopala	Jabbar Patel (Jait Re Jait)	Yashwant Dutt (Bhairu Pahilwan Ki Jai)	Smita Patil (Jait Re Jait)	

(Contd.)

Production Year	Film	Director	Actor	Actress	Music
1979	Sinhasan	Jabbar Patel (Sinhasan)	Sachin (Ashtavinayak)	Ranjana (Sushila)	
1980	22 June 1897	Jayu and Nachiket Patwardhan (22 June 1897)	Nilu Phule (Sahkar Samrat)	Usha Chavan (Ran Pakhre)	
1981	Umbartha	Jabbar Patel (Umbartha)	Girish Karnad (Akriet)	Smita Patil (Umbartha)	
1982	Shapit	Raj Dutt and Arvind Deshpande (Shapit)	Ashok Saraf (Gondhalat Gondhal)	Madhu Kambikar (Shapit)	
1983	Gupchup Gupchup	V.K. Naik (Gupchup Gupchup)	Ashok Saraf (Goshta Dhamal Namyachi)	Ranjana (Savitri)	
1984	Lek Chalali Saasarla	N.S. Vaidya (Lek Chalali Saasarla)	Ashok Saraf (Sage Soyre)	Supriya Sabnis (Navri Mile Navryala)	
1987	Dhoom Dhadaka	Mahesh Kothari (Dhoom Dhadaka)	Laxmikant Berde	??	
1994	Vazir	Sanjay Rawal (Vazir)	Vikram Gokhale (Vazir)	Sukanya Kulkarni (Varsa Laxmicha)	Shridhar Phadke (Varsa Laxmicha)
1995	Aai	Mahesh Manjrekar (Aai)	Sayaji Shinde (Aboli)	Renuka Shahane (Aboli)	Anand Modak (Mukta)
1996	Putravati	Nichiket and Jayoo Patwardhan (Limited Manuski)	Ashok Saraf (Soona Yeti Ghara)	Sonali Kulkarni (Doghi)	Shridhar Phadke (Putravati)
1997	Bangarwadi	Amol Palekar (Bangarwadi)	Mohan Joshi (Rao Saheb)	Sukanya Kulkarni (Sarkarnama)	Anand Modak (Sarkarnama)
1998	Tu Tithe Mee	Sanjay Soorkar (Tu Tithe Mee)	Mohan Joshi (Tu Tithe Mee)	Suhas Joshi (Tu Tithe Mee)	Anand Modak (Tu Tithe Mee)
1999	Bindhast	Chandrakant Kulkarni (Bindhast)	Dilip Prabhavalkar (Ratra Aarambh)	Sharvari Jamenis (Bindhast)	Shridhar Phadke (Lekroo)

National Film Awards

Production Year	Best Film	Best Director
1954	Shyamchi Aai	Acharya Pralhad Keshav Atre
1955	Mahatma Phule	Aacharya Atre
1956	Mee Tulas Tuzhya Angani	Raja Thakur
1957	Shirdiche Saibaba	Kumarsen Samarth
1958	Gruhdevta	Madhav Shinde
1959	Dhakti jau	Anant Mane
1961	Kanyadan	Madhav Shinde
1962	Prapanch	Madhukar Pathak
1962	Manini	Anant Mane
1962	Vaijyanta	Gajanan Jagirdar
1963	Ranglya Ratri Asha	Raja Thakur
1963	Gariba Gharchi Lek	Kamlakar Torne
1963	Jawai Mazha Bhala	Neelkanth Magdum
1964	Ha Mazha Marg Ekla	Raja Paranjpe
1964	Te Mazhe Ghar	Ganesh Bhatt
1965	Pathlag	Raja Paranjpe
1966	Sadhi Manasa	Bhalji Pendharkar
1967	Pavana Kathcha Dhondi	Anant Thakur
1968	Santh Wahate Krishnamai	Madhukar Pathak
1969	Ekti	Raja Thakur
1970	Tambdi Mati	Bhalji Pendharkar
1971	Mumbaicha Jawai	Raja Thakur
1972	Shantata! Court Chalu Aahe	Satyadev Dubey
1972	Ajab Tuzhe Sarkar	Raja Thakur
1973	Pinjara	V. Shantaram
1976	Saamna	Dr. Jabbar Patel
1978	Jait Re Jait	Dr. Jabbar Patel
1979	Sinhasan	Dr. Jabbar Patel
1980	22 June 1897	Nachiket and Jayu Patwardhan

(*Contd.*)

Production Year	Best Film	Best Director
1982	Umbartha	Dr. Jabbar Patel.
1983	Shaapit	Arvind Deshpande-Rajdutt
1984	Smruti Chitre	Vijaya Mehta
1985	Mahananda	K.G. Korgaokar
1986	Pudhcha Paool	Rajdutta
1987	Sarja	Rajdutt
1989	Kalat Nakalat	Kanchan Nayak
1992	Ek Hota Vidushak	Dr. Jabbar Patel
1993	Lapandav	Shravani Devdhar
1994	Mukta	Dr. Jabbar Patel
1995	Bangarwadi	Amol Palekar
1996	Doghi	Sumitra Bhave
2000	GharaBaher	Sanjay Surkar
2001	Astitva	Mahesh Manjrekar
2003	Vaastuprush	Sumitra Bhave/Sunil Sukthankar
2004	Not Only Mrs. Raut	Gajendra Ahire
2005	Uttarayan	Bipin Nadkarni
2006	Dombivali Fast	Nishikant Kamat

Bengali Cinema

The history of cinema in Bengal dates back to the 1890s, when the first "bioscopes" were shown in theatres in Calcutta. Within a decade, the first seeds of the industry was sown by Hiralal Sen, considered a stalwart of Victorian era cinema when he set up the Royal Bioscope Company, producing scenes from the stage productions of a number of popular shows at the Star Theatre, Minerva Theatre, Classic Theatre. Following a long gap after Sen's works, Dhirendra Nath Ganguly (Known as D.G.) established Indo British Film Co., the first Bengali owned production company, in 1918. However, the first Bengali Feature film, Billwamangal, was produced in 1919, under the banner of Madan Theatre. Bilat Ferat was the IBFC's first production in 1921. The New Theatre production of Dena Paona was the first Bengali talkie. A long history has been traversed since then, with stalwarts such as Satyajit Ray, Mrinal Sen and Ritwik Ghatak and others having earned international acclaim and securing their place in the movie history. Today, there are two **Bengali film industries**, one in Kolkata, India and the lesser known one in Dhaka, Bangladesh (called *Dhallywood*, a portmanteau of the words *Dhaka* and *Hollywood*).

Hiralal Sen is credited as one of Bengal's, and India's first directors. However, these were all silent films. Hiralal Sen is also credited as one of the pioneers of advertisement films in India. The first Bengali-language movie was the silent feature *Billwamangal*, produced by the Madan Theatre Company of Calcutta and released on November 8, 1919, only six years after the first full-length Indian feature film, *Raja Harish Chandra*, was released. The early beginnings of the "talking film" industry go back to the early 1930's, when it came to British India, and to Calcutta. The movies were originally made in Urdu or Persian as to accommodate a specific elite market. One of the earliest known studios was the East India Film Company. The first Bengali film to be made as a talkie was an adaptation of Tagore's short story, Dena Paona, released in 1931. It was at this time that the early heroes of the Bengali film industry like Pramathesh Barua and Debaki Bose were at the peak of their popularity. Barua also directed a number of movies, exploring new dimension in Indian cinema. Debaki Bose directed Chandidas in 1932; this film is noted for its breakthrough in recording sound. Sound recordist Mukul Bose found out solution to the problem of spacing out dialogue and frequency modulation. The contribution of Bengali film industry to Indian film is quite significant. Based in Tollygunge, an area of South Kolkata, West Bengal and is more elite and artistically-inclined than the usual musical cinema fare in India. In the past, it enjoyed a large, even disproportionate, representation in Indian cinema, and produced film directors like Satyajit Ray, who was an Academy Honorary Award winner, and the recipient of India and France's greatest civilian honours, the Bharat Ratna and Legion of Honour respectively, and Mrinal Sen, who is the recipient of the French distinction of Commander of the Order of Arts and Letters and the Russian Order of Friendship. Other prominent film makers in the Bengali film industry are Bimal Roy, the late Ritwik Ghatak, and Aparna Sen. The Bengali film industry has produced classics like 'Pather Panchali', 'Devi', 'Jalsaghar', 'Devdas', 'Neel Akasher Neechey', 'Meghe Dhaka Tara' etc. The most well known Bengali actor to date has been Uttam Kumar; he and co-star Suchitra Sen were known as *The Eternal Pair* in the early 1950's. Soumitra Chatterjee is a notable actor, having acted in several Satyajit Ray films, and considered as a rival to Uttam Kumar in the 1960's. He is famous for the characterization of Feluda in Sonar Kella and Joy Baba Felunath, written and directed by Ray. The pioneers in Bengali film music include Raichand Boral, Pankaj Mullick and K.C. Dey, all associated with New Theatres Calcutta. Other famous playback singers in Bengali film music were Hemanta Mukherjee, Manna Dey, Sandhya Mukhopadhyay and Kishore Kumar. In the 1980s, however, the Bengal film industry went through a period of turmoil, with a shift from its traditional artistic and emotional inclinations to an approach more imitating the increasingly more popular Hindi films, along with a decline in the audience and critical appreciation, with notable exceptions of the works of directors like Gautam Ghose. However, even at this time, a number of actors and actresses enjoyed popularity, including Tapas Pal, Proshenjit, Chironjeet, Rituparna Sengupta and others. However, toward the end of the 90s, with the a number of directors coming increasingly into prominence, including Rituparno Ghosh, Gautam Ghose, Aparna Sen, Sandip Ray among others, a number of popular and critically acclaimed movies have come out of the Bengali film industry in recent years. These include, Unishe April, Titli, Mr. and Mrs. Iyer, Bombaiyer Bombete, etc and signal a resurgence of the Bengali film industry.

Punjabi Cinema (Punjwood)

Punjwood is the informal name given to the Punjabi-language film industry in India. The term Pollywood is also often used in the place of Punjwood. Until now Punjwood has produced between, 900 and 1,000 movies. The average number of releases per year in the: 1970's where 9, 1980's where 8, 1990s where 6. In 1995, the number of films released was 11 (with no hits), it plummeted to 7 in 1996 and touched a low of 5 in 1997. K.D. Mehra made the first Punjabi film Sheela as Pind di Kudi, which was a super hit film, Baby Noor Jehan was introduced as actress and singer in this film. Sheela as Pind di Kudi was made in Calcutta and released in Punjab and Lahore and it ran very successfully in the circuit. Soon many more producers started making Punjabi films, as it provided to be a good preposition. K.D. Mehra then made his 2nd film Heer Sial, in which M.M. Billoo Mehra Assisted him. This film had new artistes Balo and M. Ismail and Baby Noor Jehan. This Film also ran very successfully. Due to vast Punjabi community in Lahore and Punjab, soon Lahore became a big film market. Studious opened up and many artistes, producers, directors and technicians from Bombay and Calcutta shifted to Lahore. Some prominent names were Shanta Apte, Motilal, Chandra Mohan, Hiralal, Noor Jehan, Mumtaz Shanti, Wali, Syed Attahullah Shah Hashmi, Krishna Kumar and Shanker Hussain. Many Journalists like B.R. Chopra, Ramanand Sagar has also settled in Lahore. B.R. Chopra was running his Film Magazine "Cine Herald". Ramanand Sagar was associated with "Evening News" and Syed Attahullah Shah Hashmi took out the Film Paper "Adakar"". These journalists were totally dependent on Lahore Film Industry.

In 1947, India was divided into 2 Parts: India and Pakistan (East and West). This affected the Punjabi cinema. The reason was that most Muslim artists and directors moved to Pakistan and some other Muslims, Sikhs and Hindus moved to Mumbai. The artists and directors who moved to Mumbai, made it big in Bollywood. There were many tries to keep Indian Punjabi Cinema alive. Film-makers made movies like Posti, Do Lachhian, Bhangra, etc. Some of them succeeded. Movies like Posti and Do Lachhian where hits but weren't able to revive the Punjabi cinema. And to specify why such movies became hits; there is only 1 reasons: the music and songs. The songs of movies would ran for months and years on Radio. So people became interested and really wanted to watch the films. But many didn't enjoyed Punjabi films that much. In 1964 released a big-budget romantic Punjabi film of Padam Prakash Maheshwary titled "Satluj de Kande". This film had big star like Balraj Sahni, Nishi, Wasti, and Mirza Musharraf, music by Hans Raj Behl. This was the only Punjabi Film by Balraj Sahni and was a super hit and it also earned a national award. "Satluj de Kande" was telecast thrice on National Channel of Door Darshan (Indian National TV channel). Then in 1969 released religious film Nanak Naam Jahaz Hai. Starring Prithviraj Kapoor, IS Johar, Vimmi, Som Dutt, Nishi, Suresh, David. The film was a direct ducces. The film was the first really major successful Punjabi film in Post-Independent

India with a major cultural impact on Punjabi Sikhs at home and abroad and is credited with the revival of the Punjabi Film Industry in India. People stood in km long lines to buy a ticket for the film. After Nanak Naam Jahaz Hai, movies started releasing in huge number. Hindi movie actors (who where from Punjabi descent) got interested in Punjabi movies. The next year saw releases such as Kankan De Ole (Dharmendra, Asha Parekh and Ravindra Kapoor), Nanak Dukhiya Sab Sansar (Dara Singh, Balraj Sahni, Ram Mohan and Asha Sachdev). 1971 saw no major releases. Again in 1972, Dara Singh starred in a movie. This time he paired with Prithviraj Kapoor in Mele Mitran De. 1973 saw only one major release Man Jeete Jag Jeet. This film starred Sunil Dutt, Radha Saluja and Ranjeet in lead roles. Again it was a religious film. 1974 saw many releases like Do Sher (Dharmendra and Rajendra Kumar), Bhagat Dhanna Jatt (Dara Singh and Feroz Khan), Sacha Mera Roop Hai (Manmohan Krishan) and Dukh Bhanjan Tera Naam (Shaminder Singh and Radha Saluja). The best of them was Dukh Bhanjan Tera Naam. This could have two reasons: 1. Because its a religious historical film. 2. It had many special appearances from Bollywood superstars: Sunil Dutt, Rajendra Kumar, Dharmendra, Johnny Walker, Dara Singh etc. 1975 saw 1 major release: Teri Meri Ek Jindri. Along with Dharmendra this movie introduced his cousin brother Veerendra. 1976 saw many releases: Daaj (1976), Giddha (1976), Main Papi Tum Bakhshanhaar (1976), Papi Tarey Anek (1976), Santo Banto (1976), Sardar-E-Azam (1976), Sawa Lakh Se Ek Ladaun (1976), Taakra (1976), Yamla Jatt (1976). Sawa Lakh Se Ek Ladaun was the biggest hit and starred Dara Singh. This movie ran into conflict with the Sikh political parties as the film had Khalsa Fauj soldiers wearing fake beards. The year 1977 wasn't a major one. Jai Mata Di, Saal Solvan Chadya, Sat Sri Akal, Shaheed Kartar Singh Sarabha released amongst others. Saal Solvan Chadya was a highlight because of the cameo-appearance by Rekha. Sat Sri Akal was another hit film. It starred Sunil Dutt, Shatrughan Sinha and Premnath in lead roles. In 1978 where released Udeekan, Dhyani Bhagat, Jai Mata Sheranwali, Jindri Yar Di etc. Udeekan was a drama film and was a hit. The first ever remake in Punjabi cinema was released in 1978. The film was Walayati Babu. It was remade from an older Punjabi film. Tne film is famous because the special appearance given by Amitabh Bachchan. 1979 was a big year. In this year movies like Guru Manio Granth, Jatt Punjabi, Kunwara Mama, Sukhi Pariwar, Til Til Dalekha released. Guru Manio Granth was a religious film and an instant hit. Jatt Punjabi had a big cast + special appearance by Manoj Kumar was a hit. Til Til Da Lekha was a hit. It won Punjab State Govt. award for Best Story, Writer and Second Best feature film 1979. The first-ever mystery film released. The film was Wangaar (The Challenge). It failed to become a hit. In 1980, the first Punjabi film to have achieved the national award was released. That film was Chann Pardesee. It starred Raj Babbar, Rama Vij, Amrish Puri, Om Puri and Kulbhusun Kharbanda Another film Fauji Chacha was also a hit. 1981 saw only 1 hit: Balbiro Bhabhi. This film has Veerendra in the lead role. This is the first role of Veerendra that was really appreciated. 1982 saw 2 major releases: Ucha Dar Babe Nanak Da and Sarpanch. Ucha Dar Babe Nanak Da was a religious film which was a hit because of the songs and the acting. This film established Gurdas Mann as a star. Sarpanch once again was a hit-performance given by Veerendra. In 1983 many movies released. But Putt Jattan De was the biggest hit of them. The movie was one of the first multi-starrers and had good songs. The film was a superhit. 1984 saw another hit from Veerendra in the form of Yaari Jatt Di. This film was the first one to be shot more than 50 per cent in U.K. Mamla Garbar Hai again was a hit given by Gurdas Mann. The film's songs where especially loved. 1985 saw two hit films. One was Mohammad Sadiq's Guddo. The other was Veerendra's Vairi. 1986 saw 1 major hit in the form of Long Da Lishkara, this one stars Raj Babbar, Gurdas Mann, Om Puri and Nina Deol. In 1987 two major hits from Veerendra where given: Patola and Jor Jatt Da. Punjab was shaken with the sudden assassination of Veerendra during the filming of Jatt Tey Zameen. The back-bone of Punjwood was dead. There was no real superstar more of Punjabi cinema. All other actors who gave hits in Punjabi Cinema where Bollywood actors from Punjabi descent. But Veerendra was a real superstar of Punjabi cinema. The death of Veerendra gave an opperunity to give side actors or villains like Gugu Gill and Yograj Singh to become heroes. 1988 saw nothing majors. In 1989 released critically acclaimed Marhi Da Diva. The film starred Raj Babbar, Pankaj Kapur, Kanwaljeet Singh, Parikshat Sahni and Deepti Naval. 1990 saw 2 major releases. Qurbani Jatt Di (Gugu Gill, Yograj Singh, Gurdas Mann,

Dharmendra, Raj Babbar and Priti Sapru) and Pratigya (Gugu Gill, Gurdas Mann, Priti Sapru and Dara Singh). Whilst the former one was a hit because of the star power the second one wasn't a major success despite the top-notch performances. This is Gurdas Mann's one and only villainious role till date. 1991 saw incline in cinema. With the release of Jatt Jeona Morh (Gugu Gill), which was a superhit, Punjabi cinema was believed to be revived. Also released Yograj Singh's Jagga Daku which did some moederate bussiness. But in the following years 1992 and 1993 movies weren't that successful, so Punjwood again was believed dead. Surely movies released but where movies with off repeated story lined and same violence. 1994 saw a hit in the form Kachehri which was a movie from Gurdas Mann. In 1995, the number of films released was 11 (with no hits), it plummeted to 7 in 1996 and touched a low of 5 in 1997. Till 1998 no major movie released. It was Main Ma Punjab Dee that again revived cinema. The next year already 2 Big movies released: Shaheed-e-Mohabbat and Mahaul Theekh Hai. Both where superhits and did very well business overseas as well.

In 2000 the life of Udham Singh was portrayed by Raj Babbar in film Shaheed Uddham Singh which became a huge hit. From 2000 to 2003 no major movie released. In 2003 released Jee Ayan Nu. Singer-turned actor Harbhajan Mann acted and it was directed by choregrapher-turned director Manmohan Singh. The movie was made on a big budget (for Punjwood at least)—90 lakhs, as normal flicks just cost you around 20-50 lakhs. Then in 2004, Asa Nu Maan Watna Da released. Again singer-turned actor Harbhajan Mann acted in it and it was directed by choregrapher-turned director Manmohan Singh. It was a huge hit again. 2005, released movies like Jija Ji, Des Hoyaa Pardes, Main Tu Assi Tussi, Yaaran Naal Baharan, Nalaik etc. Des Hoya Pardes was a major hit. 2006 saw movies like Dil Apna Punjabi (Again Harbhajan-Manmohan pair), Ek Jind Ek Jaan and Warish Shah. Warish Shah was so appreciated that it is being considered to be sent to the oscars. 2007 saw movies like Rustam-e-Hind, Mitti Wajan Mardi (again Harbhajan-Manmohan pair). With many directors taking keen interest and some Punjwood films doing better than big budget Bollywood films at UK box office, it seems there is some hope left for Punjwood to be revived and be an effective part of Indian Cinema as Telugu, Tamil, Hindi, Bengali, Marathi etc films are.

Superstars

- *Shivendra Mahal*: Famous supporting actor. Acted in more than 20 Punjwood movies and 17 Hindi movies. Besides that he has acted in innumerable serials in Hindi and Punjabi.
- *Veerendra*: Acted in 25 movies in his 12 years career. Gave hits like Lambhardarni, Sarpanch, Yaari Jatt Di, Batwara etc. If there is ever made a list of top 50 Punjwood flicks at least 10 will be Veerendra's. Although not so goodlooking Veerendra was a superstar because of his directorial abilities and the touching stories he wrote.
- *Yograj Singh*: Acted in about 150 movies. Mainly villain but also hero in some movies. Is still remembered for his villainous role in Badla Jatti Da. Other performances include: Kachehri and Jagga Daku.
- *Gugu Gill*: Acted in about 30-40 films. Mainly villain or hero. Still remembered as the villain in Gabroo Punjab Da.
- *Gurdas Mann*: Gave films like Ucha Dar Babe Nanak Da, Mamla Garbar Hai, Kachehri, Desh Hoya Pardes, Shaheed-e-Mohabbat and his latest Waris Shah—Ishq Da Waris. The last film in which he acted was Warish Shah. The film was India's official entry 2006 to the 79th oscars.
- *Raj Babbar*: Started in two of finest movies of the 80s, Chann Pardesee (1980) and Long Da Lishkara (1986).
- *Harbhajan Mann*: Debuted in 2003. In 4 years has acted in 4 films with the same director, Manmohan Singh. All movies are hits. Those are: Jee Ayan Nu, Asa Nu Maan Watna Da, Dil Apna Punjabi and Mitti Wajaan Mardi.
- *Meher Mittal*: Comedy king of Punjwood from 1975-1990.

Assamese Cinema

Assamese cinema was born in 1935 when Jyoti Prasad Agarwala released his movie *Joymoti*. Since then Assamese cinema has developed a slow-paced sensitive style, especially with the movies of Bhabendra Nath Saikia and Jahnu Barua. However, despite its long history, and its artistic successes, for a state that has always taken its cinema seriously, Assamese cinema has never really managed to make the breakthrough on the national scene despite its film industry making a mark in the National Awards over the years. Although the beginning of the 21st century has seen Bollywood-style Assamese movies have hit the screen, the industry has not been able to compete on the market, significantly overshadowed by the larger industries such as Bollywood.

The origin of Assamese Cinema can be traced back to the dreams and imagination of a revolutionary visionary Rupkonwar Jyotiprasad Agarwala, who was also a distinguished poet, playwright, composer and freedom fighter. He was instrumental in the production of the first Assamese Film *Joymati* in 1935, under the banner of Critrakala Movietone. Due to the lack of trained technicians, Jyotiprasad, while making his maiden film, had to shoulder the added responsibilities as the script writer, producer, director, choreographer, editor, set and costume designer, lyricist and music director. The film, completed with a budget of 60,000 rupees was released on March 10, 1935. The picture failed miserably. It is unfortunate that like so many early Indian films, the negatives and complete prints of *Joymati* are missing. Some effort has been made privately by Altaf Mazid to restore and subtitle whatever is left of the prints. Despite the significant financial loss from *Joymati* the second picture *Indramalati* was filmed between 1937 and 1938 finally released in 1939. Remaining strong in the face of adversity, Agarwala made another film after a lapse of two years titled *Indramalati.* It was his second and last film. The eminent composer and singer of Assam Bhupen Hazarika, played a stellar role in the play. With the passing away of Jyotiprasad, the Assamese film scene witnessed a temporary lull for about a couple of years. But things changed with the onset of World War II, Taking advantage of this, Rohini Kr. Baruah made a film on a relevant historical topic called *Manomati* in 1941. It was followed by films like Parvati Prasad Baruva's *Rupahi* (1946), Kamal Narayan Choudhury's *Badan Barphukan* (1947), Phani Sharma's *Siraj*, Asit Sen's *Biplabi*, Prabin Phukan's *Parghat* and Suresh Goswami's *Runumi* etc. The most remarkable film of the fifties was *Piyali Phukan* which went on to win a National award. The movie was produced by eminent film producer Gama Prasad Agarwalla under the aegis of Rup Jyoti Productions. The film was directed by Phani Sharma and music was composed by a young Bhupen Hazarika. The film was about the life of the freedom fighter Piyali Phukan, who stood against the British Rule. He was executed by the british on charges of Treason. This film technically was very advanced during that time. In 1955, a new talent Nip Barua made his directorial debut with *Smrit Paras*. His subsequent films *Mak Aaru Moram* and *Ranga Police* bagged many state awards and the silver medal at the national level. Bhupen Hazarika also produced and directed his first film *Era Bator Sur*. Prabhat Mukherjee made a film on the universality of mother-hood, *Puberan* (1959), which was shown in The Berlin Film Festival. The next notable film production was *Lachit Borphukan* by Sarbeswar Chakraborty. Bhupen Hazarika made his unforgettable musical *Shakuntala* in 1961 which proved equally successful with critics and the press winning the president's silver medal. Following this, a chain of films went into regular production and got released which included Nip Barua's *Narakasur*, Anil Choudhury's *Matri Swarga*, Brojen Barua's *Itu Situ Bahuto* and Mukta and Anwar Hussain's *Tejimala*. By the middle of the sixties, film began to be produced in Assam on a regular basis. However, between 1935 and 1970 a total of 62 films were produced. Besides the film makers already referred to, many others engaged in film making during the period included Pravin Sharma, Saila Barua, Abdul Mazid, Amar Pathak, Indukal Pattazarika, Diben Barua, Debkumar Basu, Amulya Manna, Gauri Barman, Atul Bardoloi, Sujit Singh, Nalin Duara and Prafulla Barua. During the period of 1970-82 a total of 57 Assamese films were made. New directors started emerging on the horizon. Samarendra Narayan Deb's Aranya (1970), Kamal Choudhury's Bhaity (1972) the first colour film of Assam, Manoranjan Sur's Uttaran (1973), Deuti Barua's Bristi (1974), Pulok Gogoi's Khoj (1974), Padum Barua's Ganga Chilanir Pakhi (1976), and Dr. Bhabendranath Saikia's Sandhya Raag (1977) and Atul Bordoloi's Kollol (1978) are films worth-mentioning. Notable directors of contemporary Assamese Cinema are Jahnu Baruah (who directed *Aparoopa, Papori, Haladhia Choraye Baodhan Khai, Banani, Firingoti* and *Hkhagoroloi Bohu Door*); Sanjeev Hazarika (*Haladhar, Meemanxa*) and Bhabendaranath Saikia who directed *Anirbaan, Agnisnaan, Sarothi, Kolahol, Abartan, Itihaas* and *Kaal Sandhya*. Other directors include Santwana Bordoloi who directed *Adajya* and Bidyut Chakraborty who made *Rag Birag*, both of which have won National and International Awards.

Notable Assamese Films

- Abartan (1993)
- Abhijaan (1973)
- Abhimaan (1990)
- Adajya (1996)
- Adalat (1976)
- Agnisnaan (1985)
- Ajala Kokai (1989)
- Ajali Nabou (1980)
- Amar Ghar (1959)
- Anirban (1981)
- Anthony Mor Nam (1986)
- Anutap (1973)
- Aparajeya (1970)
- Aparoopa (1982)
- Aranya (1971)
- Banahansa (1977)
- Banani (1990)
- Banjui (1978)
- Bonoria Phul (1973)
- Baruar Sansar (1970)
- Bhakta Pralhad (1958)
- Biplabi (1948)
- Bristi (1974)
- Chameli Memsaab (1975)
- Chik Mik Bijuli (1969)
- Daawor (1990)
- Dil Se (1998)
- Dr. Bezbarua (1969)
- Drishti (1990/II)
- Duranir Rong (1979)
- Era Bator Sur (1956)
- Firingoti (1992)
- Ganga Chilonir Pankhi (1975)
- Grahan (1990)
- Haladhar (1992)
- Halodhia Choraye Baodhan Khai (1987)
- Xagoroloi Bohu Door (1995)
- Indramaloti (1939)

- Itihas (1995)
- Ito Xito Bahuto (1963)
- Joymati (1935)
- Kallol (1978)
- Kokadeuta Nati Aru Hati (1984)
- Kolahal (1988)
- Konikar Ramdhenu (2003)
- Lalita (1972)
- Lati-Ghati (1966)
- Maak Aru Morom (1957)
- Maram Trishna (1968)
- Meemanxa (1994)
- Megh (1979)
- Mon-Prajapati (1979)
- Mukuta (1970)
- Narakasur (1961)
- Nayanmoni (1983)
- Nimila Anka (1955)
- Opaja Sonor Mati (1972)
- Paap Aru Prayashchitta (1977)
- Pahadi Kanya (1991)
- Papori (1986)
- Piyoli Phukan (1955)
- Pita Putra (1987)
- Ponakan (1981)
- Pratidhwani (1964)
- Pratima (1987)
- Puberun (1959)
- Ranga Police (1958)
- Ratanlal (1971)
- Roop Konwar Jyoti Parsad Aru Joymoti (1976)
- Sandhya Raag (1977)
- Sarapat (1955)
- Sarbajan (1985)
- Sarothi (1991)
- Shakuntala (1961)
- Shakuntala Aru Sankar Joseph Ali (1984)
- Shri Shri Maa Kamakhya (1983)
- Sinyor (1991)
- Siraj (1948)

- Siraj (1988)
- Smritir Parax (1955)
- Xontara (1973)
- Xonmai (1977)
- Swikarokti (1986)
- Tejimola (1967)
- Toramai (1975)
- Uttarkaal (1990)
- Gun Gun Gane Gane (2004)
- Joubone Aamoni Kore
- Tumi Mor Matho Mor
- Jown Jwole Kopalot
- Maghot Mamonir Biya
- Kanyaa Daan
- Daag
- Hiya Diya Niya
- Kadombori
- Kokadeutar Ghar Jowai (1995)
- Maharathi
- Hitlist
- Hridoyor Aare Aare
- Imaan Morom Kiyo Laage
- Morom Nodir Gabhoru Ghaat

Notable Actors and Actresses

Tara, Jamuna Baruah, Phani Sarma, Jatin Bora, Moloya Goswami, Bindiya Goswami, Geetawali Rajkumari, Chetana Das, Trisha Saikia, Jotin Borah, Ravi Sarma, Gayotry Mahanta, Hiranya Das, Hiranya Deka, Nipon Goswami, Biju Phukan, Jharna Saikia, Akashdeep, Tapan Das, Mridula Boruah, Aimee Boruah, Prastuti Parashar, Bornali Pujari, Barasha Rani Bishaya, Jerifa Wahid, Nayan Nirban, Ankur Bishaya, Pranjal Saikia, Rajiv Goswami, Purabi Sarma, Malaya Goswami, Bidya Rao, Nishita Goswami, Bishnu Kharghoria, Atul Pachoni, Divya Desai.

Tamil Cinema

The **Tamil Film Industry** is home to Tamil-language cinema based in India and is sometimes referred to as *Kollywood*. The name,

Kollywood, has derived from Kodambakkam, the area in Chennai (formerly Madras), where Kollywood films are largely produced. Tamil language movies are also filmed in Sri Lanka. Silent movies were produced in Kollywood since 1916 and the era of talkies dawned in 1931. By the end of the 1930s, the industry was booming to the extent that the State of Madras legislature passed the pioneering *Entertainment Tax Act 1939* with little opposition.

Tamil films have one of the widest overseas distribution along with Telugu and Hindi films. They have enjoyed consistent popularity among Tamil speakers in India, Sri Lanka, Singapore and Malaysia. Tamil films have recently become popular in Japan (Rajinikanth's *Muthu*, for example, screened for a record period), South Africa, Canada, and the UK. Many movies such as *Chandramukhi* and *Anniyan* were also simultaneously released in the USA. *Sivaji: The Boss*, which had released recently has also been touted as a record-breaking film for its high-budget, large opening, and reception worldwide. It also cracked into the UK's Top 10 weekend box opening movies becoming the first ever Indian movie to do so. It is also the most expensive Indian movie produced so far, largely due to the 25 Crore salary paid to Rajnikanth. Tamil films enjoy significant patronage in the neighbouring southern States like Kerala, Karnataka and Andhra Pradesh too. In Kerala and Karnataka the films are directly released in Tamil but in Andhra Pradesh they are generally dubbed into Telugu. There is a fair amount of dispersion amongst the Indian film industries. Many successful Tamil films have been remade by the Hindi and Telugu film industries. Kollywood has also remade a fair number of Hindi-, Telugu-, Malayalam-, and other-language films. It is estimated by the *Manorama Yearbook 2000* (a popular almanac) that over 5,000 Tamil films were produced in the 20th century. For a complete list of Tamil films, see the List of Tamil-Language Films. Tamil films have also been dubbed into other languages, thus reaching a much wider audience. Examples of those dubbed into Hindi include such hits as *Minsaara Kanavu*, *Roja* and *Bombay*. *Anniyan*, a recent Tamil film became the first Indian film to be dubbed into French.

There has been a growing presence of English in dialogue and songs as well. It is not uncommon to see movies that feature dialogue studded with English words and phrases, or even whole sentences. Some movies are also simultaneously made in two or three languages (either using subtitles or several soundtracks).

Quite often, Tamil movies feature Chennai Tamil, a colloquial version of Tamil spoken in Madras' i.e 'Chennai'. A visiting European exhibitor first screened (date unknown) a selection of silent short films at the Victoria Public Hall in Madras. The films all featured non-fictional subjects; they were mostly photographed records of day-to-day events. In Madras (now known as Chennai), the Electric Theatre was established for the screening of silent films. It was a favourite haunt of the British community in Madras. The theatre was shut down after a few years. This building is now part of the Post Office complex in Anna Salai. A Mr. Cohen built Lyric Theatre in the Mount Road area (now Anna Salai). This venue boasted a variety of events, including plays in English, Western classical music concerts, and ballroom dances. Silent films were also screened as an additional attraction. Samikannu Vincent, an employee of the South Indian Railways in Trichy, purchased a film projector and silent films from the Frenchman Du Pont and set up a business as film exhibitor. He erected tents for screening films. His tent cinema became popular and he travelled all over the state with his mobile unit. In later years, he produced talkies and also built a cinema in Coimbatore. To celebrate the event of King George V's visit in 1909, a grand exhibition was organised in Madras. Its major attraction was the screening of short films accompanied by sound. A British company imported a Crone megaphone, made up of a film projector to which a gramophone with a disc containing prerecorded sound was linked, and both were run in unison, producing picture and sound simultaneously. However, there was no synched dialogue. Raghupathy Venkiah Naidu, a successful photographer, took over the equipment after the exhibition and set up a tent cinema near the Madras High Court. R. Venkiah, flush with funds, built in 1912 a permanent cinema in the Mount Road area named Gaiety. It was the first in Madras to screen films on a full-time basis. This theatre is still functioning, although under different ownership. In tent cinemas, there were usually three classes of tickets: the floor, bench and, chair. The floor-ticket purchaser sat on sand to watch the movie, but he enjoyed certain advantages that other patrons did not. He could sit as he pleased, or he could turn over and take a short nap when the narrative was particularly dull and roll back again when the action was again to his liking—luxuries in which the upper class could never indulge.

In early days during 20's, Tamil Movies (silent Movies) were shot at make shift location in and around Chennai, and for technical processing they were sent to Pune or Calcutta. Later some movies featuring MKT were shot at Pune and Calcutta. In 30's AVM setup their makeshift studio in the town of Karaikudi, and in the same decade big full fledged Movie studio's were built in Salem (Modern Theatres Studio) and Coimbatore (Central Studios, Neptune and Pakshiraja). By mid 40's Chennai became the hub of Studio activity with two more movie Studios built in Chennai, Vijaya Vauhini Studios and Gemini Studios. Later AVM Studios shifted their operation to Chennai. Thus the undivided Madras Presidency being the Capital to most of South India, Chennai became the center for Tamil and notable Telugu movies. Also most of the pre-independence era drama and stage actors joining movie industry from 40's Chennai became the hub for South Indian Language Cinema. Initially, Kollywood was dominated by M.K. Thyagaraja Bagavadhar and P.U. Chinnappa in 30's and 40's, then by M.G. Ramachandran and Sivaji Ganesan from 50's till late 70's and later from 80's to till date it was dominated by Rajinikanth and Kamalhassan. These star have exclusive fanclubs that often resort to violent display of support. Distributors of films of the star are able to arrange financing of film-in-progress from banks and exhibitors without much difficulty. This club is politically influential as they are able and willing to effect swings in votes in Assembly elections.

Average annual film output in Tamil film industry has risen steadily in the 20th century.

- 1930s: 22.5 releases per year on averages
- 1940s: 22.1 releases per year on average
- 1950s: 32.6 releases per year on average
- 1960s: 43.0 releases per year on average
- 1970s: 62.5 releases per year on average
- 1980s: 104.6 releases per year on average
- 1990s: 101.2 releases per year on average

In the year 2007 a record breaking 150 movies were released as of December 31st 2007. For the purpose of entertainment taxes, returns have to be filed by the exhibitors weekly (usually each Tuesday). This is a chart of trend of box office collections of

Kollywood with figures in millions of Indian Rupees. It is running house full shows and is expected to recover the money in a short period.

Year	*Tamil Film Box Office (in Crore Rupees)*
1980	80.8
1985	156.4
1990	313.3
1995	782
2000	1,411
2005	2,320.5

The Tamil film industry accounts for approx. 1 per cent of the gross domestic product of the state of Tamil Nadu. Costs of production have grown exponentially from just under Rs. 40 lakhs in 1980 to over Rs. 11 crores by 2005 for a typical star-studded big-budget film. Similarly, costs of processing per print have risen from just under Rs. 2,500 in 1980 to nearly Rs. 70,000 by 2005.

Interestingly, The Tamil Nadu government has made provisions for an entertainment tax exemption for Tamil movies having pure Tamil word(s) in the title. This is in accordance with Government Order 72 passed on 22 July 2006. The first film to be released after the new Order was *Unnakkum Ennakum*. The original title had been *Something something Unakkum Ennakkum*, a half-English and a half-Tamil title.

There are about 2,400 cinema halls in Tamilnadu, which is the main market for Tamil film industry. Of these around 125 are located in the Chennai district. Below is a list of the most prominent exhibitors in the box office.

- Sathyam—1,266 seats (Chennai)
- Albert—1,225 seats (Chennai)
- Devi—1,212 seats (Chennai)
- Melody—998 seats (Chennai)
- Abirami—927 seats (Chennai)
- Kasi—917 seats (Chennai)
- Sangam—877 seats (Chennai)
- Maharani—733 seats (Chennai)
- Udhayam—700 seats (Chennai)
- Santham—567 seats (Chennai)

- Padmam—540 seats (Chennai)
- Suriyan—480 seats (Chennai)
- Devi Bala—369 seats (Chennai)
- Subham—306 seats (Chennai)
- Mayajaal—178 seats (Chennai)
- Inox—909 seats (Chennai)

Show rentals range from Rs. 700 in C-centres to as much as Rs. 7,000 in A-centres for an average 700-seat screen. Unlike Hollywood, superstardom is deeply ingrained into Kollywood economics, so distributors are prepared to not only finance the films of super stars with proven track records but are also, in turn, able to secure minimum guarantees for those films from exhibitors. Rise of multiplexes in the late 1990s has stunted the growth of large screens.

Cinema of Karnataka

The **Cinema of Karnataka** encompasses movies made in the Indian state of Karnataka. Most of the movies are made in the Kannada language, with a handful of them in Konkani or Tulu. Kannada films form an important component of the Cinema of India. The most popular actor in Kannada films was late Dr. Rajkumar. He has acted in over 200 movies and is a recipient of the Dadasaheb Phalke Award. Other actors, actresses, directors and producers in Kannada films include dozens like B.R. Pantulu, G.V. Iyer, Gubbi Veeranna, Balakrishna, Puttanna Kanagal, Sunil Kumar Desai and over the last few decades Vishnuvardhan, Ambarish, Shivarajkumar, Jayamala, Aarathi, Bharathi, Manjula, Ravichandran, Shankar Nag, Anant Nag, Girish Karnad, Girish Kasaravalli, M.P. Shankar, Vajramuni and Upendra. The most famous comedians in Kannada cinema have been Narasimharaju and Dwarakesh. Music directors who have made their mark in Kannada films include R. Ratna, M. Venkata Swamy, M. Ranga Rao, G.K. Venkatesh, Vijayabhaskar, the duo Rajan-Nagendra, Upendra Kumar, Sathyam, C. Ashwath, Hamsalekha, Gurukiran and T.G. Lingappa. Lyrics of Kannada film songs have been penned by Chi. Udayashankar, R.N. Jayagopal, Hamsalekha, and Doddarange Gowda among others. Playback singers in Kannada films include Dr. K.J. Yesudas, P.B. Sreenivas, S.P. Balasubrahmanyam, Rajesh Krishnan, Udit Narayan, Sonu

Nigam, Kunal Ganjawala, Shreya Ghosal, Sunidhi Chauhan, B.R. Chaya, Pallavi, Nandita, S. Janaki and P. Susheela. Dr. Rajkumar, has however sung hundreds of very melodious songs in those movies where he himself has starred as the hero, starting from the mid 1970's. There have been sad patches of Kannada Cinema—that is losing the most talented stars at their prime. Kalpana and Manjula of former years and Shankar Nag, Suneel, Nivedita Jain, Shashi Kumar (survived) of the latter, disappearing at their prime and Arati and Sudha Rani fading out due to their personal life.

1931 saw the emergence of talking pictures in the regional languages of South India with the release of *Kalidas*. In 1934, the first talky in Kannada, *Sati Sulochana*, followed by *Bhakta Dhruva* (aka *Dhruva Kumar*). Both *Sati Sulochana* and *Bhakta Dhruva* were major successes. But prospective filmmakers in Karnataka were handicapped by the lack of studios and technical crews. *Sati Sulochana* was shot in Kolhapur at the Chatrapathi studio; most filming, sound recording, and post-production was done in Madras (now Chennai). It was difficult, as well, to find financial backing for new film projects in the region; thus, very few movies in Kannada were released during the early years of Indian sound cinema. The 1950s will be remembered as the decade that introduced the doyen of Kannada cinema—Dr. Rajkumar. Rajkumar, originally known as Mutturaju was a theater artist, discovered by HLN Simha. HLN offered him a lead role in the mythological movie, Bedara Kannappa. The movie proved to be a blockbuster and signaled the arrival of a new star. It also launched comedian Narasimharaju and director G.V. Iyer. Even after the success of Bedara Kannappa, Kannada film industry remained stagnant. Lack of financiers, technicians and studios proved to be a hindrance to film making. Rajkumar, along with Narasimharaju and G.V. Iyer decided to form a partnership and produce movies. The partnership lasted for only a couple of movies. Ranadhira Kanteerava was one such successful joint venture. The majority of the films during this decade were either mythological or historical in nature. The 1970s and the '80s is heralded as the Golden Age of Kannada cinema. It was also the period that witness the birth of alternate cinema or parallel cinema. Kannada cinema spearheaded the parallel cinema movement in India along with Bengali and Malayalam cinemas.

B.V. Karanth's Chomana Dudi—an evocative film on caste distinctions, Girish Karnad's Kaadu and Girish Kasaravalli's Ghata shraddha spearheaded the Kannada parallel cinema. Vamshavruksha, Prema Karanth's Phaniyamma, Kadu Kudure, Hamsageethe, Accident, Akramana, Mooru Dhaarigalu, Tabarana Kathe, Bannadha Vesha, were some of the important movies of this decade.

Girish Kasarvalli, a gold medalist from the Pune's FTII, first film Ghata shraddha in 1977, won him the National award for best film. He has won the National award for best film four times including for his latest film Dweepa. His award winning films include Akramana (1979), Mooru Dhaarigalu (1981), Tabarana Kathe (1987), Bannadha Vesha (1989), Mane (1989), Kraurya (1996), Taayi Saaheba (1998) and Dweepa (2002). Girish Karnad's Kaadu (1973), Ondanondu Kaladalli (1978), M.S. Sathyu's Kanneshwara Rama (1977), Chithegu Chinthe (1978), Pattabhi Rama Reddy's Samskara (1970) were some the important movies of this decade. This decade also witness the rise of Puttanna Kanagal, who is widely acknowledged as the greatest director in Kannada film history. His movies like Bellimoda, Gejje Pooje, Sharapanjara Sakshatkara, Nagara Havu bought new style of film making which acted as a bridge between commercial and parallel cinema. In a bid to popularise film making, the Government of Karnataka in the 1980s granted a 50 percent tax exemption to Kannada films completely made in Karnataka and it increased the subsidy amount to Kannada films. The year 2005 witnessed stupendous box office success for Kannada film industry. Starting with Shivarajkumar starrer Jogi, which grossed Rs. 35 crore at the box office, films like Anna Tangi, Namma Basava, Amruthadhare, Deadly Soma, Nenapirali performed well at the box office. An estimated four of every five released had succeeded at the box office. In early 2005 a huge hit boosted Kannada film Industry Jogi starring Shivraj Kumar. The profits soared and there was happy mood in the Industry. There were many flicks which were moderate hits. Then came in last quarter of 2006 the huge blockbuster movie Mungaru Male, which shattered all records of the Kannada Film Industry and grossed more than 50 crores, and is released even in many other countries like USA, UK, Australia. The other huge hit of 2007 is Duniya which is still doing good at the Box Office.

Important Cinematographers of Kannada Cinema

- B.V. Madhusudhan of daari tapida maga.
- D.V. Raja Ram of Bandhana.
- B.C. GowriShankar of Om.
- S. Ramachandra Rishya Shringa, Ghatashradha.
- G.S. Bhaskar Bannada vesha, Nagamandala.
- Ramachandra Halkere Thaisaheba, Dweepa.
- G S V Seetharam of Ekaangi, aham premaasmi.

Telgu Film Industry (Tollywood)

Tollywood refers to the Telugu film industry. The origins of that name are disputed, but it is generally considered a portmanteau of "Telugu" and "Hollywood". The Telugu movie industry is based in the state of Andhra Pradesh in India. About 240 Telugu movies are released every year (approximately 3 every week). Telugu film industry is the second largest movie producer in India.. In 2005, the annual turnover reached Rs. 2.3 billion (US$57 million, as of July 17, 2007) with 700 million ticket sales. Popular movies tend to open during the three festive/holiday seasons of the region: Sankranthi, Ugadi, and Dussera. In 2004, total revenue for the Sankranthi season was around Rs. 1.5 billion (US$37 million, as of July 17, 2007). There are number of TV channels (Teja TV etc.) dedicated exclusively to feature programmes related to Telugu movies.

The Telugu film industry accounts for 1 per cent of the gross domestic product of Andhra Pradesh. Telugu films enjoy significant patronage in the neighboring southern States like Tamil Nadu, Karnataka. There is a fair amount of dispersion amongst the Indian film industries. Many successful Telugu films have been remade by the Hindi and Tamil film industries. For instance, Pokiri which was a Telugu film starring Tollywood heartthrob Mahesh Babu, was remade into Tamil and now being remade in Hindi with Salman Khan as the lead actor. Tollywood has also remade a fair number of Hindi, Tamil and other language films. The state of Andhra Pradesh has more than 2700 theaters, of which 150 are in the city of Hyderabad alone. The Tollywood film distribution is divided into 12 areas:

Area	Cities
Nizam	Hyderabad [Bhagyanagaram] Rangareddy Medak Nalgonda Nizamabad (Induru) Warangal Adilabad Khammam Mahabubnagar (Palamuru) Karimnagar (Srirampuru) Raichur (Karnataka)
Rayalaseema	Kurnool Cuddapah Anantapur Chittoor Bellary (Karnataka)
Nellore	
Guntur	Guntur Prakasam
Krishna	
East Godavari	
West Godavari	
Vizag	Vishakapatnam Vijayanagaram Srikakulam
Tamil Nadu	
Karnataka	
Orissa	
Overseas	

The Telugu film industry originated with the silent film in 1921, with the production of *Bhisma Pratighna*. The film was directed by Raghupati Venkaiah and his son R.S. Prakash. The two would go on to produce and direct dozens of films throughout the decade, casting theater actors in major roles. They established a long-lasting precedent of focusing exclusively on religious themes; *Nandanar*, *Gajendra Moksham*, and *Matsyavatar*, three of their most famous productions, centered on religious figures, parables, and morals. In 1931, the first Telugu film with audible dialogue, *Bhakta Prahlad*, was produced by H.M. Reddy. Popularly known as 'talkies', films with sound quickly grew in number and fanbase. In 1934, the industry saw its first major commercial success with *Lavakusa*.

Directed by C. Pullaiah and starring Parupalli Subbarao and Sriranjani in lead roles, the film attracted unprecedented numbers of viewers to theaters and thrust the young film industry into mainstream culture. By 1936, the mass appeal of film allowed directors to move away from religious and mythological themes. That year, under the direction of Krithiventi Nageswara Rao, *Prema Vijayam*, a film focusing on social issues, was released. Its success prompted the production of dozens of other immensely successful 'social films', notably 1939's *Vandemataram* and *Malli Pelli*. Touching on societal problems like the status of Untouchables and the practice of giving dowry, Telugu films increasingly focused on contemporary living: twenty-nine of the ninety-six films released between 1937 and 1947 had social themes. The outbreak of World War II and the subsequent resource scarcity caused the British Raj to impose a limit on the use of filmstrip in 1943 to 11,000 feet, a sharp reduction from the 20,000 feet that was common till then. As a result, the number of films produced during the War was substantially lower than in previous years. Nonetheless, prior to the ban, an important shift occurred in the industry: independent studios formed, actors and actresses were signed to contracts limiting who they could work for, and films moved from social themes to folklore legends. 1942's *Balanagamma* typified these changes: the film featured fantasy elements of cultural lore, was produced by Gemini Studios, and its producers added a restricting clause to the lead actress' contract. By 1947, nearly all films were produced by studios with contracted actors.

The budgets for Telugu movies typically range from 20 to 40 crores per film. Pre-lease revenues for popular films can range from 12 to 20 crores per film and post-release business for these movies can be 25-40 crores depending on the success of the movie. The Telugu film industry has a reputation for producing many singers, such as Ghantasala, S.P. Balasubrahmanyam, P. Susheela, S. Janaki. S.P. Balasubrahmanyam holds the record for singing the most number of songs (approximately 39,000).

Well-known stars of Telugu film industry have devoted fan followings in the southern India. Nandamuri Taraka Rama Rao, Akkineni Nageswara Rao, Krishna, Krishnamraju, Shoban Babu, Chiranjeevi, Balakrishna, Nagarjuna Akkineni, Venkatesh, Pawan Kalyan, Mahesh Babu, Jr. NTR are very popular and enjoy a significant fan following among the Telugu movie audience.

- 80 Telugu films were made in the first five years after the release of Bhakta Prahlada.
- A long-time Chief Minister of Andhra Pradesh, N.T. Rama Rao, was a popular actor of Telugu Cinema.
- Chiranjeevi, well known as Mega Star is the most popular actor in Tollywood and one of the highest paid actors in India

Malayalam Cinema

Malayalam cinema refers to films made in the Indian state of Kerala in Malayalam language. It forms a significant component of Indian cinema. Malayalam cinema remains the most popular medium of entertainment of the people of Kerala. Malayalm cinema is known for its socialistic leanings and it is the most realistic of Indian film industries. So obviously, at a different league from the Bollywood, which occasionally makes superhits out of films with out any commercial formulas. Movies like Namukku Parkkan Munthirithoppukal is an example. Malayalam movies are widely copied to Hindi, Tamil, Telugu and Kannada. Malayalam movie Manichitrathazhu was copied as Apthamitra in Kannada, Bhool Bhulaiya in Hindi and Chandramukhi in Tamil and Telugu.

The first Malayalam film, titled *Vigathakumaran* was released in 1928. It was a silent film, produced and directed by a businessman, J.C. Daniel who had no prior film experience. The second film *Marthanda Varma* based on a novel by C.V. Raman Pillai, was produced in 1933. But it was never released due to some legal disputes. *Balan* released in 1938 was the first talkie in Malayalam. Its screenplay and songs were written by Muthukulam Raghavan Pillai and directed by S. Nottani. It was produced at Chennai (then Madras) in the neighbouring state of Tamilnadu. Malayalam films continued to be made almost exclusively by Tamil producers till 1947 when the first major film studio, Udaya was established in Kerala. Malayalam Cinema has always taken its themes from very relevant social issues and has been intervened with the fields of literature, drama and politics from the very beginning. Jeevithanauka (1951) was a musical drama which spoke about the ego clashes in a joint family, the norm of the day. This movie was widely accepted and popular and can be mentioned as the first "Super Hit" seen by Malayalam Cinema. This success of the movie turned out to be sweet and sour at the same time. Although this success accelerated malayalam movie making, films that were produced after Jeevithanouka took up after this "success formula", hampering true creativity for a very long time. In 1954, *Neelakkuyil* captured national interest by winning the President's silver medal. Scripted by the well-known Malayalam novelist Uroob and directed by P. Bhasbaran and Ramu Kariat, it is often considered as the first authentic Malayali film. Another notable production was *Newspaper Boy* (1955) which had elements of Italian neorealism. This film is noteworthy as the hard work of a group of amateur college students and spoke of the story of a printing press employee and his family hit by extreme poverty. *Chemmeen* (1965), directed by Ramu Kariat and based on a story by Thakazhi Sivasankara Pillai went on to become immensely popular and won the national award. It had music by Salil Chowdhury, songs by Manna Dey and editing by Hrishikesh Mukherjee. The first colour film in Malayalam was *Kandam Becha Coat*.

The 70s saw the emergence of a new wave of cinema in Malayalam. The growth of film society movement in Kerala introduced the works of the French and Italian New Wave directors to the discerning Malayali film enthusiasts. Adoor Gopalakrishnan's first film *Swayamvaram* (1972) brought Malayalam cinema to the International film arena. In 1973 M.T. Vasudevan Nair who was by then recognized as an important author in Malayalam, directed his first film *Nirmalyam*, which won the President's Gold Medal for the best film. G. Aravindan followed Adoor's lead with his *Uttarayanam* in 1974. K.P. Kumaran's 'Adhithi' (1974) was another film which was acclaimed by the critics. John Abraham, K.R. Mohanan, K.G. George, and G.S. Panikkar were products of the Pune Film Institute who made significant contributions. During the late 70s, a good proportion of the youth started seeing Malayalam Cinema as a medium of expression and thought of it as a tool to revitalize the society. A noted Director, Aravindan was famous in Kerala as a cartoonist before he started making films. His important movies include *Kanchana Seeta* (1977), *Thampu* (1978), *Kummatty* (1979), *Chidambaram* (1985), *Oridathu* (1986), and *Vasthuhara* (1990).

Adoor Gopalakrishnan made *Elipathayam* in 1981. This movie was widely acclaimed and won the British Film Institute award. His other movies include *Mukhamukham* (1984), *Anantharam* (1987)

Mathilukal (1989), *Vidheyan* (1994), *Kathapurushan* (1995), and *Nizhalkkuthu* (2003). Padmarajan made his early works in this period including the movie *Koodevide?* (1983) P.A. Backer and Bharathan are other names worth mentioning.

Most critics and audiences consider this period from as the golden age of Malayalam cinema. The Malayalam cinema of this period was characterised by detailed screenplays dealing with everyday life with a lucid narration of plot intermingling with humour and melancholy. This was aided by brilliant cinematography and lighting as in motion pictures like Perumthachan (1990), directed by Ajayan with Santosh Sivan as the cinematographer. These films are also remembered for their warm background music by composers like Johnson, as in the motion picture Namukku parkkan munthiri thoppukal (1986) by Padmarajan. Many of the movies released during this time narrowed the gap between art cinemas and commercial cinemas in the Malayalam film industry, as in *Oru Vadakkan Veeragatha* (1989). These were paralleled with movies like *Kireedam* (1989) directed by Sibi Malayil and written by Lohitadas, *Mathilukal* directed by Adoor Gopalakrishnan (1989), 'Amaram'(1991) directed by Bharathan, *Kaakothikaavile Appoopan Thadikal* (1988) directed by Kamal and 'Sargam' (1992) directed by Hariharan. The period had an abundance of movies rich in creative humour from directors like Priyadarshan, Sathyan Anthikkad and Kamal. The era also saw well crafted comedy by the Duo Siddique-Lal, (Ramji Rao speaking (1989) and *In Harihar Nagar* (1990). Other notable contributions of this period include *His Highness Abdullah* (1990) directed by Sibi Malayil, *Piravi* (1989) by Shaji N. Karun, *Abhayam* (1991) directed by Sivan, and the motion picture *Daisy* (1988) an expressive depiction of separation and longing set in a Boarding school, directed by Prathap K. Pothan.

Films made during this period continued to stand out for their brilliance in storytelling and appeal. These include 'Bharatham' (1991) by Sibi Malayil, *Ulladakkam* (1991) directed by Kamal, Kaalapaani (1996) by Priyadarshan, and the award winning 'Manichitrathazhu' (1993) by Fazil. 'Sphadikam' (1995) directed by Bhadran was well received by the viewers as was 'Desadanam' (1997) by Jayaraaj. Some works stood out as strong in evocative power reminiscent of the earlier period, like *Swaham* (1994) directed by Shaji N. Karun, the first Malayalam film entry into the Cannes

International Film Festival. Malayalm movies have seen a rare downward journey of softcore pornographic films, which was commonly known as Shakila made commercial gains. This gave malaylam movies a very bad name among general public on other parts of India who are unaware of the high standards Malayalam Movies followed till then. But These Softcore Porn Movies were never a part of mainstream cinema. Family viewers simply stoped watching cinema in theatre. They left glued to their TV sets watching golden era movies aired by Malayalam Satellite channels like Asianet. The Malayalam film industry in recent times has been affected by the spread of satellite digital television and film piracy. Slapstick comedy is the predominant theme. *Meesamadhavan* (2002) by Lal Jose and *Kunjikkoonan* directed by Sasi Shankar (2002) are examples. However notable exceptions to these were *Chinthavishtayaya Shyamala* by Srinivasan (1998), *Vanaprastham* (1999) directed by Shaji N. Karun, *Maduranombarakaatu* (2000), *Meghamalhar* (2001), *Perumazhakaalam* (2004) and *Karuthapakshikal* (2006) directed by Kamal. Sequels have been made of a number of successful films. These include *Ravanaprabhu* (*Devasuram*) and *Nerariyan CBI* (*Oru CBI Diarykurippu*). Generally movies at this period were of low quality. Malayam cinema has seen a rare dearth of talent. At the same time, Tamil movies had seen a surge of new talent in script writers, directors and actors alike. This resulted in increased popularity of Tamil and Hindi movies in Kerala. Several Film theatres were closed rural Kerala and were converted to Marriage Halls.

Malayalam movies have seen a real comeback in 2005. New directors such as Lal Jose, Roshan Andrews, Blessy and Anwar Rasheed brought back original scripts to Malayalam movie. Notable Movies of this era are Udayananu Tharam, Note Book, Classmates, Thanmatra, Kazhcha, Palunku, Keerthi Chakra, Raja Manikyam, Vinoda Yatra, Rasa thanthram, Arabi Kadha and Kadha Paryumbol. This era has seen new promising actors like Prithviraj, Narain, Jayasurya, Meera Jasmin and Kavya Madhavan along with stalwarts Mohan Lal and Mammooty.

AMMA

The major actors and actresses of the Malayalam Cinema has recently formed an organization to safegaurd their interests and to fight against piracy. The Association of Malayalam Movie Artists better know as *AMMA* (literal meaning: Mother) aims to act against piracy, safegaurd the interests of member actors and actresses and act as a common forum to raise concerns and address issues. The organization is generally regarded as successful. The activities of "AMMA" include endowments, insurance schemes, and committees on wages and benefits on revision, fund for research, pensions, education loans for their children etc. for the members. The organization has recently entered into Film production to raise funds for its activities.

Other Organisations

- Malayalam Cine Technicians Association (MACTA)
- Kerala Film Chamber of Commerce
- Malayalam Film Chamber of Commerce
- Kerala Film Producers' Association
- Kerala Film Distributors Association
- Kerala Cine Exhibitors Federation
- Kerala Film Exhibitors Association

A crisis hit Malayalam film industry in early 2004 when the AMMA participated in a couple of stage shows, despite protests from the Kerala Film Chamber of Commerce. A 4 moth long long stand-off followed, with both sides remanined adamant on their stands, despite attempts to ease situation from the State Government. The stand-off came to an end when both sides loosened their stands as they started to suffer from the crisis and rebel action.

3

Introduction to Film-making : Elements and Dimensions

FILM-MAKING

Film-making is the process of making a film, from an initial story idea or commission through scriptwriting, shooting, editing and finally distribution to an audience. Typically it involves a large number of people and can take anywhere between a few months and several years to complete. Film-making takes place all over the world in a huge range of economic, social and political contexts, using a variety of technologies and techniques.

Stages of Film-making

Film-making consists of five main stages:

- *Development*: The script is written and drafted into a workable blueprint for a film.
- *Pre-production*: Preparations are made for the shoot, in which cast and crew are hired, locations are selected, and sets are built.
- *Production*: The raw elements for the finished film are recorded.
- *Post-production*: The film is edited, sound effects, music and any computer effects are added, and the film is completed.
- *Sales and Distribution*. The film is picked up by a distributor and reaches its audience.

Development

This is the stage where an idea is fleshed out into a viable script. The producer of the movie will find a story, which may come from books, plays, other films, true stories, original ideas, etc. Once the theme, or underlying message, has been identified, a synopsis will be prepared. This is followed by a step outline, which breaks the story down into one-paragraph scenes, concentrating on the dramatic structure. Next, a treatment is prepared. This is a 25 to 30 page description of the story, its mood and characters, with little dialogue and stage direction, often containing drawings to help visualize the key points.

The screenplay is then written over a period of several months, and may be rewritten several times to improve the dramatization, clarity, structure, characters, dialogue, and overall style. However, producers often skip the previous steps and develop submitted screenplays which are assessed through a process called script coverage. A film distributor should be contacted at an early stage to assess the likely market and potential financial success of the film. Hollywood distributors will adopt a hard-headed business approach and consider factors such as the film genre, the target audience, the historical success of similar films, the actors who might appear in the film and the potential directors of the film. All these factors imply a certain appeal of the film to a possible audience and hence the number of "bums on seats" during the theatrical release. Not all films make a profit from the theatrical release alone, therefore DVD sales and worldwide distribution rights need to be taken into account.

The movie pitch is then prepared and presented to potential financiers. If the pitch is successful and the movie is given the "green light", then financial backing is offered, typically from a major film studio, film council or independent investors. A deal is negotiated and contracts are signed.

Pre-production

In pre-production, the movie is designed and planned. The production company is created and a production office established. The production is storyboarded and visualized with the help of illustrators and concept artists. A production budget will also be drawn up to cost the film.

The producer will hire a crew. The nature of the film, and the budget, determine the size and type of crew used during film-making. Many Hollywood blockbusters employ a cast and crew of thousands while a low-budget, independent film may be made by a skeleton crew of eight or nine. Typical crew positions include:

- The director is primarily responsible for the acting in the movie and managing the creative elements.
- The assistant director (AD) manages the shooting schedule and logistics of the production among other tasks.
- The casting director finds actors for the parts in the script. This normally requires an audition by the actor. Lead actors are carefully chosen and are often based on the actor's reputation or "star power."
- The location manager finds and manages the film locations. Most pictures are shot in the predictable environment of a studio sound stage but occasionally outdoor sequences will call for filming on location.
- The production manager manages the production budget and production schedule. He or she also reports on behalf of the production office to the studio executives or financiers of the film.
- The director of photography (DP or DOP) or cinematographer creates the photography of the film. He or she cooperates with the director, director of audiography (DOA) and AD.
- The art director manages the art department, which makes production sets, costumes and provides makeup and hair styling services.
- The production designer creates the look and feel of the production sets and props, working with the art director to create these elements.
- The storyboard artist creates visual images to help the director and production designer communicate their ideas to the production team.
- The production sound mixer manages the audio experience during the production stage of a film. He or

she cooperates with the director, DOP, and AD.
- The sound designer creates new sounds and enhances the aural feel of the film with the help of foley artists.
- The composer creates new music for the film.
- The choreographer creates and coordinates the movement and dance—typically for musicals. Some films also credit a fight choreographer.

Production

In production the movie is created and shot. More crew will be recruited at this stage, such as the property master, script supervisor, assistant directors, stills photographer, picture editor, and sound editors. These are just the most common roles in film-making; the production office will be free to create any unique blend of roles to suit a particular film.

A typical day's shooting begins with an assistant director following the shooting schedule for the day. The film set is constructed and the props made ready. The lighting is rigged and the camera and sound recording equipment are set up. At the same time, the actors are wardrobed in their costumes and attend the hair and make-up departments.

The actors rehearse their scripts and blocking with the director. The picture and sound crews then rehearse with the actors. Finally, the action is shot in as many takes as the director wishes.

Each take of a shot follows a slating procedure and is marked on a clapperboard, which helps the editor keep track of the takes in post-production. The clapperboard records the scene, take, director, director of photography, date, and name of the film written on the front, and is displayed for the camera. The clapperboard also serves the necessary function of providing a marker to synched up the film and the sound take. Sound is recorded on a separate apparatus from the film and they must be synched up in post-production.

The director will then decide if the take was acceptable or not. The script supervisor and the sound and camera teams log the take on their respective report sheets. Every report sheet records important technical notes on each take.

When shooting is finished for the scene, the director declares a "wrap." The crew will "strike," or dismantle, the set for that scene. The director approves the next day's shooting schedule and a daily progress report is sent to the production office. This includes the report sheets from continuity, sound, and camera teams. Call sheets are distributed to the cast and crew to tell them when and where to turn up the next shooting day.

For productions using traditional photographic film, the unprocessed negative of the day's takes are sent to the film laboratory for processing overnight. Once processed, they return from the laboratory as *dailies* or *rushes* (film positives) and are viewed in the evening by the director, above the line crew, and, sometimes, the cast. For productions using digital technologies, shots are downloaded and organized on a computer for display as dailies.

When the entire film is in the can, or in the completion of the production phase, the production office normally arranges a wrap party to thank all the cast and crew for their efforts.

Post-production

Here the film is assembled by the film editor. The modern use of video in the film-making process has resulted in two workflow variants: one using entirely film, and the other using a mixture of film and video.

In the film workflow, the original camera film (negative) is developed and copied to a one-light workprint (positive) for editing with a mechanical editing machine. An edge code is recorded onto film to locate the position of picture frames. Since the development of non-linear editing systems such as Avid, Quantel or Final Cut Pro, the film workflow is used by very few productions.

In the video workflow, the original camera negative is developed and telecined to video for editing with computer editing software. A timecode is recorded onto video tape to locate the position of picture frames. Production sound is also synched up to the video picture frames during this process.

The first job of the film editor is to build a rough cut taken from sequences (or scenes) based on individual "takes" (shots). The purpose of the rough cut is to select and order the best shots.

The next step is to create a fine cut by getting all the shots to flow smoothly in a seamless story. Trimming, the process of shortening scenes by a few minutes, seconds, or even frames, is done during this phase. After the fine cut has been screened and approved by the director and producer, the picture is "locked," meaning no further changes are made. Next, the editor creates a negative cut list (using edge code) or an edit decision list (using timecode) either manually or automatically. These edit lists identify the source and the picture frame of each shot in the fine cut.

Once the picture is locked, the film passes out of the hands of the editor to the sound department to build up the sound track. The voice recordings are synchronised and the final sound mix is created. The sound mix combines sound effects, background sounds, ADR, dialogue, walla, and music.

The sound track and picture are combined together, resulting in a low quality answer print of the movie. There are now two possible workflows to create the high quality release print depending on the recording medium:

1. In the film workflow, the cut list that describes the film-based answer print is used to cut the original colour negative (OCN) and create a colour timed copy called the colour master positive or interpositive print. For all subsequent steps this effectively becomes the master copy. The next step is to create a one-light copy called the colour duplicate negative or internegative. It is from this that many copies of the final theatrical release print are made. Copying from the internegative is much simpler than copying from the interpositive directly because it is a one-light process; it also reduces wear-and-tear on the interpositive print.
2. In the video workflow, the edit decision list that describes the video-based answer print is used to edit the original colour tape (OCT) and create a high quality colour master tape. For all subsequent steps this effectively becomes the master copy. The next step uses a film recorder to read the colour master tape and copy each video frame directly to film to create the final theatrical release print.

Finally the film is previewed, normally by the target audience, and any feedback may result in further shooting or edits to the film.

Distribution

This is the final stage, where the movie is released to cinemas or, occasionally, to DVD, VCD or VHS (though VHS tapes are less common now that more people own DVD players). The movie is duplicated as required for theatrical distribution. Press kits, posters, and other advertising materials are published and the movie is advertised.

The movie will usually be launched with a launch party, press releases, interviews with the press, showings of the film at a press preview, and/or at film festivals. It is also common to create a website to accompany the movie. The movie will play at selected cinemas and the DVD is typically released a few months later. The distribution rights for the film and DVD are also usually sold for worldwide distribution. Any profits are divided between the distributor and the production company.

Independent Film-making

Film-making also takes place outside of the studio system and is commonly called independent film-making. Since the introduction of DV technology, the means of production have become more democratized. Film-makers can conceivably shoot and edit a movie, create and edit the sound and music, and mix the final cut on a home computer. However, while the means of production may be democratized, financing, distribution, and marketing remain difficult to accomplish outside the traditional system. Most independent film-makers rely on film festivals to get their films noticed and sold for distribution. However, the Internet has allowed for relatively inexpensive distribution of independent films; many film-makers post their films online for critique and recognition. Although there is little profitability in this, a film-maker can still gain exposure via the web.

LOW-BUDGET FILM-MAKING

Low budget film-making involves:

1. MMM/Low Budget/Shooting on Film
2. Movie Making Manual—Writing Low Budget

SHORT FILMS AND ART OF FLIRTING

Short films implies:

1. Movie Making Manual—Submitting to a broadcaster
2. Movie Making Manual—Why Make a Short
   - The Concept
   - The script: The script is a basic layout of the scenes, dialogue and actions in the film.
   - Financing it
   - Assembling a team
   - Headline text
   - Pre-production
   - Production
   - Post-production
   - The Screening
   - Cannes
   - Selling the film
   - Searching for sponsorship
   - Lessons learned

MOVIE MAKING MANUAL: AN OVERVIEW

Introduction to Movie Making

- What is movie making?
- Staffing and casting

Development

- Writing
  - Theory
  - Writing
  - Rewriting

- Screenplay format
- Treatments
- Synopsis
- Logline
- Pitching
- Certification
- Downloading scripts
- Writing low budget

- Protecting your ideas
- Funding and budgetting
    - Funding plans
    - Grants
    - Tax Breaks
    - "Elements"
- Contracts and law
    - Copyright

Pre-production

- Overview
- Budgeting and scheduling
- Pre-production
    - Acquiring film stock
    - Storyboarding
    - Casting Directors
    - Location scouting
    - Funding and budgetting contents
    - Scheduling contents
- Paperwork
    - Call sheet
    - Scene breakdown
    - Release form
- Contracts and Law
    - Crew contract
    - Cast contract
    - Release form

Production

- Overview
  - Production overview
- Technical
  - Cinematography
  - Actors contents
  - Blocking
  - Lighting
  - Power sources
  - Sound recording
  - Stills photography
  - Character animation
- Directing and Managing a Set
  - Directing contents
  - Shooting styles
  - Clapper board and keeping notes on set
  - Directing actors
  - Keeping the crew happy

Post-production

- Overview
  - Post Production overview
- Audio
  - Music/Film Scoring
  - Sound design
  - Foley
  - ADR
- Visual: What is Editing
  - How to edit a dramatic scene
  - Visual effects
  - Animation (for visual effects)
  - Colour grading
  - Digital intermediate
  - Subtitles
  - Which format to finish on?

- HD Links
- For Celluloid
  - Telecine

Film Distribution and Marketing

- Overview
  - Film distribution and marketing overview
- Sales, Exhibition and Distribution
  - Film marketing
  - Distributing direct
  - Selling online
  - Digital cinema distribution
  - Submitting to a broadcaster
  - Putting videos online
  - Burning a DVD

EDUCATING ABOUT FILM MAKING PROCESS IN BRIEF: A CASE STUDY

The first student to complete the basic filmmaking course (pre-production) is Mohamed Alsayed of Cairo, Egypt. The final assignment of the course is to create an animatic (which is a movie of the storyboards produced with the free version of FrameForge 3D Studio.)

Wikiversity Film School Courses in Narrative Film Production

Course 1 : Basic Filmmaking (pre-production)
Course 2 : Film editing introduction
Course 3 : Film scoring for dramatic scenes
Exercise : Script writing for high school dramas
Project : The storyboard artwork project
Future : Poser/DAZ Studio animation

These courses are only for dramatic motion pictures (movies with a script and dialog). These courses are not for documentaries, event video, corporate video, educational programmes, or multimedia.

Anyone can Learn to be a Filmmaker

Filmmaking is Easy: Filmmaking is not rocket science. Everything about filmmaking is extremely easy to learn. Anyone can do it if they wish.

The challenge of learning filmmaking: The challenge is filmmaking requires learning a huge number of skills. If you want to be an independent filmmaker, you must learn the equivalent of 20 different careers.

Telling a Story: In a dramatic motion picture, the story is told by many people. The cinematographer tells the story with the camera. The lighting person tells the story with lighting. The film composer tells the story with music. The actors tell the story with action and dialog. The editor tells the story with editing. The sound effects person tells the story with sound.

And as an independent filmmaker, you have to learn to all of these skills. If you fail to learn even one of these skills, people will notice and be turned off by your movie. You must learn everything!!!!

What do We Do?

Make a Tiny Movie: In the filmmaking class, we create a short motion picture. It is less than a minute long so it is very simple.

Where to Start?

Filmmaking, Editing, and Scoring: Budding filmmakers should start with the basic filmmaking course. For the first lesson, you will format a very short motion picture script. After that, take the pop quiz where you tell me how you would begin to film this scene.

If you want to be a film composer (but you are not a musician), screen writer, or a film editor, you can go directly to the courses in film editing or film scoring or the script writing exercise.

Learning Filmmaking Software

Intel Processor: First, you need to do is learn about the computer software for filmmaking. See below for a list of the software you will need. Most is free!

Designed for the Macintosh: The Film Scoring course is designed for Apple's GarageBand with Jam Pack: Symphony Orchestra

The Film Editing course is designed for Apple's Final Cut Pro or Adobe Premiere.

Linux: Where possible, free Linux software is listed. However, there is still no standard movie file format for Linux and nothing which matches the quality and usefulness of Apple's GarageBand for film scoring.

Therefore, Linux is currently not a good choice for filmmakers.

Cost

Lessons: These filmmaking courses are free. The only requirement is you submit your homework assignments so others can benefit. (see right)

The Disks: If you do not wish to purchase the required disks from the Star Movie Shop, you can borrow the disks from the instructor. You will have one month before you must return each disk.

Software: I always try to select programmes which are free.

Sharing Your Work

Your Homework Assignments: Your completed assignments must be submitted under the Free Documentation License or as Public Domain.

This allows what you have learned to be shared by others.

Free Filmmaking Software at Wikivesity Film School

There is some of free software used at Wikiversity Film School. Sometimes, this software is demo versions or simplified versions of software but this is good enough to complete these lessons. Using free software, you can learn a tremendous amount about filmmaking.

FrameForge 3D Studio Free Demo Version

Basic filmmaking (pre-production): The heart of the Wikiversity Film School's basic filmmaking course (pre-production) is

FrameForge 3D Studio 2 Demo Version. This is the most educational programme used at Wikiversity Film School. And the demo version is free for both the Macintosh and Windows operating system.

This programme simulates the motion picture camera, the movie set, and the actors. The programme is useful for experimenting with the different lenses on your motion picture camera. And the final output of FrameForge 3D Studio 2 Demo Version is completely frame accurate (including depth of field effects) ready to give your cinematographer for creating all the shots of your movie.

The free demo version is limited to 20 uses. Other limitations apply. However, this is more than enough to complete your assignments at Wikiversity Film School. Download this free programme today and begin learning how to use it.

Apple's GarageBand

Film Scoring: All film scoring lessons at Wikiversity Film School is done using Apple's GarageBand which is free with each new Macintosh PC.

Starting in 2008, if you are going to by a PC, you might as well purchase a Macintosh PC.

You will also need the musical instruments of the symphony orchestra. Some sources of musical software instruments of the symphony orchestra are free (such as the packages from Boldt) and some are not. I recommend Apple's Jam Pack: Symphony Orchestra. I have not tried Apple's new Jam Pack for voices which might also be useful.

- Filmmakers should not use Apple's Logic 7 which is poorly designed and exceedingly awkward.

Film Dailies

Film Editing: The filmmaking, film editing and film scoring courses use disks from the Star Movie Shop. The Star Movie Shop is not open to the public. It is only open to serious film students.

The disks contain unedited scenes from television dramas for editing and scoring on the Macintosh computer. This is the real thing. Most film dailies require QuickTime. Files can be converted to other formats for Windows using additional software (not provided.)

Except for the actual film dailies, all the contents of these disks is distributed under the NGU Open Source Document License.

Animation: Starting in 2009, Wikiversity Film School will have a simple course in 3D animation. This will use the free programmes of DAZ Studio and Bryce 5.5.

If you have Poser and Vue, you can use those programmes but they are not free.

DAZ Studio and Bryce take time to learn so if you are interested in working with 3D, you should download these free programmes and begin to learn them.

Other Useful Programmes

- ArtRage2 Free is used for matte painting and creating the movie poster. This is a simple and fun artistic painting programme. Feels very natural. Extremely useful. If you need any kind of digital painting with traditional artist materials, this is your first choice. This is the free version which is fully working but more limited than the full version which is also remarkably inexpensive.
- GIMP is a free paint programme comparable to Adobe Photoshop. Surprisingly mature programme but definitely not to the level of Photoshop. Requires X-11. If you do not have Adobe Photoshop 4 or later, this programme is absolutely necessary for some of the classes at Wikiversity Film School.
- Audacity is a free useful utility for working with audio and converting audio to OGG files. It is a bit awkward but it is free.
- Tux Paint is a free fun paint programme for kids. It has the added advantage of using rubber stamps and creating matte paintings easily. Has the unique feature of doing rough storyboards with special storyboard artwork. Also useful for one of the lessons about learning matte painting at Wikiversity Film School for kids.

Course 1: WikiU Film School Course 01: Learning the Basics of Filmmaking

Lessons in Basic Filmmaking Course

- Formatting the Script
- Pop Quiz—What is the first shot?
- Creating the thumbnail storyboards
- Creating the 3D storyboards
- Entrance Exam disk
- Learning about camera lenses
- Record the dialog for the animatic
- Intro to narrative filmmaking
- Draw the movie poster for 'Star Wars'
- Understanding dailies
- Create a matte painting
- Understanding editing
- Pop Quiz—Creating the moods (film scoring)
- Understanding "L-Cuts"
- Create the animatic

Course 1—"Basic Filmmaking" starts by showing you all the pre-production steps for making a short motion picture.

- Begin learning filmmaking by formatting the script using the free demo version of Final Draft (or CeltX for people who have Linux.)

Your Instructor Says:

- Please use the free demo version of Final Draft rather than CeltX.
  1. The free Final Draft demo has fewer bugs than the beta version of CeltX.
  2. You will learn much more from Final Draft because it has many more features than CeltX.
  3. It takes longer to learn to use Final Draft than CeltX but Final Draft has better instructions.

Purpose and Goal of This Filmmaking Course

The purpose of this course is to learn the steps needed to prepare to make a motion picture. This is called "Pre-Production".

The final product of this course is a movie of the storyboards which is called an "Animatic".

The heart of this course is the free demo version of FrameForge 3D Studio. You must use this programme to create the high-quality storyboards needed for the animatic.

Download the free demo version of FrameForge 3D Studio today and take a look.

Note: As we walk through all the steps of making this movie, you will prepare yourself for entering film school.

The Story

The Story of Our Motion Picture: The story is simple. A young person and an old person talk about the meaning of the motion picture "Star Wars". That is how the story gets the name "Seduced by the Dark Side!".

Time to Completion

Work at Your Own Pace: There are many steps to make a movie. Go at your own pace. Eventually, you will need to complete all the courses at the Wikiversity Film School to complete this movie.

The Software

The Software is Free: Most of the software for this course is free. We use trial version and free versions when we can.

The Most Important Programme: This course centers around the FREE demo version of FrameForge 3D Studio. Once you learn to use this programme, you will find it very helpful for your entire filmmaking career.

The Steps of This Course

1. *Script Formatting*: You format the script with the free demo version of Final Draft.

2. *Select the First Two Frames*: You decide how you want the movie to start.
3. *Thumbnail Storyboards*: You download the storyboard sheet and quickly draw the thumbnail storyboards.
4. *High Quality Storyboards*: You create the storyboards with FrameForge 3D Studio.
5. *Study Lenses*: Before you create the storyboards, you need to study the effect of the camera lens.
6. *Draw the Movie Poster Prop*: Before you create the storyboards, you need to create the poster for the storyboards.
7. *Record the Dialog*: You need to record the dialog for the animatic.
8. *Select the Music*: You must decide the moods of the story.
9. *Create the Matte Painting*: You must create a matte painting for the last (or the first) storyboard for the scene.
10. *Create the Animatic*: Finally, you make a movie of the storyboards.
    - Completing this course will be easier if you have also take the film editing and film scoring courses.

Course 2: Fundamentals of Narrative Film Editing

Course: Introduction to Film Editing

Exercise : Fun scene—Edit "The Promotion"
Lesson 1 : Overview of editing a conversation
Exercise : Fun scene—Edit "Missing"
Lesson 2 : Analyze film dailies—24 unedited scenes

Exercise : Edit Missing—Edit "Watching"
Example : The story of Penny and Eggbert
Lesson 3 : How and why of L-Cuts
Lesson 4 : Editing for film scoring
Lesson 5 : Creating your own editing workshops

This Course is for Editing a Dramatic Scene

Which type of editing?: This course covers only one (1) type of film editing: editing scripted dialog (drama).

For people who want to make narrative motion pictures, editing a **dramatic conversation** is the most important and the most challenging form of film editing.

Not for Documentaries nor Multi-media: This course is only for editing of a dramatic conversation. If you are interested in other documentaries nor multi-media, do **not** take this course.

Editing a conversations is **completely backwards** to editing everything else.

Real hands-on Editing: This course quickly goes through all the basics of editing a dramatic scene from TV dramas.

These lessons gives you hands-on experience editing actual motion pictures and television dramas. It's the real thing!

Required Disks: Each lesson requires a disk. After the first disk, I will loan you the disks but you must return them. To get the first one, see the qualification to the left.

What are Practice Scenes?

Practice scenes are the film dailies from actual motion pictures or television dramas. These are unedited scenes which have been digitized, ready for editing on your computer.

Drama, not Documentaries: These scenes are not from documentaries. Instead, they contain scripted dialog from narrative productions. That means a dramatic conversation.

Editing a dramatic scene is totally different from editing a documentary which is a completely different technology using completely different methods. If you want to learn to edit documentaries, corporate video, event video or multimedia, these lessons will only confuse you.

Editing for Motion Pictures: Narrative film editing gives you an understanding of the basic concepts of telling a dramatic story. Once you have learned to edit a conversation, you are ready for more advanced editing of motion pictures.

Course 3: Film Scoring: Introduction

This school is: Narrative film production—Wikiversity Film School and School of Music—Wikiversity Film School

This course is: Film scoring for musicians

The pages in the course is: 1. Introduction to film scoring

2. *Exercise*: The sound of fear
3. *Exercise*: Other moods from a single note
4. *Exercise*: The sound of joy
5. *Exercise*: Other moods from delicate rhythm
   Fun pop quiz: Music which tells a story
6. *Exercise*: Creating a mood or story with a melody
   Creative pop quiz: *The Spy Story*—Who is who?
   FREE: Entrance Exam disk for film editing and scoring
7. *Exercise*: Creating a motive
8. *Exercise*: Creating continuity
9. *Exercise*: Foreground/Background music
   Watch a movie: *George Lucas In Love*
   Film scoring with actual scenes from television dramas
10. *Exercise*: What is a "Spotting Session"?—*Only A Dream*
11. *Exercise*: Write two musical cues for *Home Wrecker*
    More Musical Theory
    Exercise: Butchering Midi
12. *Exercise*: How would you score *Green Tea Smoothie*?
13. *Exercise*: Write a film score for *Blindman's Bluff*
    Exercise: Write a film score for *Seduced by the Dark Side!*

The Ideal Student

This course is only for people who want to make musical sound effects.

The Wrong Student

If you enjoy writing songs, do not take this course.

If you ever attended a music school, do not take this course.

If you enjoy playing music, do not take this course.

About This Course

Which Kind of Film Scoring?: This course teaches you how to score a conversation from a narrative motion picture or narrative television drama.

This course teaches how to use musical sound effects to create moods for dramatic scenes where people are talking. That is all!

Creating the mood for a conversation is the most challenging job of a film composer. Everything else is much easier. That is why the course focuses on just this one kind of film scoring-conversations.

Film Scoring Made Easy: Film scoring is easy. Anyone can do it.

You just need someone to tell you the theory and then show you how to apply it to real scenes from television dramas.

The Secret of Film Scoring

All you have to do is learn **the secret of film scoring**:

1. The only purpose of a film score is to create the moods for a scene.
2. Single notes are best. (Usually, a single note is all that will fit.)
3. Delicate rhythms also work well. (No drums or other percussion, including piano)
4. Melodies can do lots of special things.

Preparing the Viewer Emotionally

Explaining the story with music: This course deals with dramatic TV shows (cop, lawyer, medical shows). This is a medium where sounds are used to cue the viewer emotionally. That is your job!

The best way to do this is to keep your music short and simple. That is why this course is emphasizes the basics. You simply add moods to a scene.

I cannot stress this enough. This course is **not** about making music. Instead, this course is about creating **moods**.

In this course, you create most of your film score by creating musical sound effects, not music. That is all that is needed.

Don't get carried away with your own brilliance. Please keep it simple!

The Disks are on Loan

This disks for this course come from the Star Movie Shop.

I can loan them to you if you promise to return each disk in one month. (All of the disks are not copy protected.)

Otherwise, you must purchase the disks from them.

You Begin at the Beginning

Start with the Basics

I can teach you film scoring. But you must start with the basics.

For the moment, forget about John Williams and Danny Elfman.

Instead, think Schroeder (of the "Peanuts" cartoons). Just a 5-year-old kid pounding on a toy piano to create Musical Sound Effects.

These musical sound effects create moods. That is your goal. To create moods for your audience.

Requirement for this course: To take this course, you must become a 5-year-old kid who likes to create wonderful moods just by pounding on your Midi keyboard.

The Theory of Film Scoring

Mood, Mood, Mood: The only purpose of music in a motion picture is to explain the moods of the scene.

The composer tells the audience what they should be feeling when they watch the movie. That's it!

Therefore, you have to learn to create moods with your music.

Most Important: It is not the music which is important but only the mood which it creates.

Most of the time, your music must be kept short and simple. Musicians have very little time and space in a motion picture. Most musicians/composers find this very frustrating. Get over it.

It is not About You: Film scoring is not about your music. Film scoring is only about creating the moods that the director needs in his movie. If you can accept this, you can be a great film composer.

So keep it simple. Just create moods.

Required Software

Symphony Orchestra: For this course, you should be able to create realistic sound of a symphony orchestra on your computer. Lots of programmes do this. Even GarageBand with Jam Pack:

Symphony Orchestra or the **free** Boldt packages can do this very well.

Expertise in MIDI: Before you begin these lessons, you must have already mastered your music creation software. You must be able to do midi sequencing with software instruments inside your computer.

How to Score a Scene

What are the Moods?: Go through each scene, sentence by sentence, and decide what the audience should feel.

If the audience does not automatically feel that way, you must create that mood with your music.

The Actors' Words are Most Important: Do not put strong music on top of dialog. The exception is dialog that you do **not** want the audience to listen to carefully or you want the audience to strain to listen to.

What Part of the Story is not Clear?: If any part of the story is not clear, you must explain the story to the audience using music that tells a story.

If something is happening off screen and the sound effects do not tell the whole story, you must **tell the story** with a melody.

Create Continuity: When possible, create continuity throughout the motion picture using your music (with a motif).

Transitions: Use music to transition from one scene or one action to another.

Course 4: Basic Filmmaking for High School Drama Departments

Filmmaking for High School Drama Departments

A Film and a Play: Wikiversity Film School is developing a new way for drama departments to create short motion pictures at the same time they produce a school play.

The idea is to create a 5-minute motion picture using the same set, lights, costumes and props as the current school play. After the school play begins its run, rehearsals on a short movie can begin with new actors. Once the play is over, the shooting of the movie can begin. Since the set and the lights and the costumes are all ready, filming can be done very quickly during the weeks that follows the closing of the play.

Once the short movie is filmed, the raw footage can be put on DVD-Video disks for people around the world to edit.

To do this, schools need 5-minute motion picture scripts which can be filmed on stage for the most popular school plays.

Script Writing

We need you to write a script which a high school drama department will turn into a 5-minute motion picture.

But not just any script. Your script must use the same movie set, lights, costumes, and props for popular schools plays such as:

1. Grease
2. Peter Pan
3. The Sound of Music
4. Little Red Ridinghood
5. Rumplestiltsikn
6. Cinderella
7. Christmas Carol
8. Fiddler on the Roof
9. Romeo and Juliet
10. Annie
11. Music Man
12. Death of a Salesman
13. Our Town
14. Godspell
15. You're a Good Man, Charlie Brown

The Situation

It has been 15 years since digital video came to personal computers. Yet today, few high school drama departments create their own motion pictures. (I have only heard of one in Lawrence, Tennessee.)

There must be an easier way for drama departments to begin making movies.

Each year, high school drama departments put on outstanding plays by extremely talented students. These plays have beautiful and expensive stage sets, very extensive lighting, and wonderful costumes.

So why not use all of this to make a very short motion picture once the play is finished?

Right now, the missing ingredient is a movie script for each of the popular school plays.

Once we have scripts, we can begin to create the storyboards and all the rest of the pre-production elements for the movie.

Course 5: Digital Puppet Animation

Lessons in Digital Puppet Animation

Introduction	:	Introduction to Digital Puppets
Lesson	:	Character animation with digital puppets
Lesson	:	Scenery Generation
Lesson	:	Compositing characters and scenery
Lesson	:	Dialog recording
Lesson	:	Film scoring
Lesson	:	Film editing

Mostly Free Software

In this course, we will create a movie using Digital Puppets and a scenery generator.

For this course, I will recommend software which is free or very low cost. If you want to do more, contact me before you buy anything.

Basic Requirements

- DAZ Studio for character animation—free
- Bryce 5.5 for scenery generation—free
- After Effects (not free) for compositing

Digital Puppet Animation

History: Digital Puppets (also know as Poser figures) is a unique form of 3D animation. We will use digital puppets to create a motion pictures based on everything you have learned so far.

Prerequisites: To begin this class, you must have completed all the other courses. This is because you will need the animatic which you created in the course on Basic Filmmaking which relies on the editing course and the film scoring course.

Animation vs. Live Action: When you attend film school, you will learn all about live action filming. You will learn to work in a team and become a team player.

Therefore, for this course, you will work alone to create the entire motion picture by using digital actors on your personal computer.

Casting

The first step will be to find the digital actors you want for your motion picture. This requires the same care as casting live action actors. You need to find the characters which help tell the story you want to tell.

When you select the characters, these characters will greatly shape the meaning of the motion picture.

Also the selection of the characters for your motion picture will decide what kind of voices you need for the characters.

As an example, look at the list of possible characters for this movie. See how each of the options gives a completely new feeling to the motion picture.

Digital Puppet Magazine

For background information on Digital Puppets, download some of the old copies of this magazine.

Storyboard Artwork Project

In this project, you create educational materials for schools. If you like to draw human figures or if you have Poser or DAZ Studio, you can join.

The artwork that you will create in this project turns Tux Paint into a storyboarding programme. The artwork is a human figure viewed from many angles. Once you have drawn the artwork, you mask the figures so they can be used as "stamps" in Tux Paint for kids to create storyboards for motion pictures.

These special stamps allow Tux Paint to work like a simple version of Storyboard Quick and Storyboard Artist.

Hopefully, this project teaches you everything you need to know to create storyboarding stamps for Tux Paint. If you need more information, please contact the co-ordinator for this project.

The Lessons in the Project

Here are four lessons to help you get started creating stamps for Tux Paint:

1. The artwork needed for storyboarding
2. How to create stamps for Tux Paint
3. 2D: How to create artwork for storyboarding in Tux Paint using 2D software
4. 3D: How to create artwork for storyboarding in Tux Paint using 3D software

Optional: There are also optional lessons for creating props and background scenery.

(A) How to create blank storyboard frames for Tux Paint (optional)
(B) How to create background scenery and props for Tux Paint Storyboards (optional)

Completed Rubber Stamps for Tux Paint: Rubber stamps for storyboarding.

Tux Paint

Tux Paint is a fun drawing programme for kids. It allows kids to add pictures called "Stamps" to their artwork.

Storyboard Quick and Storyboard Artist also uses stamps to draw storyboards but unlike Tux Paint, these programmes are not free.

These special stamps are pictures of people in various poses. Storyboard Quick uses hand drawn pictures of people while Storyboard Artist uses pictures from Poser.

Anyone who likes to draw figures or is learning to use Poser or DAZ Studio can participate. All they have to do is create poses of people in various positions.

2D Human Figures

Hand Drawn Artwork

We need artists who can draw human figures from many different angles. If you are interested, you can practice by drawing the same figure from 3 or more angles. This can be stick figures, realistic artwork, or cartoon art. We need them all.

- ArtRage Free
- ArtRage 2
- Painter
- Photoshop, etc.

3D Human Figures

We need artist who can render 3D human figures from many angles. If you are interested in learning to use 3D programmes, you can practice by drawing the same figure from 5 or more angles.

- DAZ Studio
- Poser

Blank Storyboard Frames

Storyboard Work Sheet for Tux Paint: Once the artwork is created and masked, we need a storyboard worksheet in Tux Paint ready for children to be painting on. These sheets can be done with:

- Adobe Photoshop
- Adobe Illustrator
- Freehand

4

Aspects Related to Pre-Production, Production and Post-Production

PRE-PRODUCTION: MEANING AND IMPLICATION

Pre-production is the process of preparing all the elements involved in a film, play, or other performance.

In the film industry, pre-production usually only commences once a project has been developed and is greenlit. At this stage a project will generally be fully financed and have most of the key elements such as principal cast, director and cinematographer in place, as well as a screenplay which is satisfactory to all the financiers.

During pre-production, the script is broken down into individual scenes and all the locations, props, cast members, costumes, special effects and visual effects are identified. An extremely detailed schedule is produced and arrangements are made for the necessary elements to be available to the film-makers at the appropriate times. Sets are constructed, the crew are hired, financial arrangements are put in place and a start date for the beginning of principal photography is set. At some point in pre-production there will be a read-through of the script which is usually attended by all cast members with speaking parts, all heads of departments, financiers, producers, publicists, and of course the director.

Even though the writer may still be working on it, the screenplay is generally page-locked and scene-numbered at the beginning of pre-production to avoid confusion. This means that even though additions and deletions may still be made, any particular scene will always fall on the same page and have the same scene number.

	Pre-production	Production
The Filmmaking Paper Trail:	Screenplay | Breaking down the script | Script breakdown sheet | Production strip | Production board | Day out of Days | One liner schedule | Shooting schedule | Film budgeting	Daily call sheet | Daily editor log | Daily progress report | Film inventory report (daily raw stock log) | Sound report | Daily production report (DPR) | Cost report

UNTITLED STUDIO PRE-PRODUCTION

For clarification, Currently Untitled Studio means just that, not that CUS is the name of the studio. The name will be changed as work progresses. In either case, this is a case study/log of events concerning production of a series of shorts undertaken by DorianGray (director) and a group of volunteers.

Note: The first few weeks of work are not dated, or have only been dated by the accuracy of memory. Specific items such as previous ideas, names, and storylines/scripts will not be mentioned or changed for privacy, liability and copyright reasons. These will possibly be changed as work progresses/finishes.

Development

- Finding a story
- Begging for backing
- Contracts

Pre-Production

- Storyboarding
- Casting
- Location scouting
- Budgeting
- Schedule
- Paperwork

Production

- Cinematography etc.
- Sound recording
- Tracking and management

Post-Production

- Soundtrack
- Editing
- Formatting

Exhibition and Release

- Exhibition
- Distribution

FILM PRODUCTION OVERVIEW

Who are These People?

First there is the movie's producer. The producer hires the line producer to be in charge of the crew but the producer is still going to be hanging around the movie set each day.

The line producer must hire all the people on the crew. And the line producer must also worry about keeping the crew happy!

The producer hired the movie's director. Over the years, the role of director has changed. And depending on how the deal was set up, the director can have other titles and duties as well. In the simplest case, the director simply controls the performance of the actors and focuses the actors. The director must be good at directing actors. The director will do the blocking for the scene. Each director has his own shooting style.

The cinematographer is in charge of everything related to creating and capturing the image on film (or digital video, etc.). Therefore, the cinematographer must worry about lighting, the camera, the lenses, film stock, cameras and formats, power sources, the film, filteration etc. and everything which effects the look of the movie. The cinematographer is in charge of the camera crew and renting a camera, no matter if it is film, HD and DV. If your movie is low budget, guess who worries about Shooting on Film on a low budget? One way to save money is [.../Short Ends | short ends]. The cinematographer is responsible for monitoring and measuring exposure. The cinematographer must do all the in-camera special effects such as filming or faking rain or shooting underwater. For more information on learning to be a cinematographer, here is a list of books. Other things to consider are [Movie Making Manual/HDV I HDV vs. DVCproHD].

To do the sound recording, the sound mixer records the dialogue while the boom operator holds the microphone over the actors but out of sight of the camera (hopefully). The slate person operates the clapper board and quietly through this entire process, a still photographer takes the stills.

The Daily Grind

Each day, according to the call sheet that was distributed the night before, the actors arrive very early in the morning for makeup and costumes. Last night, the actors have memorized their lines for today based on the scene list in the call sheet.

In the meantime, the director, producer and studio executives are looking at the film dailies from yesterday to see what went right and what went wrong.

At the same time, the light people are finishing the rough setup of the lighting. And the construction crew is finishing any last minute changes to the movie set.

Finally, everyone gets together and begins blocking the scene and final rehearsals (if any.)

If lighting adjustments are needed based on the blocking, the actors go to their trailers while their stand-ins stay to help with the lighting.

Finally the filming of the scene begins. Long before now, the director has broken down the scene into a series of shots. For each shot, the cinematographer positions the camera and the boom operator positions the microphone.

Filming Procedure

When everyone is ready, the Cinematographer yells, "Set" to mean that the everything on the set is ready.

The tape recorder for the boom microphone is turned on when the director yells, "Roll Sound".

When the audio tape recorder has reached the proper speed, the sound mixer yells, "Rolling".

Then the director yells, "Roll Camera". The camera is started. The camera is turned on after the audio tape recorder because the film is more expensive than the audio tape.

When the Camera is rolling, the camera operator will yell, "Rolling".

Then the director will yell, "Slate" and the slate operator will announce which scene this is (having first gotten that information from the script supervisor). This same information is written on the slate of the clapper board. The reason for announcing the scene number is for the lab technician who will listen to the audio tape to find the start of the correct scene when the lab operator syncs the audio to the picture that night.

Then the slate operator will close the clapper sticks with a loud clapping sound so that the camera sees the closing of the clapper sticks and the audio tape records the noise of the sticks hitting together.

Then the director will inform the actors that they can begin the scene.

When the director feels like it, the director will yell, "Cut". If the movie is being shot on 35 mm film which is very expensive, and the director likes the actor's performance and the cameras performance, the director will also yell, "Print" which means that this is a good take and everyone including the script supervisor, the sound person and the camera assistant will circle this take number on their logs or notes.

If the director feels like it, he will ask everyone do to this again. If the director is satisfied, then director will yell, "Next" and everyone will set up for the next shot. If the same scene will be filmed from a different angle, the script supervisor will create a number Take Number usually by adding an alphabetic letter to the take number. Take 32A is will be roughly the same as Take 32 but from a different camera angle.

If there are multiple takes,

If the slate is not at the beginning of the shot, it will be at the end of the shot but upside down.

If the movie has a really low budget and the audio or the camera are not running accurately, there might be two slates, one at the beginning and one at the end so the audio can be stretched to fit the video. (This is very rare but realize it is possible.)

Visiting the Movie Set

The best way to see all of this is to visit the movie set. If you donot have the time to become a Production Assistant, take the tours of movie studios. Some tours can be very interesting.

Hollywood Studio Tours

While the Universal Studio Tour is more entertainment than actual examples of filming, you can pick up tickets to filming as you leave Universal Studio Tour area. Most are for Sitcoms which are filmed totally different from a motion picture. Yet they are very educational and entertaining to watch.

At one time, the best tour in Hollywood (and the most expensive) was at Warner Bros. Their website does not work well but you can try it at Warner Bros. If you have been on this tour recently, please tell us.

NBC Studio has a ticket office which gives out free ticket. However, these are mostly for sitcoms. If anyone has been to the filmings in LA, please give us a list of where you go to get tickets and what is available currently.

Japan

Do not overlook the studio tours in other lands. Eiga Mura, the Toei Studio Movie theme park in the northwest part of Kyoto is great fun. Years ago, you could actually see post-production if you waited and watched very carefully in one of the distant buildings. If anyone has gone visited this movie village recently, please describe what you saw. Here is an article on this movie village in 2005. Many of the movie are filmed in plain sight of the crowds of tourists. Great fun!

India

Ramoji Film City in Hyderabad does have a tour facility. The main hub of Indian Cinema is Mumbai—A unguided tour of Film City, off the Western Express Highway in Goregaon (E), Mumbai is a good place to start off with. Spread over acres and acres of lush green forests on mountains there are sets of various film and TV productions at any point in time with shoots going on. One of India's largest film processing labs, Adlabs is located here along with sets of Balaji (India's tele soap factory) and many others. One can also move from here to Mehboob Studios, Bandra where there are often lavish sets of various film songs are set up. Then on its a process of ask the locals and try your luck.

England

I believe that Pinewood Studios has a studio tour. Anyone been there? Please tell us more.

Visiting the Movie Set by Watching Film Dailies

You can also get an understanding of the way that movies are filmed if you watch film dailies. You see everything that the camera sees for all of the circle takes.

Watching the Movie Set—Film Dailies on eBay

Sometimes these tapes (given as souvineers to the cast and crew) become available on eBay. If you also plan to edit the scenes for practice, be sure to get only originals, not copies.

Watching the Movie Set—Digitized Film Dailies

If you have no other way to watch what happens on the movie set of television dramas, look at Disk #2 from the Star Movie Shop which shows how 24 different scenes were filmed from a variety of television dramas. It is amazing to watch how perfectly the actors repeat their lines. After only one night of memorization and one mornings rehearsal, they hit their mark perfectly. Note: If you shoot your own movie, the dailies will never look as good as dailies from a television drama which is filmed fast and efficiently after years of practice for both the cast and crew. Your first day of filming on a low budget movie with a new crew and inexperience actors will look more like a disaster movie than a motion picture set.

The Different Tasks of Production

This section will be expanded shortly. It will include such wonderful jobs as "Craft Services". Guess what that is!!!

Animated Motion Pictures

If you are making an animated movie, the production is done differently. Animation for an animated motion picture is done during production (not post-production) and is very different from the animation which is done for visual effects in post-production.

POST-PRODUCTION

Post-production occurs in the making of audio recordings, films/ movies, photography and digital art, videos and television programmes. It is the general term for all stages of production occurring after the actual recording and ending with the completed work.

Post-production is in fact many different processes grouped under one name. These typically include:

- Editing the picture/TV programme.
- Editing the soundtrack.
- Writing and recording the soundtrack music.
- Adding visual special effects—mainly computer generated imagery (CGI) and digital copy from which release prints will be made (although this may be made obsolete by digital cinema technologies).

Typically, the post-production phase of creating a film takes longer than the actual shooting of the film, and can take several months to complete.

Other film production stages include (very broadly)—writing the screenplay, script development (rewriting), financing, pre-production, the actual shooting and film distribution/marketing.

BLOCKING

Blocking is the act of walking the actors through the scene before it is shot in order to make sure the lighting is sufficient and the camera is able to get the desired focus required. That is close: Blocking is for all departments to be sure that they are prepared for the scene to be shot. Taking the extra 3-5 minutes to block a scene can save your time, money and patience later. It is not uncommon for blocking to last days for a big scene, such as the scene in Jarhead where the soldiers all met in a tent "in country". Sam Mendes blocked that scene for 4 days before they shot it. Still closer: Blocking a scene for film also must afford the camera the most aesthetically interesting compositions that flow before the lens. It is not only the movement of actors and props to achieve optimum efficiency on the set.

LIGHTING

Lighting Conventions

Broadcast, Video, and Film Productions share common lighting conventions. Due to the fact that most lighting tools were originally developed for film, with a few tools introduced for video, the equipment carries ratings and specifications standardized for film. All the lighting tools found in a decently equiped video production studio have direct relatives (usually just larger, brighter and more expensive) in a film production studio.

Electricity

Every lighting fixture uses electricty. How much it requires and in what form varies on the application of the light(s). The electrical description consists of Voltage, Amperage, and Wattage. Commonly studio lights use 115±(plus or minus) 5 Volts (V) or 225±5 V. The amperages (ampres or amps) and wattages (Watts or W) vary depending on the fixture, bulb type, and light output. 115 V lights range from 10 W (LEDs) up to 2000 W-2500 W (Halogen-Quartz), 225 V range also from 10W to 4500 W-5000 W.

Terminology

Bulbs

Refers to the actual light source. Most bulbs consist of a filament, insulating gas, and a glass encasement.

Fixtures

The case that holds the bulb, and often serves the purpose of directing the light. Fixtures range from bulb holders, to elaborate mechanisms capable of all but picking one's nose.

Mounts

A device that holds the light where you want it to be. Some clamp to overhead lighting grids, while others are stands.

Power

Or power source/supply. Where is light getting its juice?

Lighting Equipment

Lighting equipment consists of a great deal more than just sockets with bulbs. Lighting equipment (briefly) consists of bulbs, fixtures, dimmers/power units, mounts, light control/quality.

Bulb Types

Video/Film recording lights use many different bulb types. Some are standards from Edison (tungsten) but others are cutting edge of the 2000s (LED). Most bulb types use a filament-ignition process to produce light. A wire of some electrically excitable material is put under voltage in a oxygen-depleted environment, causing it to 'burn' without lighting afire. Flourescent bulbs and LEDs function rather differently from filament bulbs.

Tungsten

A tungsten light is basically a more powerful version of a common household light bulb. While a household light bulb may only take a few hundred watts at most, lights that are used to light film sets are easily 1000 watts (1 K) and often over 20,000 watts (20 K). The tungsten light bulb naturally produces an orange hue, similar to indoor lights. Tungsten lights have a colour temperature ranging from 3200 to 3400 Kelvin. One typically uses a CTB filter to balance the colour temperature with outdoor or HMI light.

Redheads: Redheads are a specific type of open-faced light made by Ianiro. They are very compact and come in 600 and 650 watt versions. They are also known as Mickey-Moles (when made by Mole-Richardson). The term is often used to loosely describe smaller, open-faced lights.

Blondes: Blondes are a 2 K open-faced light. Because they are open-faced, they tend to put out more light than a 2 K fresnel.

Halogen-Quartz

Halogen-Quartz bulbs, often known as 'Halogens' or 'Quartz' are a staple of lighting. Halogens rarely posses a colour temperature outside of 3200°K. These same bulbs are often used in car headlights, portable worklights, and recently in house-decor lighting. The bulbs come in wattages ranging from 15 W-3500 W. Additionally they are manufactured in a wide range of enclosures, bases, and connectors. Common are the "T", and bayonet base. Halogens emit significant amounts of heat during operation, so much so that oils on the glass surface of the bulb case lead to uneven heat distribution and rupturing (through thermal shock to the glass) or heat build-up and exploding gas within the bulb.

HMI

An HMI light is used very often to light film sets. One requires a ballast in order to power and creates a loud noise when turning on, so it is set protocol to yell "striking" in order to warn others on set to both ignore the noise and avoid looking at the light. The HMI light is a different type of light bulb than the more common tungsten. An HMI emits ultra-violet lights and emits a blue hue. HMI lights produce a colour temperature around 5600 Kelvin. One typically use a CTO filter to balance the colour temperature with indoor or tungsten light.

Fluorescent

Fluorescent bulbs were not used for lighting film and video until recently. This was because of problems with flicker and a tendency to emit more of a greenish hue. The fluorescent lights used in film now are made to be flicker-free and come in both daylight and tungsten balanced bulbs. "Kino-flo" is one of the major companies involved in making fluorescent bulbs and fixtures for film and video production. Fluorescent lights tend to be very soft, but do not put out much light in comparison to other lighting instruments.

LED

Until the last five to ten years Light Emitting Diodes (LEDs) have seen little implimentation. Recent advances in production costs and chemical advances used in the diode junctions have led to inexpensive led 'bulbs' as well as even colour temperatures in multiple bulbs. LEDs are manufactured in all colours, and white comes in many colour temperatures; 3200 K being the most common, but ranging from 3000 K to 5600 K+. Diodes, due to their engineered design tend to have a very directional light. The front lens is parabolic, focusing the light to a small dot even several meters away.

Light Control, Quality and Appearance

Lighting Shape/Area

There are a number of tools used to control where light falls. Often these are used to prevent light falling where it is not needed. In other circumstances a pattern created by the light is desired.

Barn Doors: Perhaps the most common form of lighting area shaping, barn doors are found around the front outside of the fixture. Most commonly there are four barn doors forming a square around the fixture, but the numbers vary for specialty applications.

Basically, barn doors block the light from hitting an area of the set or frame you do not want them to. They swing towards and away from the fixture opening.

Gobos: Gobos shape the light. Many gobos appear to be shapes cut in a cookie sheet (and indeed many are) but they consist of a material able to withstand the heat put out by the fixture, with shapes cut out for the light to travel through.

Think of gobos as jack o' lanterns.

Blackwrap: Blackwrap is essentially aluminum foil, but covered in black paint. It is often used to block light and kill any spill from a light. Blackwrap can be shaped however you like to affect where the light falls. It is useful in narrowing larger lights to point lights or spots or making lights non-circular. It is very inexpensive, light weight and more flexible than barn doors. However, it will burn on too hot a light, so watch for smoke.

Lighting Intensity

Flags: A flag can be any item that blocks light. A standard flag on set can be of varying sizes. The standard flag is attached to a small metal handle and short rod that can be attached to a C-Stand to place it so that it blocks the light from hitting something in the shot. Flags can be used to help prevent certain shadows from hitting certain walls and also be used to mimic doors and the such.

Types of flags include singles and doubles to cut down hard light. Solids to block light. Silks to diffuse light.

Focus: Adjusting the focus on a focusable light changes the distance between the actual bulb and a lens at the end of the light. This affects how diffuse the light is. Closer to the lens spreads the light out more, whereas farther back makes it closer to a spot. Try to do this before the light gets too hot, so you can adjust it without burning yourself.

Neutral Density Filters: Neutral density filters are a variety of gel (or camera filter) which reduces all colours of light equally, making a light less intense without altering its colour. This can be added on top of colour gels or used on its own to make a light less intense.

Lighting Quality

Gels: Gels are thin and translucent. They come in rolls that can be cut into a more manageable size when needed. While a gel can be any colour, there are two main colours which are referred to as Colour Temperature Orange (CTO) and Colour Temperature Blue (CTB). These two types of gel are respectively orange and blue, with varying degrees of darkness broken up into 1/8, 1/4, 1/2, and Full. Full is the darkest and 1/8 is the lightest. When asking for a gel, one may say "I'd like a quarter CTO put on this light."

Gels are attached to a light in order to alter their colour temperature. Tungsten lights produce an orange hue, while HMI's produce a blue hue. If filming outside with tungsten lights, gels would be needed to match the colour temperature of the daylight if the DP wanted all the light to be the same colour temperature. Daylight produces a blue hue like an HMI light, so CTB would be needed to be placed on all the tungsten lights. Gels are attached to lights with clothespins, also called "C-47's."

Besides CTO and CTB, to work with fluorescent lights or a "kino flo", there are "plus green" and "minus green" gels. Since fluorescent lights produce a green hue, a minus green gel would remove the green hue from a fluorescent light and a plus green gel would help match a non-fluorescent light to a fluorescent.

Attaching: Some lights have clips for attaching gels, but the most common method of attaching them is via wooden clothespins (also referred to as C47s, pegs, or bullets). These clothespins will begin to smoke before the gels, so you can prevent your gels from being ruined, and they also don't conduct heat, so they can be manipulated even on a very hot light. They can also be reversed to give them a longer mouth, allowing you to use them to pull scrims from hot fixtures. Once reversed, they often go by C-74's or "scrim pullers."

General Lighting

Here is the nitty-gritty of the page. Although different formats have varying needs in both quantity and quality of light, the underlying yet critical concepts of lighting are fairly applicable to any medium.

Lighting Digital Video

Dynamic Range: There are many differences between DV and film, but one that particularly stands out regarding lighting is dynamic range.

Most DV and video cameras have a relatively low dynamic range. (I.ex. the Sony PD150 has about 4-5 stops, and Kodak's 50D film has up to 11). This means the range between the completely black and the whitest white is very low. One therefore has to keep this in mind while lighting. This has been an integral part of cinematography since the beginning. Controlling so one can see details in the darkest area of an image, and also in the brightest. One can always adjust the contrast in post (Colourgrading). This style of working is called shooting for post. (The DV standard has an OK light intensity resolution, so adjusting contrast in post is not as difficult as adjusting colour.)

White Balance: As the DV standard has a low colour-resolution, it is important to control and know how to filter and white balance the image on set. It has been proved difficult to adjust colour in post with a good result, although it has been done. Regarding lighting, be aware of the possibilities the white balance setting on the camera have, and use gels on the lamps, and sometimes on windows to create a neutral image.

In return for these shortcomings, DV-cameras can be more light-sensitive than most film stocks, and therefore require less light intensity, to give the same image. (PD150 is about 320ASA versus Kodak's 50D's 50ASA. One would need about 8 times more light, to get the same image at the same F-stop). Although high ASA film is available.

MUSIC VIDEO

Music videos includes details regarding

1. Movie Making Manual—Exhibition of Music Videos
2. Movie Making Manual—Submitting Music Videos
3. Movie Making Manual—Why Make a Music Video

DIGITAL VIDEO

Introduction to Digital Video Production Manual

- Why is this a separate book?

History of Video

- You cannot know where you are going until you know where you have been.

Production Process

- Process Overview
- Development

- Preproduction
- Production
- Postproduction
- Distribution

POWER SOURCES

On a film set, the power source is usually managed by the Electrical Department. Depending on where you are shooting and the volume of power the production requires, many different power sources are used. Typically you are either using Stage Power, House Power, A Tie-in, or a Generator.

Stage Power

When filming on a sound-stage large amounts of power are typically provided as part of the facility, although this is not always the case. Typically, power is provided in the form of 3-phase 110 V with Cam-Lock hook-ups.

House Power

House power refers to power that is already an installed within a location. For example, if you are shooting in an apartment, House Power refers to exiting power installed in the apartment. House power is generally not preferred because: lighting equipment can require more power than is available, circuit-boxes can be difficult to locate in the event of a overload, a relatively large amount of power is usually used which increases the power-bill for that cycle.

Tie-ins

A Tie-in is a method of tapping directly into the power that feeds a building from the city power-grid, thereby bypassing the limits of the circuits that are installed in the building.

A Tie-in is a dangerous activity which requires experience and skill. Improper methods can result in damage to city power-grids and death.

Generator

Generators are used in Motion Picture Production to provide power to all the departments of the production, the most demanding on which is the lighting department. Typically generators are used when filming on location, as power is normally provided when filming on a sound-stage.

SOUND RECORDING

Types of Microphone

- Dynamic: Most common/cheapest.
- Condenser: Most require Phantom Power. Known for producing more detail, especially in the upper frequencies.
- Ribbon: Was rare, becoming more common. Catching speed as being 'smooth' on guitars.
- Also: Mic Patterns.

Electronics You should be Aware of

Balanced versus Unbalanced

Balanced audio connections use 3 wires for sending each channel: a plus phase, a negative phase, and a ground. The sending device sends its output over both the plus phase and the negative phase. But (and here is the clever bit) the signal is inverted on the negative phase. The receiving device then inverts the negative phase back (to match the positive phase) and adds it to the positive phase. Any noise picked up along a stretch of wire will be out of phase with itself (once the destination reverts the negative phase) and be cancelled out.

In short: Balanced is practically immune to noise (like "mains hum") and so you should use balanced connections as often as possible. It is absolutely vital to use balanced connections for long lengths of wire (lengths over a meter) and in situations where there is lots of electro-magnetic interference (EMI) like on a film set. (Those 20kW HMIs, for example!)

Grounding

Shielding

Phantom Power

Phantom power is used for condenser microphones that need power to run. It is also used to power direct boxes. Direct boxes turn unbalanced signal into balanced signal for reducing and preventing hum. You will most often see phantom power in 48 V. You can get phantom power from a source such as many sound consoles, especially if you have a recording console. If you do not have it built into your console, you can buy a portable unit that takes up an outlet and has an xlr in and xlr out (with 48 V power).

Mixing

As a quick rule of thumb for a TV mix, dialogue should average 3.5/4 ppm on a meter i.e. around -20/-18dB. You should record it like this and mix at these levels. Peak dialogue shouts etc should not really go above 6 ppm (-10dB). If you are recording or mixing for TV nothing should peak over 7 ppm (-6dB). And those peaks should last a minimal amount of time. Music is mixed at the dubbing mixer's discretion, so that it works with the programme and fits with the dialogue, but should not peak above 6.5 ppm. A limiter would usually be placed across the output to ensure nothing goes above 7 ppm.

If you are mixing for DVD or Theatre release you would use the full digital scale. Dialogues should still average -20/-18dB however your fx peaks can go the full range to 0dB but not over!

So you would have two mixes one for TV and one for DVD.

The BBC's audio delivery specification states:

> "Peak sound levels (when measured on a BS 5428 Peak Programme Meter) within the programme must not exceed PPM 6: that is, no greater than +8dB with respect to the reference level of -18dBFS."

In other words there should be no less than 10db of 'headroom' between the highest level you can record and your programme's highest peak.

It is preferable to have sound with "hiss" rather than distortion. Distortion cannot be fixed, background noise can be somewhat fixed.

What to Record on?

The Video Camera

I have recorded onto camera quite a few times—the skinny is that you can get great audio from the cameras with XLR inputs and also:

The Canon XL1 has not got phantom power—you need an external mic power supply.

The DVX-100a has small audio controls which are more difficult to manipulate, a little movement seems to make a big difference in level.

One of the two DVX100a's I've used had a buzz only when the DV tape was installed. Very annoying, but the other one was quiet.

The Sony PD170 has a good set of audio controls—especially the ch1/ch2 link function when using one microphone (two channels are better than one!)

The PD100 has needs a +48/XLR hot shoe attachment, otherwise it sounds fine.

It is wise to back up audio, and slate scenes without pausing, when using DV cameras—back up on DAT. On a recent 3 camera shoot, I had a total of 6 audio tracks, one into the DVx100a, one into a Canon Optura PI (fine little camera!), but with 1/8" connector and one into a Sony tcd-08 DAT—the DAT won as the best overall sound with the lowest noise and cleanest sound, BM.

DAT

DAT-Heads concerns itself with Digital Audio Tape decks, with an emphasis on their use for the recording and distribution of live music.

MiniDisk

ATRAC 3 is a proprietary lossy perceptual audio codec developed by Sony and used for minidisc and other Sony products such as the PlayStation Portable. Uncompressed PCM offers higher quality, and therefore field recording with a portable DAT or hard disk recorder is almost always preferrable to a minidisc recorder.

Hard Disk

Hard Disk recording has quickly become the industry standard (aside from analog tape.) Benefits include: Non-linear editing—no need to rewind or fast-forward to find different songs. Cost—You can buy a hard drive with well over a hundred gigs, for around a hundred bucks. 100 gigs can hold 300 hours of uncompressed single-channel audio, making it a very cheap way to record.

Wild Track

When on location you should always record a "wild track." This should be a few minutes of the ambient noise from your location (the sound of traffic in the distance, birds singing etc). You should ask the assistant director to tell the entire crew to be quiet so you get an undisturbed track.

Why bother? In the edit it is very useful (and often absolutely required) to keep a wild track running in the background to smooth over the changes from cut to cut.

A Wild Track is an audio only recording of an actor's lines while the camera is not rolling. There are no sync marks or visible slates. These wild recordings are used to replace dialogue from a filmed take that may be un-usable for various reasons. Perhaps a plane flew over during the scene. The Wild Track or Wild Line will be used in part or in whole to replace the on-camera dialogue. It is also used for Off-camera lines that need to be recorded on-mic. Many times Wild lines are used to replace compromised recordings made during a Wide master shot where the microphone could not be placed in the optimal position. Because the shot is wide, lip-sync of these lines is not as critical and sync errors are not as visible as for a close up.

"Room Tone" or "Presence" is a wild recording of just the ambient sound of a location (no one speaking). It is used in post production to cover unwanted sounds (like the director's verbal instruction during the take). To record Room tone you should place the same microphone in the same position as it was during the dialogue take. Record at the same level used for the actual take but have everyone remain still and quiet.

SHOOTING STYLES

Blair Witch Project

The Blair Witch Project is different in its shooting style in many ways:

- The whole film is presented as if it were an unedited documentary, filmed by the protagonists, and as such the shooting style resembles that of an amateur documentary or a home movie.
- This includes shaking shots when the characters are running and more or less useless or irrelevant shots when the characters are just fooling around with the cameras.
- A large part of the movie is in black and white, as one of the cameras that the protagonists carry with them only shoots in this format. This adds to the realism of the movie.

Ken Loach

The films of Ken Loach have an incredible authenticity and 'realness' to them. How does he achieve this?

Taken from "Loach on Loach"

- Never use ADR
- Run the entire scene for every shot, do not break the scene down into little "shot length" segments.
- Light the entire scene so you are not artificially telling the audience "This is the lead actor for this scene, the others are less important"
- Do not give the actors marks (indeed, you do not have to because you are lighting the entire scene)
- Actors should have vulnerabilities

Dogme/Dogma

From Bright Lights Film Journal: *Copyrights lawyers are out of luck.*

Anyone can obtain a Dogme certificate if he (or she) shoots a film in accordance with the ten rules known as "The Vow of Chastity."

The Vow of Chastity

- Shooting on location (no imported props or sets)
- Sound and image produced together
- A handheld camera
- Natural light
- No optical work or filters
- No superficial action (murders, weapons)
- No temporal or geographic alienation
- No genre films
- Film format must be Academy 35 mm.
- No signature; the director must not be credited.

Alfred Hitchcock

A man dedicated to suspense and intrigue:

Emotion is the ultimate goal of each of his shots. Hitchcock believed that emotion came directly from the actor's eyes. By bringing us closer or tearing us away he used camera angles to jerk us into the feeling of his moments.

The camera should be just like a person looking around for something out of place in a room. This allows the audience to feel like they are involved the action. Scenes can often begin by panning a room showing close-ups of objects that explain plot elements.

Hitchcock also loved to keep us on our toes by throwing in shots fast and close after being slow and far...

STILL PHOTOGRAPHY

Stills photography involves taking photos of the film-making process. These are often used for promoting the film and as a documentary record. This area of film production is often overlooked on smaller budget films or some photographs are taken by members of the crew, but for promotional and documentary uses; good quality and professional images are a must. If the film budget canot stretch to a professional photographer, many photographers will do work to use in their portfolios, and for the experience.

Equipment

Both film and digital have their respective advantages and disadvantages. Digital photography provides instant results, and combining this with a notebook computer means the results can be viewed instantly by the photographer, crew and cast. The choice often comes down to personal preference, but is sometimes dictated by the stills photographer's brief. Medium and large format cameras are often used for a higher quality image although 35 mm is usually sufficient, and is often used for speed and ease of use. Large format cameras—considered superior in terms of image quality—is a slower medium, and often hard to use on a busy set. Generally the equipment will suit the type of shots required. If the shots are "reportage" style, then 35 mm is advantagous. High-quality cast/set shots can be taken on medium/large especially for very large poster/billboard reproductions.

Publishing Stills Photos Online

If you have your own webspace then it is very easy to install a free gallery package and publish your photos online. Some excellent free gallery packages include:

- Gallery
- Coppermine

Examples of Production Stills

- Jack Kelly's film production stills gallery

CHARACTER ANIMATION

There are two kinds of animation used in the making of a motion picture. Animated movies have a special produced and the animation is done in production. This section covers the procedure for creating an animated movie.

Animation is also done in Post Production as part of visual effects. For visual effects, go to Animation for Visual Effects.

Overall Procedure of an Animated Motion Picture

An animated motion picture starts out like any other motion picture. Pre-production is the same...and that includes storyboarding. The only difference is storyboarding for an animated motion picture is much more intense. In live action filming, the storyboards are only an approximation. In an animated motion picture, the storyboards eventually become the keyframes of the animation.

Dialogue Recording

All textbooks on making an animated motion picture explain that before the animation can begin, the dialogue of the script must be recorded by the actors. The textbooks say that only after the actor's dialogue has been recorded does work begin on the animation.

The problem in this method does not work. Actors have too much trouble visualizing who they are and their surroundings in an animated movie. Their performance is terrific when they can see the animation but not good when they cannot see anything.

Therefore, in almost all cases, the dialogue must be recorded **a second time** after the animation is finished. To see that this is true, go through the "making of the movie" articles for all the successful animated movies and you will learn that they recorded the dialogue a second time while the actors watch the animation.

Dialogue Recording vs. ADR Session

To keep the two recording sessions separate, I will call the first recording of the dialogue, the "Dialogue Recording". And the second recording of the dialogue after the movie is almost finished, the "ADR Session" since the second recording of the dialogue is very much like a normal ADR session with a few exceptions.

Dialogue Recording Procedure

There are two different ways to record the initial dialogue for an animated motion picture:

One Actor at a Time: The first way is the easy way. This is to bring in each actor, one at a time, and record that persons dialogue.

This recording session is with the director who will coach the actor by either reading the other character's dialogue or will explain each scene to the actor.

Multiple Actors: This is much more difficult. Two or more actors are brought into the recording studio and if possible, put into separate (isolated) recording booths connected to the same recording console. The actors can hear each other as they record their dialogue together. This way, the two actors interact with each other but their voices are recorded on separate tracks.

If the two actors are in the same recording booth, and if the actors happen to be speaking at the same time (as people often do in a heated conversation), this become locked into the dialogue recording. There can be no adjustment during the editing of the movie.

Therefore, recording each actor on a separate track is preferable.

The other Steps of Making the Animated Movie

Here are the steps for creating the animated movie once the dialogue has been recorded:

Animatic Creation Procedure

Using the still images from the storyboard, an animatic is created using the recorded dialogue. Another way to explain this is the movie is made using just still pictures along with the dialogue as well as with a temp film score and rough sound effects.

Timing Procedure

Once the dialogue is recorded and the animatic completed, the dialogue must be timed. For each scene, each syllable of the dialogue must be timed from the beginning of the scene. This is needed for the animators to create the animation and rough lip sync.

Animation Procedure

Once the timing of each scene is complete the animation is started. For 3D animation, each shot is rendered just like a motion picture shot on film with live actors. Then these shots are edited together.

This is very different from 2D animation where each frame is carefully planned out and no extra frames are created. In 3D animation, about 10 per cent of the rendered frames are removed (trimmed off the two ends of the shot) during editing.

If ADR will be used, the actual lip sync can still be very rough or not at all.

Editing Procedure

For 3D animation, a regular digital video editing programme (such as Final Cut Pro) is used to edit the movie. The sound effects and the musical score are added now. The musical score might even have been created before the editing so that the movie will be edited to match the film score.

Dialogue Recording Procedure

Once the animation is done and the movie has been edited, all the actors return, one at a time, to an ADR session where the actors see everything that is happening on the screen and they react to it.

Lip Sync Timing Procedure

Now the final timing of the lip sync is calculated. Then the animation for the mouth movements is done to match the timing. Some animation software have faster ways to do this. This is the last step in the animation process.

Types of Animation

There are two kinds of 3D character animation:

General Purpose 3D Animation Programmes

This is done with programmes such as Maya, LightWave, and 3D Studio Max. In this case, all characters in the movie are custom made. All the movie sets and the scenery are created from scratch.

Special Purpose 3D Animation Programmes

This is done with specialized programmes such as Poser and DAZ Studio. In this case, most all the characters are purchased off the shelf from companies such as RuntimeDNA. Frequently, specialized programmes are also used to create the movie set. These programmes are Vue and Bryce. For low budget animation, the movie sets will be rendered as multi-layered still images which are composited with the character animation and (at the same time) animated with Adobe AfterEffects.

- Examples of animation motion pictures created with general purpose 3D animation programme are Polar Express and Aero-Troopers. Polar Express uses realistic human figures while Aero-Troopers uses cartoon-like characters which are easier to animate.
- Examples of animation motion pictures created with special purpose 3D animation programme can be seen overseas in television dramas.

5

Cinematography and Movie Making : Crucial Dimensions and Aspects

CINEMATOGRAPHY

Cinematography [from Greek: *kinesis* (movement) and *grapho* (to record)], is the discipline of making lighting and camera choices when recording photographic images for the cinema. It is closely related to the art of still photography, though many additional issues arise when both the camera and elements of the scene may be in motion.

History

The first attempt at cinematography can be traced back to the world's first motion picture film, *Roundhay Garden Scene*. It was a sequence directed by Louis Le Prince, French inventor and showman, on October 14, 1888 in the garden at *Oakwood Grange* in Roundhay, Leeds, West Yorkshire, England. This groundbreaking event happened seven years before the Lumière Brothers' *Sortie de l'usine Lumière à Lyon* made the first paid exhibition on December 28, 1895 at Le Grand Café, in Paris, France. This date is known as the birth of cinema since it was the first time the cycle of production-distribution-exhibition happened. The European city soon became the motion picture capital of the world.

Cinematography is an art form unique to motion pictures. Although the exposing of images on light-sensitive elements dates back to the late 1600s, motion pictures demanded a new form of photography and new aesthetic techniques.

In the infancy of motion pictures, the cinematographer was usually also the director and the person physically handling the camera. As the art form and technology evolved, a separation between director and camera operator emerged. With the advent of artificial lighting and faster (more light sensitive) film stocks, in addition to technological advancements in optics and various techniques such as colour film and widescreen, the technical aspects of cinematography necessitated a specialist in that area.

In 1919, in Hollywood, the new motion picture capital of the world, one of the first (and still existing) trade societies was formed: the American Society of Cinematographers (ASC), which stood to recognize the cinematographer's contribution to the art and science of motion picture making. Similar trade associations have been established in other countries, too.

The ASC defines cinematography as a creative and interpretive process that culminates in the authorship of an original work of art rather than the simple recording of a physical event. Cinematography is not a subcategory of photography. Rather, photography is but one craft that the cinematographer uses in addition to other physical, organizational, managerial, interpretive and image-manipulating techniques to effect one coherent process.

Aspects of Cinematography

Numerous aspects contribute to the art of cinematography.

Film Stock

Cinematography can begin with rolls of film or a digital imaging sensor. Advancements in film emulsion and grain structure have led to a wide range of film stocks available to cinematographers. The selection of a film stock is one of the first decisions they must make during any film production.

Aside from the film gauge selection—8 mm (amateur), 16 mm (semi-professional), 35 mm (professional) and 65 mm (epic photography, rarely used except in special event venues)—the cinematographer has a selection of stocks in reversal (which, when developed, create a positive image) and negative formats along with a wide range of film speeds (varying sensitivity to light) from ISO 50 (slow, least sensitive to light) to 800 (very fast, extremely sensitive to light) and differing response to colour (low saturation, high saturation) and contrast [varying levels between pure black (no exposure) and pure white (complete overexposure)].

Advancements and adjustments to nearly all gauges of film created the "super" variety wherein the area of the film used to capture a single frame of an image is expanded, although the physical gauge of the film remains the same. Super 8 mm, Super 16 mm and Super 35 mm are all formats that utilize more of the overall film area for the image than their "regular" non-super counterparts.

The larger the film gauge, the higher the overall image resolution clarity and technical quality.

In the realm of digital imaging, various film stocks are no longer applicable, but the cameras themselves feature image adjustment capabilities that go far beyond the abilities of one particular film stock. The cameras can be adjusted to varying degrees of colour sensitivity, image contrast, light sensitivity and so on. One camera can achieve all the various looks of different emulsions, although it is heavily argued as to which method of capturing an image is the "best" method. It should be mentioned that the digital method of image adjustments (ISO, contrast etc) are executed by estimating the same adjustments that would take place if actual film were in use and are thus vulnerable to the cameras sensor designers perceptions of various film stocks and image adjustment parameters. Sensors generally have an optimal ISO rating past which faster speeds will result in noticeable increases in image noise, thus compromising the quality.

The Lab

Laboratory work can also offer a considerable variance in the image produced. By controlling the temperature and varying the duration in which the film is soaked in the development chemicals and by skipping certain chemical processes (or partially skipping them), cinematographers can achieve very different looks from a single film stock in the laboratory.

Filters

Filters, such as diffusion filters or colour-effect filters, are also widely used to enhance mood or dramatic effects. Most photographic filters are made up of two pieces of optical glass glued together with some form of image or light manipulation material between the glass. In the case of colour filters, there is often a translucent color medium pressed between two planes of optical glass. Colour filters work by blocking out certain colour wavelengths of light from reaching the film. With colour film, this works very intuitively wherein a blue filter will cut down on the passage of red, orange and yellow light and create a blue tint on the film. In black and white photography, colour filters are used somewhat counter intuitively; for instance a yellow filter, which cuts down on blue wavelengths of light, can be used to darken a daylight sky (by eliminating blue light from hitting the film, thus greatly underexposing the mostly blue sky), while not biasing most human flesh tone. Certain cinematographers, such as Christopher Doyle, are well known for their innovative use of filters. Filters can be used in front of the lens or, in some cases, behind the lens for different effects.

Lens

Focal Length

The camera does what a human eye does. That is, it creates perspective and spatial relations with the rest of the world. However, unlike one's eye, a cinematographer can select different lenses for different purposes. Variation in focal length is one of the chief benefits of such an advantage. Cinematographers can choose between a range of wide angle lenses, "normal" lenses and telephoto lenses, as well as macro lenses and other special effect lens systems such as borescope lenses. Wide-angle lenses have short focal lengths and make spatial distances more obvious. A person in the distance is shown as much smaller while someone in the front will loom large. On the other hand, telephoto lenses reduce such exaggerations, depicting far-off objects as seemingly close together and flattening perspective. A zoom lens allows a camera operator to change their focal length within a shot or quickly between setups for shots. As prime lenses offer greater optical quality and are "faster" (larger aperture openings, usable in less light) than zoom lenses, they are often employed in professional cinematography over zoom lenses. Certain scenes or even types of film-making, however, may require the use of zooms for speed or ease of use, as well as shots involving a zoom move.

Depth of Field and Focus

Focal length also affects the depth of field of a scene—that is, how much the background, mid-ground and foreground will be rendered in "acceptable focus" (only one exact plane of the image is in precise focus) on the film or video target. Depth of field (not to be confused with depth of focus) is determined by the aperture size and the focal distance. A large or deep depth of field is generated with a very small iris aperture and focusing on a point in the distance, whereas a shallow depth of field will be achieved with a large (open) iris aperture and focusing closer to the lens. Depth of field is also governed by the format size. 70 mm film has the least depth of field for the same focal length lens than does 35 mm. 16 mm has even more and most digital video cameras have more depth of field than 16 mm. As videographers try to emulate the look of 35 mm film with digital cameras, this is one issue of frustration—excessive depth of field with digital cameras and using additional optical devices to reduce that depth of field.

In *Citizen Kane*, cinematographer Gregg Toland used tighter apertures to create very large depth of field in the scenes, often rendering every detail of the foreground and background of the sets in sharp focus. This practice is known as deep focus. Deep focus became a popular cinematographic device from the 1940s onwards in Hollywood. Today, the trend is for more shallow focus.

To change the plane of focus from one object or character to another within a shot is commonly known as a *rack focus*.

Aspect Ratio and Framing

Aspect Ratio

The aspect ratio of an image is the ratio of its width to its height. Beginning in the 1910s, motion pictures settled on a ratio of four to three (four units wide to three units high). Often written as 4:3, this ratio may be reduced to 1.33:1 and this aspect ratio is commonly known as 1.33. The introduction of sound-on-film narrowed the aspect ratio briefly, before the Academy ratio of 1.37 was introduced in 1932 by means of thickening the frame line. For years, cinematographers were limited to this shape of image, but in the 1950s, thanks to the unanticipated popularity of Cinerama, widescreen ratios were introduced in an effort to pull audiences back into the theater and away from their home television sets. These new widescreen aspect ratios granted cinematographers a wider frame within which to compose their images. Many different proprietary photographic systems were invented and utilized in the 1950s to create widescreen movies, but one dominates today: the anamorphic process, which optically squeezes the image to photograph twice the horizontal area to the same size vertical as standard "spherical" lenses. The first commonly used anamorphic widescreen format was CinemaScope, which used a 2.35:1 aspect ratio, although it was originally 2.55:1. CinemaScope was used from 1953 to 1967, but due to technical flaws in the design and its ownership by Fox, several third-party companies, led by Panavision's technical improvements in the 1950s, now dominate the anamorphic cine lens market. Changes to SMPTE projection standards altered the projected ratio from 2.35:1 to 2.39:1 in 1970, although this did not change anything regarding the photographic anamorphic standards; all changes in respect to the aspect ratio of anamorphic 35 mm photography are specifically correlative to camera or projector gate sizes, not the optical system.

After the "widescreen wars" of the 1950s, the motion-picture industry settled into 1.85:1 (which is a cropped version of 1.37:1) as a standard for theatrical projection in the United States and the United Kingdom. Europe and Asia opted for 1.66:1 at first, although 1.85:1 has largely permeated these markets in recent decades. Certain "epic" or adventure movies utilized the anamorphic 2.39:1.

In the 1990s, with the advent of high-definition video, television engineers created the 1.78:1 (16:9) ratio as a mathematical compromise between the theatrical standard of 1.85:1 and television's 1.33:1, as it was not physically possible to safely create a television tube with a width of 1.85:1. Until that point, nothing had ever been originated in 1.78:1. Today, this is a standard for high-definition video and for widescreen television.

Lighting

Most likely the single most important aspect of cinematography is lighting. Light is necessary to create an image exposure on a frame of film or on a digital target (CCD, etc). The art of lighting for cinematography goes far beyond basic exposure, however, into the essence of visual storytelling. Lighting contributes considerably to the emotional response an audience has watching a motion picture. The control of light quality, colour, direction and intensity is a major factor in the art and science of cinematography.

Camera Movement

One aspect of cinematography that strongly separates it from still photography (aside from having a moving subject) is the ability to move the camera, which represents the audience's viewpoint or perspective, during the course of filming. This movement plays a considerable role in the emotional language of film images and the audience's emotional reaction to the action on the screen. From the most basic movements of panning (horizontal shift in viewpoint from a fixed position; like turning your head side-to-side) and tilting (vertical shift in viewpoint from a fixed position; like tipping your head back to look at the sky or tilting your head down to look at the ground) to dollying (placing the camera on a moving platform to move it closer or farther from the subject), trucking (placing the camera on a moving platform to move it to the left or right), craning (moving the camera in a vertical position; being able to lift it off the ground as well as swing it side-to-side from a fixed base position), and a combination of all of the above.

Cameras have been mounted to nearly every imaginable form of transportation. Most cameras can also be handheld, that is the camera operator literally holds the camera in their hands and moves from one position to another while filming the action. Personal stabilizing platforms came into being in the late 1970s through the invention of Garrett Brown, which became known as the Steadicam. The Steadicam is a body harness and stabilization arm that connects to the camera that allows the operator to move naturally while completely isolating the movements of their body from the movements of the camera. After the Steadicam patent expired in the early 1990s, many other companies began manufacturing their concept of the personal camera stabilizer.

Special Effects

The first special effects in the cinema were created while the film was being shot. These came to be known as "in-camera" effects. Later, optical and digital effects were developed so that editors and visual effects artists could more tightly control the process by manipulating the film in post-production.

Frame Rate Selection

Motion picture images are presented to an audience at a constant speed. In the theater, it is 24 frames per second, in NTSC (US) Television, it is 30 frames per second (29.97 to be exact), in PAL (Europe) television it is 25 frames per second. This speed of presentation does not vary.

However, by varying the speed at which the image is captured, various effects can be created knowing that the faster or slower recorded image will be played at a constant speed.

For instance, time-lapse photography is created by exposing an image at an extremely slow rate. If a cinematographer sets a camera to expose one frame every minute for four hours, and then that footage is projected at 24 frames per second, the event that took four hours to record will now take 10 seconds to present (1 frame per minute for 4 hours equals 240 frames, projected at 24 frames per second equals 10 seconds). This compresses the event that took place in four hours into just 10 seconds. At this speed, one can present the events of a whole day (24 hours) in just one minute. The inverse of this, if an image is captured at speeds above that at which they will be presented, the effect is to greatly slow down (slow motion) the image. If a cinematographer shoots a person diving into a pool at 96 frames per second, and that image is presented back at 24 frames per second, it will take four times as long to watch the dive as it did for it to actually happen.

In motion pictures the manipulation of time and space is a considerable contributing factor to the narrative storytelling tools. Film editing plays a much stronger role in this manipulation, but frame rate selection in the photography of the original action is also a contributing factor to altering time.

"Ramping" is a process whereby the capture frame rate of the camera changes over time. For example, if in the course of 10 seconds of capture, the capture frame rate is adjusted from 60 frames per second to 24 frames per second, when played back at the standard film rate of 24 frames per second, a unique time-manipulation effect is achieved. For example, someone pushing a door open and walking out into the street would appear to start off in slow-motion, but in a few seconds later within the same shot the person would appear to walk in "realtime" (normal speed). The opposite speed-ramping is done in *The Matrix* when Neo re-enters the Matrix for the first time to see the Oracle. As he comes out of the warehouse "load-point", the camera zooms into Neo at normal speed but as it gets closer to Neo's face time seems to slow down, perhaps visually accentuating Neo pausing and reflecting a moment, and perhaps alluding to future manipulation of time itself within the Matrix later on in the movie.

Role of the Cinematographer

In the film industry, the cinematographer is responsible for the technical aspects of the images (lighting, lens choices, composition, exposure, filtration, film selection), but works closely with the director to ensure that the artistic aesthetics are supporting the director's vision of the story being told. The cinematographers are the heads of the camera, grip and lighting crew on a set, and for this reason they are often called directors of photography or DPs.

Directors of photography make many creative and interpretive decisions during the course of their work, from pre-production to post-production, all of which affect the overall feel and look of the motion picture. Many of these decisions are similar to what a photographer needs to note when taking a picture: the cinematographer controls the film choice itself (from a range of available stocks with varying sensitivities to light and colour), the selection of lens focal lengths, aperture exposure and focus. Cinematography, however, has a temporal aspect (see persistence of vision), unlike still photography, which is purely a single still image. It is also bulkier and more strenuous to deal with movie cameras, and it involves a more complex array of choices. As such a cinematographer often needs to work co-operatively with more people than does a photographer, who could frequently function as a single person. As a result, the cinematographer's job also includes personnel management and logistical organization.

Evolution of Technology: New Definitions

Traditionally the term "cinematography" referred to working with motion-picture film emulsion, but it is now largely synonymous with videography and digital video due to the popularity of digital cinematography.

Modern digital image processing has also made it possible to radically modify pictures from how they were originally captured. This has allowed new disciplines to encroach on some of the choices that were once the cinematographer's exclusive domain.

SLATE

The clapper board (AKA Clap slate) is a well-recognized icon of filming, but serves many purposes beyond its appearance. A clapper board is made up of two parts: the slate and the clapper.

The slate's most obvious purpose is the documentation, it provides on what scene is being filmed, when it was filmed, what take it was, which film reel it was, etc. The "clapper" provides an easily identified audio marker, which is useful when filming with multiple cameras and you must synchronize them during post-production, and is more commonly used to synchronize the sound and picture since they are usually recorded on separate devices. The black-and-white stripes on the clapper provide a reference for setting the white balance on the camera.

Increasingly in the modern digital age, the clapper becomes less useful as footage can be digitally marked by the camera and audio synchronization is no longer a problem due to the digital nature of the footage. However, for the sake of your editor, you may wish to continue using a clapper to make any possible problem easier to fix.

How to Use a Clapper Board?

While a clapper board seems simple, its use is more complex than it looks. When motion picture film is developed, the laboratory technician who is developing the film, printing the film, and syncing the audio to the film, must have all the necessary information to sync the audio to the picture. If you want to see your dailies the first thing in the morning and you want everything to work properly, you must never confuse the laboratory technician.

Verbal Slate

While the clapper board provides information for the picture, there must also be a verbal slate for the audio. This verbal slate must provide the scene and take number for the laboratory technician. The verbal slate must also make it clear if multiple cameras are used. The verbal slate must also make it clear if multiple tracks of audio are used. "Stereo Split" means one track of a stereo track has the audio from one microphone and the other track has audio from the other microphone.

A and B Cameras

If there are two or more cameras, sometimes a common slate is used. Both the slate and the verbal slate must make this clear.

Using a common slate is not good because it can be confusing. With a common slate, there is no camera number ("Camera A" vs. "Camera B") and no film reel number. Therefore, each camera should have its own slate. The slate information for one camera must never be seen by the other camera. The same rule applies for showing the clapper closing. Therefore, when one camera is slated, someone puts their hand over the lens of the other camera to block the view of the other camera's slate.

Tail Slates

Sometimes, when it is impossible to use a clapper board at the beginning of a shot, someone will yell "Tail Slate" at the beginning of the shot and at the end of the shot, the slate will be clapped upside down so that the film laboratory will know that this is the slate at the end of a shot rather than the slate for the beginning of the next shot. The verbal slate is always done at the same time as the clapper board.

Any Pulse Will Do

On shots where a clapper board is not practical, the actors will use their arms as a huge clapper. The film laboratory can easily see when the actor's hands come together. This noise is loud enough and concentrated enough to be accurate for syncing the audio to the picture.

Wildtrack

If there is no clapper for a shot, then the sound is wild. The laboratory technician might try to do a rough sync. Or the technician will create a separate section of the dailies for the audio from wildtracks. When you hear a wild track on the dailies, you see only a card saying Wildtrack as you hear the audio.

Re-syncing Sound

For motion picture film, the closing of the clapper (as seen on the film) must be aligned with the audio pulse (which shows up on the audio tape as a blip). Since audio travels at about 40 feet per frame of motion picture film (1/24th of a second), the audio pulse should be less than one frame after the closing of the slate unless the microphone is far from the camera (and the audience). Yet, when you watch dailies made using digital slates in Hollywood, you will find that most film laboratories sync the audio so it is late by one or two frames because the electronics in the slate are slow. Therefore, before you begin editing your movie, you must resync each take based on the actual clapper closing and the pulse on the audio track.

DV Camcorders

DV Camcorders often are supplemented with a separate audio recording device in order to record better sound quality. In this case it is nessasary to use a clapper in the beginning (or at the end if you are tailslating) in order to sync the sound up with the video.

Watch Dailies

If you want to see how the clapper board is used, simply look at film dailies from motion pictures and television dramas. You can buy motion picture and television drama dailies on tape at almost any second-hand video store in Hollywood.

CREW

Food

Never underestimate the importance of good food. If your crew is working for free then you must feed them well and at well defined times. If you are going to overrun then stop and ask your crew if they mind working for another hour before lunch. Always try to provide hot food. Sandwiches are your last resort.

Good food need not cost a lot. See if you can get your Mum involved or your best friend's mate who is an out-of-work chef. Remember also that some of your cast and crew (especially the clapper-loader) may have to work though their food breaks and so will need easy-to-eat food. Oh, and do not forget to check on allergies.

Check here for advice on good food which is affordable and works on set—Ultra Low Budget production Recipies.

Also remember to have a snack table (called craft services table in the USA). This may seem insignificant, however, film sets bring together very different personalities and egos, both technical and artistic, in very intense situations over a short period of time. Tempers will flare. They always do. Humans when upset or dealing with any extreme emotion in all cultures like to do one thing: put something in their mouth. A drink, a smoke, a chocolate, a thumb…whatever. The craft services table provides this option. Coffee, tea, water, donuts, pastries, chocolates, sweets, juice, and fruit. Do not underestimate it. Try to put the emphasis on healthy food like fruit rather than chocolates and crisps—junk food may give a quick 'high' but would not sustain that high so your crew will become irritable as the day progresses.

Another option (if you are lucky) is to get a deal with a local restaurant or pizza place, perhaps exchanging discounts on food for product placement in your film or advertising in the credits, brochures or your film's website. Local pizza places are a good first stop. This can get costly if done too often. Some consider this option selling out, which is fair, however, it is not a bad way to get some grub for the crew.

No matter what your position on set try to offer others a tea or coffee whenever you can. As a runner you will quickly gain the enthusiasm of others by offering tea and coffee. As a more senior crew member you will show that you are not a snobby nosed, status-obsessed fool in it only for the power, but a good natured human who likes to get along with people and do the best job possible.

But—be warned—never eat in front of a hungry camera crew. Why? The camera crew do not have the option of quickly picking up a sandwich because their hands must be kept very clean whilst on set and handling camera kit. Once, on my first ADing job, I was casually nibbling on a sandwich when the DoP gave me a loud and public telling off. You have been warned!

Hours

Do not overwork your crew. Your job as a film-maker is to get the very best out of your cast and crew—as a producer or director you actually do 'very little' hands-on film-making. So the best thing you can do is create a productive, exciting and comfortable environment for your cast and crew. The one thing that will destroy the mood on set (and destroy your film) is exhaustion. If your schedule demands 20 hour days then cut the script or increase the number of shooting days.

It is important to remember that the hours worked also include the 'wrapping out' time: not all crew just walk away when 'wrap' is called, spark (electricians), camera crew, grips, makeup, wardrobe and others still have a lot of work to pack up from the day and clean and prepare for the next day. So an estimated wrap time of say, 22.00 hours really means an end of shooting at 21.00 to allow for the wrapping-out. Expecting a 12 hour on-camera day to then be followed by an hour's worth of putting away the gear is a surefire way to spark a mutiny!

Communication

Give the cast and crew as much information as possible, especially when things are going wrong. If you can then print and distribute the schedule to every crew member at the start of each day, if not far earlier. If you are going run over schedule then first explain the situation to your crew, then ask very nicely if they mind working longer and then tell your crew the new estimate wrap time.

Drugs

You can not stop everyone from taking loads of drugs but do your best to dissuade your cast and crew.

Drugs and alcohol on set will void most insurance policies. You must get your crew to never ever take any kind of extreme mind altering substances while anywhere near set. I would advise firing anyone that does not heed this warning. This has nothing to do with moral or social issues it has to do with running a business. Until the insurance contracts change no drugs or alcohol on set.

Drinking

This is a dodgy one. Going out for drinks every night of the shoot is a good way to get to know everyone. But do not over do it. What you do as a director or producer is up to you. You will certainly increase your chances of getting on well with your cast and crew if you go out drinking with them. But, then again, you have probably got to spend every evening preparing the next day's shot list.

DIRECTION

- Casting Directors
- "Elements"
- Directing Actors
- Storyboarding

DIRECTING ACTORS

Clint Eastwood never shouts "action!", as he thinks it shocks actors and disturbs their concentration. Instead, he waits until the camera is rolling, and then says, "when you are ready..."

If you have done the casting correctly and your actor has the ability—let them express it. An actor will respond far better if they are given a degree of freedom to bring their creativity to the process. A good director will encourage this without, however, letting it go too far. The challenge here is to find the balance between allowing the actor to express themselves and serving the scene. The scene is part of a greater whole and their performance should be in balance with the other elements of the film.

Casting Actors

Next to having a great screenplay and a clear vision, casting great actors is the best thing you can do to improve the odds of your film succeeding. Casting good actors is 80 per cent of the directing process because once you have cast actors who understand what they are doing, the director's job is almost done. External reference on Auditioning and Casting actors

Inexperienced Actors

Inexperienced actors nearly always err on the side of overacting, putting too much into the role. Your task is often to convince them to be more naturalistic. Be clear and do not baffle them with technical terms. Explain how tight the shot is and their range of movement within the frame and they should be able to gauge how to behave. One very effective way to get truthful acting from inexperienced actors is to let them improvise their own lines around a specifically designed situation. It works! Guaranteed.

Another rule of thumb is to compliment generally, but criticize specifically. For example, telling an actress that you liked how she flipped her hair will cause her to do it again and again in subsequent takes, and it would not look as natural as it did the first time. Just tell her how great she did and hopefully she will unconciously continue what she was doing. However, you will want to be precise (but gentle) when pointing out the things you are certain you do not want.

If you have not done it already, making a backstory for the characters is always useful.

Troubleshooting

These tricks should be a last resort; the best way to work is through honest and open communication. Being sneaky can sometimes lose you the trust of your cast.

There is a great story about an actor who was so nervous he was having trouble remembering his lines and was getting flustered. The director gave him a coin to flip and asked him to keep flipping it throughout the scene. This successfully made the actor less self conscious and the scene flowed after that.

If an actor continually overdoes it, quietly start the camera, keep it rolling and do a "walkthrough" of the scene. Some of the footage might be quite usable.

ACTORS

Actors and film-making involve:

(i) Casting Directors
(ii) "Elements"
(iii) Directing Actors

FILM EDITING

Film editing is the connecting of one or more shots to form a sequence, and the subsequent connecting of sequences to form an entire movie. Film editing, by definition, is the only art that is unique to cinema and which defines and separates film-making from almost all other art forms (such as: photography, theater, dance, writing, and directing). The job of an editor is not merely to mechanically put pieces of a film together, nor to just cut off the film slates, nor merely to edit dialogue scenes. Film editing is an art form which can either make or break a film. A film editor works with the layers of images, the story, the music, the rhythm, the pace, shapes the actors' performances, "re-directing" and often re-writing the film during the editing process, honing the infinite possibilities of the juxtaposition of small snippets of film into a creative, coherent, cohesive whole.

Film Editor

A film editor is a person who practices film editing by assembling footage into a coherent film. Film editors often are responsible for pulling together all of the elements of story, dialogue, music, sound effects, visual effects, rhythm and pace of a film. In the making of a film, the editors usually play a dynamic and creative role.

History of Film Editing Technology

Film editing evolved from the process of a film editor physically cutting and taping together pieces of film, using a splicer and threading the film on a machine with a viewer such as a Moviola, or "flatbed" machine such as a Kem or Steenbeck.

Before the widespread use of non-linear editing systems, the initial editing of all films was done with a positive copy of the film negative called a film workprint (cutting copy in UK). Today, most films are edited digitally (on systems such as Avid or Final Cut Pro) and bypass the film positive workprint altogether. In the past, the use of a film positive (not the original negative) allowed the editor to do as much experimenting as he or she wished, without the risk of damaging the original.

When the film workprint had been cut to a satisfactory state, it was then used to make an Edit Decision List (EDL). The negative cutter referred to this list while processing the negative, splitting the shots into rolls, which were then contact printed to produce the final film print or answer print. Today, production companies have the option of to bypass negative cutting altogether. With the advent of digital intermediate or "DI," the physical negative does not necessarily need to be physically cut and hot spliced together; rather the negative is optically scanned into computer(s) and a cut list is conformed by a DI editor.

Edwin S. Porter

Edwin S. Porter is generally thought to be the American filmmaker who first put film editing to use. Porter migrated to the United States as a young sailor and worked as a mechanic before joining the film laboratory of Thomas Alva Edison in the late 1890s.

Early Edison films were short films that were typically shot in one long static locked down shot. When Edison's motion picture studio wanted to increase the length of the short films he came to Porter. Porter made the breakthrough film *Life of an American Fireman* in 1902. The film was among the first that had a plot, action, and even a closeup of a hand pulling a fire alarm.

Other films were to follow. Porter's ground-breaking film, *The Great Train Robbery* is still shown in film schools today as an example of early editing form. It was produced in 1903 and was one of the first examples of dynamic, action editing (the piecing together scenes shot at different times and places and for emotional impact unavailable in a static long shot). Being one of the first film hyphenates (film director, editor and engineer) Porter also invented and utilized some of the very first (albeit primitive) special effects such as double exposures, miniatures and split-screens.

Post-production

The Editor's Cut

There are several editing stages and the editor's cut is the first. An editor's cut (sometimes referred to as the "assembly edit" or "rough cut") is normally the first pass of what the final film will be when it reaches picture lock.

The film editor usually starts working while principal photography (shooting) starts. In the first stage of editing the film editor will usually work alone (save for his or her own team of assistant editors, associate or co-editors and/or visual effects and music editors). Likely, prior to cutting, the editor and director will have seen and/or discussed "dailies" (raw footage shot each day) as shooting progresses. Screening dailies gives the editor a ballpark idea of the director's intentions.

Because it is the first pass, the editor's cut might be somewhat longer than the final film. The editor continues to refine the cut while shooting continues, and often the entire editing process goes on for many months and sometimes more than a year, depending on the film.

The Director's Cut

When shooting is finished, the director can then turn his or her full attention to collaborating with the editor and further refining the cut of the film. This is the time that is set aside where the film editor's first cut is molded to fit the director's vision, and before the studio and/or producers are generally allowed to have input. In the United States, under DGA rules, directors receive a minimum of ten weeks after completion of principal photography to prepare their first cut.

While collaborating on what is referred to as the "director's cut," the director and the editor go over the entire movie with a fine tooth comb; scenes and shots are re-ordered, removed, shortened and otherwise tweaked. Often it is discovered that there are plot holes, missing shots or even missing segments which might require that new scenes be filmed.

Because of this time working closely and collaborating—a period that is normally far longer, and far more intimately involved, than the entire production and filming—most directors and editors form a unique artistic bond.

The Producers vs. the Director

Often after the director has had his or her chance to oversee a cut, the subsequent cuts are supervised by one or more producers, who represent the production company and/or movie studio. At times, the final cut of films produced by the major studios is the one that most closely represents what the studio wants from the film and not necessarily what the director wants. Because of this, there have been several conflicts in the past between the director and the studio, sometimes leading to the use of the "Alan Smithee" credit signifying when a director no longer wants to be associated with the final release.

Continuity

Often a film editor is blamed for improper continuity. For example, cutting from a shot where the beer glass is empty to one where it is full. Continuity is, in fact, very nearly last on a film editor's list of important things to maintain. Continuity is typically the business of the script supervisor and film director, who are together responsible for preserving continuity and preventing errors from take to take and shot to shot. Generally speaking, the editor utilizes the script supervisor's notes during post-production to log and keep track of the vast amounts of footage and takes that a director might shoot. However, to most editors what is more important than continuity is the editing of emotional and storytelling aspects of any given film—something that is much more abstract and harder to judge—which is why films often take much longer to edit than to shoot. Often a film editor will used this to focus on the theme of the film.

Methods of Montage

In motion picture terminology, a montage (from the French for "putting together" or "assembly") is a film editing technique.

There are at least three senses of the term:

1. In French film practice, "montage" has its literal French meaning and simply identifies a movie's editor.
2. In Soviet film-making of the 1920s, "montage" was a method of juxtaposing shots to derive new meaning that did not exist in either shot alone.
3. In classical Hollywood cinema, a "montage sequence" is a short segment in a film in which narrative information is presented in a condensed fashion. This is the most common meaning among laymen.

Soviet Montage

Lev Kuleshov was among the very first to theorize about the relatively young medium of the cinema in the 1920s. For him, the unique essence of the cinema—that which could be duplicated in no other medium—is editing. He argues that editing a film is like constructing a building. Brick-by-brick (shot-by-shot) the building (film) is erected. His often-cited Kuleshov Experiment established that montage can lead the viewer to reach certain conclusions about the action in a film. Montage works because viewers infer meaning based on context.

Although, strictly speaking, U.S. film director D.W. Griffith was not part of the montage school, he was one of the early proponents of the power of editing—mastering cross-cutting to show parallel action in different locations, and codifying film grammar in other ways as well. Griffith's work in the teens was highly regarded by Kuleshov and other Soviet film-makers and greatly influenced their understanding of editing.

Sergei Eisenstein was briefly a student of Kuleshov's, but the two parted ways because they had different ideas of montage. Eisenstein regarded montage as a dialectical means of creating meaning. By contrasting unrelated shots he tried to provoke associations in the viewer, which were induced by shocks.

Montage Sequence

A montage sequence consists of a series of short shots that are edited into a sequence to condense narrative. It is usually used to advance the story as a whole (often to suggest the passage of time), rather than to create symbolic meaning. In many cases, a song plays in the background to enhance the mood or reinforce the message being conveyed. Classic examples are the training montages in Sylvester Stallone's *Rocky* series of movies.

Continuity Editing

What became known as the popular 'classical Hollywood' style of editing was developed by early European and American directors, in particular D.W. Griffith in his films such as *The Birth of a Nation* and *Intolerance*. The classical style ensures temporal and spatial continuity as a way of advancing narrative, using such techniques as the 180 degree rule, Establishing shot, and Shot reverse shot.

Alternatives to Continuity Editing (Non-traditional or Experimental)

Early Russian film-makers such as Lev Kuleshov further explored and theorized about editing and its ideological nature. Sergei Eisenstein developed a system of editing that was unconcerned with the rules of the continuity system of classical Hollywood that he called Intellectual montage.

Alternatives to traditional editing were also the folly of early surrealist and dada film-makers such as Luis Buñuel (director of the 1929 *Un chien andalou*) and René Clair (director of 1924's *Entr'acte* which starred famous dada artists Marcel Duchamp and Man Ray). Both film-makers, Clair and Buñuel, experimented with editing techniques long before what is referred to as "MTV style" editing.

The French New Wave film-makers such as Jean Luc Godard and François Truffaut and their American counterparts such as Andy Warhol and John Cassavetes also pushed the limits of editing technique during the late 1950s and throughout the 1970s. French New Wave films and the non-narrative films of the 1960s used a carefree editing style and did not conform to the traditional editing etiquette of Hollywood films. Like its dada and surrealist predecessors, French New Wave editing often drew attention to itself by its lack of continuity, its demystifying self-reflexive nature (reminding the audience that they were watching a film), and by the overt use of jump cuts or the insertion of material not often related to any narrative.

Editing Techniques

Stanley Kubrick noted that the editing process is the one phase of production that is truly unique to motion pictures. Every other aspect of film-making originated in a different medium than film (photography, art direction, writing, sound recording), but editing is the one process that is unique to film. In Alexander Walker's *Stanley Kubrick Directs,* Kubrick was quoted as saying, "I love editing. I think I like it more than any other phase of film-making. If I wanted to be frivolous, I might say that everything that precedes editing is merely a way of producing film to edit."

In his book, *On Film Editing,* Edward Dmytryk stipulates seven "rules of cutting" that a good editor should follow:

- "Rule 1. *Never* make a cut without a positive reason.
- "Rule 2. When undecided about the exact frame to cut on, cut *long* rather than short" (Dmytryk, 23).
- "Rule 3: Whenever possible cut 'in movement' " (Dmytryk, 27).
- "Rule 4: The 'fresh' is preferable to the 'stale' " (Dmytryk, 37).
- "Rule 5: All scenes should begin and end with continuing action" (Dmytryk, 38).
- "Rule 6: Cut for proper values rather than proper 'matches'" (Dmytryk, 44).
- "Rule 7: Substance first—then form" (Dmytryk, 145).

According to Walter Murch, when it comes to film editing, there are six main criteria for evaluating a cut or deciding where to cut. They are (in order of importance, most important first):

- *Emotion*—Does the cut reflect what the editor believes the audience should be feeling at that moment?
- *Story*—Does the cut advance the story?
- *Rhythm*—Does the cut occur "at a moment that is rhythmically interesting and 'right'" (Murch, 18)?
- *Eye-trace*—Does the cut pay respect to "the location and movement of the audience's focus of interest within the frame" (Murch, 18)?
- *Two-dimensional Place of the Screen*—Does the cut respect the 180 degree rule?
- *Three-dimensional Space of Action*—Is the cut true to the physical/spatial relationships within the diegesis?

Murch assigned notional percentage values to each of the criteria. Emotion, with 51 per cent, outweighed the combined value of all the other criteria.

SCREENPLAY

A screenplay or script is a written plan, authored by a screenwriter, for a film or television programme. Screenplays can be original works or adaptations from existing works such as novels. A screenplay differs from a script in that it is more specifically targeted at the visual, narrative arts, such as film and television, whereas a script can involve a blueprint of "what happens" in a comic, an advertisement, a theatrical play and other "blueprinted" creations.

The major components of a screenplay are action and dialogue, with the "action" being "what we see happening" and "dialogue" being "what the characters say." The characters, when first introduced in the screenplay, may also be described visually. Screenplays differ from traditional literature conventions in ways described below; however, screenplays may not involve emotion-related descriptions and other aspects of the story that are, in fact, visual within the end-product.

For more details on the contents of screenplays, see Screenwriting.

In the United States, the Writers Guild of America (WGA) has final control on whom may be awarded screenwriting credit for a screenplay in a union production. The WGA is one of several organizations in the U.S. and worldwide which recognize screenplays with awards.

A script for television is sometimes called a teleplay.

Writing on Spec or Assignment

Screenplays can be written either on "spec" (speculative) or as assignment ("Commissioned"). The Variety slanguage dictionary defines "spec script" as "a script shopped or sold on the open market, as opposed to one commissioned by a studio or production company."

Writing on Assignment

Assignments are commissioned by production companies or studios on the basis of pitches from producers or writers, or literary properties they already own. Most established writers do most of their work on assignment and will only "spec" scripts which they think no-one will pay them to write, or if they cannot find assignment work.

There are exceptions: some very famous writers only write on spec because they know that they can get a better price for their work this way. Other writers spec scripts that they care deeply about so that they do not have to bend to the whims of executives and producers.

An assignment may be for an original screenplay, or for an adapted screenplay based on another work such as a novel, film, short story, comic book, magazine article or, increasingly, video game. It may also, however, be for a rewrite of an existing script, and in fact this is how a large proportion of writers in the modern studio system make their living. Rewriting scripts is an art in itself and an extremely lucrative one at that: it is not unknown for trusted writers in the higher echelons of the industry to receive $200,000 a week (2004 numbers) for their efforts. $50,000 per week is not uncommon.

Rewriting is difficult because executives often have very clear ideas about what is wrong with a script, however, they are usually unable to provide detailed prescriptions for ways it can be fixed. This is not surprising, because screenwriting is not the expertise of the executive, but of the screenwriter. The writer is therefore usually expected to come up with a detailed prescription for how the script can be improved, and then execute this in a timely fashion. During the process of choosing a writer to rewrite a script the executives may ask several writers for their 'take' and choose the one who appears to have the greatest likelihood of moving the script forward to the point where it may be greenlit for production.

Before 'going to script' a writer may be asked to write a treatment, an outline, or a step outline describing the script in various granularities of detail. Some writers resist this process and will do anything to avoid it and get down the writing the script itself; others embrace the process and even deliver fairly elaborate treatments, the so-called scriptments. It is fair to say that producers tend to be wary of the former and pleasantly surprised by the latter.

Spec Scripts

Many Spec scripts (short for speculative) are written independently by screenwriters in hopes of optioning and eventually outright selling them to producers or studios. Other spec scripts are written by writer-directors who plan to direct the film themselves. Many so-called "art films" films fall into this latter category, whereas the former category tends to be filled with "high concept" scripts—mostly action or comedy, to which a star or A-list director can be attached. However, most of the hundreds of thousands of spec scripts penned each year are written by unknowns who are trying to attract attention and find it difficult to generate the kind of "buzz" that more established scribes count on to sell their scripts.

The Development Process

Once a studio has purchased or commissioned a script, it goes through the process of revisions and rewriting until all stakeholders are satisfied and ready to proceed. It is not uncommon for a script to go through many, many drafts on its journey to production. Very few scripts improve steadily with each draft, and when a certain avenue has been exhausted the writer will often be replaced and another brought in to do a rewrite.

Occasionally it becomes impossible to satisfy all such parties, and the project enters development hell.

If a studio decides it does not wish to proceed to production with the script, the project enters 'turnaround.' Another studio may purchase the script from its original owner, but the script is encumbered with the development costs the studio has already incurred. At a certain point, it may simply be uneconomic for anyone to purchase the script, even if it is a very good one. This goes part of the way to explaining why some of the best scripts in Hollywood remain unproduced.

The Shooting Script

Once a script has been approved for production, camera directions and notes may be inserted by the Director, and each scene is assigned a number to provide a convenient way for the various production departments to reference individual scenes. When a scene is omitted, its number is retained labeled with "omitted", so that it would not be assigned to any newly added scenes.

When the shooting script is distributed, its pages are locked, meaning that any subsequent revisions will apply to the first set of revision pages. When revisions are distributed, the pages are swapped into the outstanding drafts, and the script is once again locked. The process is repeated for each new round of revisions.

Each round of revisions is distributed on different coloured paper. The progression of colours varies from one production to the next. Since rewrites often continue throughout principal photography, most shooting scripts evolve into a rainbow of gold, pink, blue, green and cherry pages.

Transcripts

A screenplay is different from a transcript. A transcript is simply a copy of what dialogue finally appeared onscreen, without regard to the original script, the stage directions or action. A full post-production transcript may also include descriptions of the action on-screen, but since it is generally not written by a professional writer but either a production assistant or a fan, it may not be particularly entertaining to read.

Many published screenplays available at booksellers or downloaded from the internet are in fact glorified post-production transcripts rather than shooting scripts. Transcripts and screenplays often differ radically because scenes are frequently re-ordered or dropped entirely during the editing process. Moreover, actors may change lines or simply improvise dialogue, and many directors will make their own changes to the script on the fly during rehearsal or shooting.

It can be extremely revealing to compare a shooting script with the film as finally distributed.

Screenwriting Software

Detailed computer programmes are designed specifically for screenplays, and many have templates for teleplays and stageplays. These programmes have been designed to create industry standard screenplays and are used by professional screenwriters. What should be remembered is that all such software is an aid in the formatting of a screenplay and not the actual creation of it. A number of these programmes offer access to online screenwriter communities where feedback from fellow screenwriters is available. Some examples of screenwriting software are: Celtx, Dreama Script, Final Draft and Montage. Furthermore, screenwriting software is available for handheld devices (Palm OS, and Windows Mobile/Pocket PC).

6

Television Production: Elements, Steps and Stages

TELEVISION PRODUCTION

This helps people use both field and studio television production facilities to communicate over public and government access cable television channels. It has become clear over the years (as it should have been in the beginning) that lighting is the same for painters as it is for still photographers as it is for today's videographers. We are still trying to imitate the sun and the shadows it creates. Principles of composition have not changed since the ancient Greeks, digital video notwithstanding. In the same vein, the principles of editing remain as constant as the principles of storytelling no matter how old or how modern the medium might be.

There are essentially two ways of doing television. Programmes are shot either in a specially designed television studio using several cameras which are fed into a control room and assembled in "real time," or they are shot using a single camera on location and assembled later in an editing room or on a computer. Obviously, almost all non-professional video is shot using a single camera. That makes it what the pros call "electronic field production," or EFP.

In electronic field production, the director is like a composer of music, creating and assembling images and impressions, fitting them together carefully, weighing the quality and importance of each as he goes. He works much as a film director would, in a linear fashion from one shot to the next, one scene to the next. He is dealing with only one picture and one situation at a time. Since the programme will be edited later, he can shoot out of sequence, repeat shots, and record extra shots to be included later. Electronic field production allows for a richness of scene and artistic creativity born sometimes out of necessity and sometimes out of opportunities suggested by the location itself.

Professionals spend most of their time planning, scripting, and organizing their productions. The amount of time spent actually recording the programme is surprisingly short compared to the time spent preparing for it. Each programme goes through several important stages, from development of the concept through planning and scripting, then on to set design or location scouting, acquisition of performers and rehearsal. Along the way, the producer schedules his equipment, finds a competent crew, and brings all of the necessary elements together for actual production of the programme.

Television is an amalgam of many diverse disciplines. Professional productions often depend on the skill and cooperation of many people, as well as the ability of the producer and director to bring these people together in a cooperative effort. On the other hand, with digital technology, it is also possible to be a "one man band," performing all of the various functions yourself, and produce a "broadcast quality" programme. While this book will deal with many of the techniques of production, it does not pretend to tell you how to do anything. After all, rules are made to be broken. Or ignored. Still, picking the mind of a professional television producer will help you get better results every time you pick up a camera.

Beginning in June of 2006 we have added a discussion forum for issues related to this web site and television production in general. The forum can be found at www.tv-handbook.com/ discussion

Television production involves:

(i) The Camera
(ii) Lighting
(iii) Composition
(iv) Basic Audio
(v) Basic Video
(vi) Organization of Materials
(vii) Additional Video
(viii) Rights and Responsibilities
(ix) Editing and Programme Continuity
(x) Getting the Word Out

The Camera

We are well on our way to the world of fully automatic "point and shoot" television cameras. Smart cameras are great most of the time and they certainly cut down on the common mistakes most people (even pros) make from time to time. When automatic operation does not work, though, the results can be pretty bad. Knowing what the conditions were that fooled your "smart" camera will help you to know when to turn these features off and do it the old-fashioned way. But before you do, you need to know what cameras do and how they work.

The television camera changes light into an electronic signal that can be stored (using video tape, optical disks, or computer memory, transmitted, and displayed on a television receiver or monitor. Television cameras are probably easier to operate well than film or still cameras because you can watch and control the camera output as you record. There are few electronic controls, and the manual controls on the lens will be familiar to anyone who has used a good still or motion picture camera. Since video cameras can, as a rule, produce sharper, clearer pictures than the recording media they were designed to work with, the quality of your camera is seldom an excuse for fuzzy pictures. Understanding how to use the camera correctly will help you avoid poor results.

Lens Controls

The modern television lens has three controls: iris, focus, and zoom. On a fully automatic camera you may not have to adjust the focus or iris except under unusual conditions, but you should know what is going on so you can use manual settings with confidence.

1. *Iris*. The ring closest to the camera body controls the amount of light passing through the lens to the light-sensitive surface of the pickup tube or chip. It is called the iris, aperture, or f-stop control and is marked off in f-numbers. The lowest f-stop lets in the most light, and the highest f-stop lets in the least. Some lenses even have a "C" setting after the highest f-stop which means the lens is completely closed, letting no light through at all.

More light——————Less light
1 1.4 2 2.8 4 5.6 8 11 16 22 32
STANDARD F-NUMBERS

Each standard f-stop lets half as much light through the lens as the f-stop below it.

If the camera gets too little light, the image will look fuzzy and drab, even though it may be in focus. The camera image may lag behind quick changes in the picture and the picture will be grayish, with little contrast.

Too much light will produce too much contrast. Details in both the very bright and the very dark parts of the picture will be lost. Bright spots may grow "halos" or "bloom." So-called "point sources" of light may cause light vertical stripes on CCD cameras.

The correct setting is between these extremes, generally about one f-stop higher than the f-stop at which the bright parts of the picture lose details and grow halos, or "bloom." To find this point, begin with the lens in the closed or highest f-stop position and open it slowly until you start losing details in the brightest parts of the picture. Then reduce the amount of light coming through by going down to the next highest f-stop.

Indoors it is often necessary to add light to get a good picture. Outdoors on bright sunny days it may be necessary to reduce the light reaching the pickup tube even more than the lens will allow. This is done by adding a neutral density filter between the lens and lens hood. A two power (2X) filter has the same effect as using the next highest f-stop, while a four power (4X) filter gives the effect of going up two f-stops.

2. *Zoom.* The center ring on most lenses is the zoom control. Most cameras use a rocker switch beside the lens. This allows you to change the focal length of the lens through a range from wide angle (short focal length) to telephoto (long focal length). It is common for inexpensive zoom lenses to have a range of about six to one. That is, the longest focal length is about six times the shortest. Zoom lenses for television cameras with two-thirds inch pickup tubes or chips range from about 12 mm to 75 mm, with a normal focal length of about 33 mm.

A wide angle setting makes the subject smaller as the angle of view is increased. Distances from the camera are exaggerated, with objects nearer the camera appearing abnormally large. This is especially true of people who are too close to a wide angle lens. Straight lines near the edges of the picture are often bent with an effect known as barrel distortion.

A telephoto setting makes the subject larger as the angle of view is reduced. Distances from the camera are compressed. More than one feature film director has used this effect to make an action (like running toward the camera) seem to take much longer than it should.

The normal lens settings offer the most natural perspective to the viewer. It is possible to change the focal length of a zoom lens during a shot by "zooming" in or out. Inexperienced camera operators often over-use this capability. The main value of the lens is in controlling the field of view of the camera when it is inconvenient or impossible to change the distance from the subject to the camera.

3. *Focus.* The focus control is the ring farthest from the camera body, on the front of the lens. Distance settings are marked in meters and in feet. While a non-zoom (fixed focal length) lens is focused simply by turning the ring until the image is sharp; the zoom lens must be zoomed in to the smallest angle of view and the largest image size to adjust focus. The lens should then be zoomed out to the widest angle of view and the smallest image size to make sure the image stays in focus through the entire zoom range. If the image stays sharp, the lens will remain focused at any focal length as long as the distance from the subject does not change.

Depth of field is the range of distances in front of the lens in which objects appear to be in acceptable focus. It is longer for short (wide angle) lenses than for long (telephoto) lenses, and it increases as you use higher f-stops. It is often wise to use a higher f-stop when lighting conditions permit, if you expect the distance between the camera and the subject to change often while you are taping, since you will have less trouble keeping the subject sharply focused with greater depth of field.

While all cameras with zoom lenses must control iris, focal length, and focus, the functions of the three rings described here may be automated or provided by remote control.

Most lenses also have a "macro" setting on the zoom ring. This changes the characteristics of the lens to let you focus on objects right up to the front of the lens.

Electronic Controls

Some or all of the following controls may be automatic or preset and thus not adjustable by the user.

1. ***Pedestal.*** Also called the "set-up" control, sets the level of the darkest parts of the picture. On portable cameras it is generally automatic or totally absent.

2. *Gain.* Also called "level," this control sets the level of the brightest parts of the picture. It can be used to reduce the level when too much light is striking the pickup tube, but it will not make the picture brighter without making it grainy or snowy if the pickup tube or chip is not getting enough light. Automatic gain controls can be extremely sensitive to even small bright parts of the picture, driving medium and darker parts into black. They may also bring dark parts up into the medium range if there is not enough light for a good picture.

3. *White Balance.* If you use outdoor film with normal indoor lighting (no flash) everything comes out orange. The color temperature of sunlight is very different from an incandescent light bulb. Most consumer cameras now sense the overall colour temperature and adjust colour electronically. In older or professional cameras it may be necessary with each change in location or lighting to "tell" the camera how to interpret colour. This is done by showing the camera a white card, which represents the total absence of colour. Controls on the camera are then used to minimize the colour output of the camera.

4. *Viewfinder.* There are often controls to adjust a camera viewfinder. To state the obvious, these controls have absolutely nothing to do with the actual output of the camera. It is helpful to adjust the viewfinder under controlled conditions so it shows a faithful representation of actual camera output. Otherwise, if you want viewfinders to tell you the truth, they should never be adjusted just to make a "pretty" picture.

Television Lighting

Television is a means of changing patterns of light into electrical signals for storage or transmission and then recreating those patterns on a screen. In order to do this well, the television camera must be presented with properly illuminated scenes. The three important considerations are overall level, contrast range, and colour temperature.

Level

Lighting levels for television are generally set by adjusting the incident light, or the light striking the subject. The unit of measure for incident light is the foot candle, which is the amount of light produced by a standard candle at a distance of one foot. Lighting measurements are made using an incident light meter, which has a white plastic cover over the sensing element and a logarithmic scale calibrated in foot candles. To measure the useful incident light for television, the meter is held near the subject and pointed toward the camera.

The minimum acceptable level for colour television depends on the ability of the lens to transmit light to the camera, the sensitivity of the pickup tube or chip, and the amount of depth of field you need. For high-quality pictures you need something between fifty and two hundred foot candles. Most cameras can be operated in light ranging from the minimum up to ten thousand foot candles, or fairly bright sunlight. Where lighting conditions fall outside this range, steps must be taken to bring the lighting level into line with the capabilities of the camera. With too little light, additional lighting must be added. With too much, special neutral density filters must be used on the camera.

Absolute Rock Bottom

You will see cameras advertised as 2 LUX or 4 LUX cameras. 2 LUX is equal to .19 foot candles. 4 LUX is about .37 foot candles. I was suspicious, so a number of years ago I set up an ordinary candle one foot away from a white square on a black background. I tested two cameras. The first was a popular CCD camera requiring four LUX for minimum illumination. The second was a broadcast camera using Saticon pickup tubes. At a nominal one foot candle the CCD camera produced 40 IRE units of video, but the amount of noise in the picture was very objectionable. At four foot candles the CCD camera produced 100 IRE units with an acceptable noise level. The broadcast camera produced 20 IRE units at one foot candle with the "boost" set at 18 dB. At four foot candles, it produced 46 dB at 0 boost and 95 dB at 9dB boost. At four foot candles the broadcast picture was obviously superior to the picture from the consumer camera.

The difference at one foot candle is essentially the willingness to tolerate more noise in the CCD camera, giving it more apparent sensitivity under extremely low light situations. To mask some of the noise at low light levels, consumer cameras often use a setup, or black level, of zero IRE, rather than the 7.5 IRE broadcast standard. Some cameras that automatically boost the signal in low light situations can also be run in manual mode where you can control how much boost you want to use.

Lighting levels of five to fifteen foot candles are common in homes, while office settings tend to range from fifty to sixty foot candles. Keeping the reservations in the preceding paragraph in mind, consumer camcorders should have plenty of light for acceptable pictures in either setting.

Contrast

Contrast refers to the difference in brightness from the darkest parts of a scene to the brightest.

Useful contrast for NTSC television is determined by the amplitude of the video signal. The NTSC standard calls for a "peak to peak" amplitude of one volt at 75 ohms impedance. Only seven tenths of a volt is used for the luminance, or black and white part of the signal.

Common digital video signals are 24 bit colour, with eight bits each for red, green, and blue. This scheme allows for 256 individual shades from dark to light for each colour. Since 24 bit colour allows for over sixteen million colours, the limited number of shades available for each colour is not usually a problem, although the luminance steps may be visible in monochromatic scenes.

If there is too little contrast many receivers will produce a flat, grayish picture. If there is too much contrast, details in the brightest and darkest parts of the picture will be lost and the picture will look too harsh.

Since contrast is actually light reflected from the subject, it is measured using a reflectance light meter. The meter is held near a variety of very light and very dark parts of the subject and pointed toward each part of the subject to be measured. The ideal contrast range for NTSC television is about twenty to one. This corresponds to a difference of about four and one half f-numbers between the darkest and brightest parts of the picture on a reflectance light meter. In practice, actual contrast ranges are rarely measured using a meter. A subjective analysis based on camera output is generally sufficient.

Colour Temperature

The third consideration is color temperature. Every source of light has a characteristic colour. This color is related to its "temperature." Lower colour temperatures tend to be red or orange while higher temperatures tend to be green or blue. Colour temperatures are measured in degrees Kelvin. Some examples:

Colour Temperature

Temperature	*Source*	*Color*
1950	Candlelight	Orange
2870	Normal Incandescent	Orange
3200	Most Photo or TV Lights	Orange
3400	Some Photo Lamps	Orange
3500-4000	Fluorescent Lamps	Green
5500	Midday Sunlight	Blue

The eye "remembers" how things are supposed to look and interprets colour accordingly, regardless of the colour temperature of lighting sources. A white sheet of paper seems white whether viewed under an incandescent lamp or sunlight. The eye can even adjust for "correct colour" when two light sources of different colours are present in the same scene. Sunlight streaming into a room which is also lit by incandescent lamps does not make objects it strikes appear bluish.

Television cameras are not so versatile. They must be set up to render colour in a way that is pleasing to the eye. They can do this only if all of the important lighting sources within a scene have the same colour temperature. A combination of filters and electronic adjustments is used to adapt colour cameras to each new lighting situation. Most cameras can adjust automatically to typical colour temperatures. They cannot resolve conflicts when major picture elements are lit at different colour temperatures.

Organization of Materials

The materials needed to produce a television programme fall into two broad categories. The first consists of the material itself, including the script, on-camera talent, sets, and props. The second consists of the videotape, equipment, and crew which will be involved in production. It is the job of the producer to see to it that both come together at the time of production. Even if you are just shooting home movies, you can appreciate the difficulty in getting the "cast" and your equipment together and ready all at the same time. In the world of professional film and video the problems are the same, only bigger.

Planning and Pre-production

The first step in planning a production is usually called a "treatment." This is nothing more than a brief description of the way the material is to be organized and the programmatic goals of the production. For example:

This programme is designed to present the services provided by Moving Pictures, including programme production, tape duplication, and computer graphics and animation.

This might be followed by an outline showing sequences in the order in which they will appear in the final programme and detailing the objectives for each sequence.

I. Open with variety of location shots.
II. Brief description of range of services.
III. POC explains advantages of television over other media.
IV. Examples of too small—too large—too far away—too dangerous concepts.
V. Examples of narrations in different languages.
VI. Computer animation and graphics examples.
VIII. Closing statement.

The next step is a shot sheet, or storyboard. While a shot sheet describes each shot in writing, a storyboard does the same thing using pictures.

While these storyboard frames were taken from actual video, pictures can be stick figures, cartoons, or (in some cases) professionally painted panels. If it works, its just fine.

Finally, a full script may be written, containing all of the audio and video information to be presented in the programme (See Table 6.1).

Not all of these steps are appropriate to every production. In electronic field production the producer will scout each location involved to determine whether lights will be needed, whether sufficient power is available, how any lights will be placed, where the camera will be set up, and how sound recording will be handled. He should visualize each shot, making sure any problems can be overcome and ensuring that the shot will fit into the programme without breaking any of the rules of continuity.

Table 6.1

TITLE: PRODUCER:	DRAFT NO:	PAGE NO:
VIDEO		AUDIO
Copyright Warning		
CU aerial shot	MUSIC UP	
Key MP Production & Services Music. Over CU aerial shot		
POC at Vesuvius intro		
Fire truck in parade		
Wiring, Ill Bell Champaign office		
WS of special "easy to ride" bicycle at Parkland College	MUSIC UNDER	
"Time Pinnacle" laser show		
WS Skylights in Danville Village Mall.	NARRATOR: MOVING PICTURES is a television production company.	
MP at Business Expo	We make television programmes for business and government.	
Danville Village Mall	We also provide a full range of services related to making and showing television programmes.	
Key over stack of labeled tapes	from tape duplication to	
Tape Duplication	consulting to	
Facilities Design for Production	designing and building both production and	
Playback	playback facilities.	
POC in edit suite	POC: At MOVING PICTURES we make pictures that move; images on videotape that move in the literal sense, but also move your audience to understanding or to action. You have a number of ways to communicate with your various audiences.	

For any production that might be shown to the public, the producer should get permission to use each location and make sure that he has a release form for each person he intends to use as on-camera talent at each location. People appearing incidentally in a shot need not sign release forms, provided the taping is done openly in a public place. Even when taping in public places it is a good idea to inform concerned authorities of your intentions to avoid any misunderstandings or problems such as crowd control or interference with other activities at the same location.

If the script calls for the use of any potentially copyrighted materials, it is the responsibility of the producer to acquire the right to use the material, or, failing that, find substitute material for which he can acquire rights. It is important for the producer to anticipate his distribution needs when buying rights, since he could find he has the rights to distribute in one way and needs to distribute in another. For example, having performance rights for a play is not the same as having recording rights to turn it into a television programme. And owning a recording of a song in no way gives you the right to use that recording as a part of a programme. Special rights called "synchronization rights" are needed to do that.

Additional Video

Note: Of all the chapters in this book, this is most subject to change as television production moves from the use of tangible forms of image storage, such as slides or prints, to electronic storage. While slides and prints are still important sources of pictorial images, in the generation and use of titles and text, we have not used or even seen anything other than computer-generated text since the mid nineteen eighties.

Titles and Artwork

Graphic material is very important in many types of programmes. Certainly almost any sort of show looks more polished and professional if it has, at least, opening titles, and credits for the major members of the production crew at the end. Other types of written and graphic material may also be needed.

There are four main ways to incorporate graphic information into a television programme.

The *Character Generator* is a computer that produces printed material digitally and converts it into a form which is directly usable as a video source.

Graphics can also be produced on *Live Cards,* usually cardboard sheets about 11 x 14 inches, which are shot by a camera.

Slides can be produced photographically in a variety of ways from the same sort of originals used for live cards and can then be projected into a special camera using a device called a film chain or projected onto a white surface and shot by a camera.

Computers are used to generate most of the graphics now used in television at all levels.

Character Generator

Character generators differ significantly in their versatility and ease of use, but mostly tend to look the same, consisting of a console with a typewriter-style keyboard and, usually, a dedicated video monitor, there are a number of special keys on the keyboard which control specific functions of the character generator, such as page advance, character size and type style, automatic centering, and perhaps other options. There is always a set of keys to position (up, down, left, right) a cursor which appears on the character generator's own monitor (but not in the signal sent to the switcher) and indicates exactly where on the screen the next letter will appear.

Most character generators allow for only a small number of characters on the screen at once; ten lines of thirty figures each is typical. Actually, this is not a disadvantage. Small characters are difficult to see given the limited resolution and large viewing distances of TV sets in the home. This general principle applies to all graphics work for television: keep it simple, make all important elements large, and try to present complicated graphics in several pages, if needed, instead of all at once. The output of a character generator is usually inserted over other video by means of a key or matte.

As character generators become more sophisticated (and expensive), they may offer some of these additional features: Most units can store more than one "page" of graphics and allow you to recall them in order, or randomly, by pressing keys. The ability to roll (vertically) or crawl (horizontally) lettering across the screen is useful; rolling credits are common at the ends of programmes, and crawls are often used to make announcements during a programme at the bottom of the screen. Some machines offer a disk or tape cassette storage system which allows pages of characters to be stored for recall at any time, also extending the page-storage capability of the character generator enormously. Finally, more sophisticated character generators offer a wide variety of sizes and styles (and sometimes colors) of characters, variable italicization, outlines, shadows, and even the ability to create custom characters or logos for regeneration later. Less expensive machines may offer only one or two sizes of a single type font; the very cheapest do not even have lower-case letters.

The major disadvantage in the use of character generators for television graphics is that they are at their best only when presenting rather simple textual information. If you have in mind any kind of charts or graphs, or the use of some special type style, you will have to use something else.

Live Cards

Before computer graphics we used live artwork cards in front of a camera to present graphics and photographs. Modestly stiff multi-ply cardboard in cards about 11 by 14 inches were the most common background material for live cards. This material is available at art supply houses in a variety of colours and textures.

Lettering on live cards can be done with dry transfer letters, again available at art and school supply stores. This material is provided in large sheets containing several complete alphabets of a particular type font. There are other lettering systems too, sometimes faster or cheaper but seldom as good-looking as well done dry transfer work.

In making up live cards, it is important to assure that everything you need will be seen on the television screen and that no extraneous material gets in. Always allow a 1-1/2 to 2 inch border on all sides of a live card to give some leeway in camera positioning and framing. This area should be completely clear of dirt, pencil marks and other distractions, as should, of course, the main picture area itself. Also, remember that the dimensions of the television screen are four units wide by three units high. A six by eight inch area in the center of an 11 by 14 card would be a very safe one in which to compose your graphics. Usually type no smaller than 24 point (1/3 inch high) would be used in a space of that size.

Slides

Any 35 mm still camera can be used to generate slides for use in television. In any photographic work for television, remember that the television system always crops the image slightly, so you will see less on the TV screen than appears in the original slide or film. The 35 mm slide format also has a slightly different aspect ratio than the TV screen; the pictures are wider. Thus, anything at the extreme edges of the picture will not be reproduced.

Digital still cameras normally have a 1.33 aspect ratio and almost all have more than the 640 × 480 pixels used in SD television graphics.

It is wise to allow a border of about 20 per cent of the picture area on each side when framing in the still camera's viewfinder to allow for this image cutoff. This same precaution applies when shooting live-action photographs for use in television. Some very expensive 35 mm cameras have interchangeable focusing screens and make available a screen marked with the appropriate television "safety" areas.

Here are the most important restrictions on the use of still photographs in television:

1. *Observe the safe action area*: As mentioned above, a border of about 20 percent is needed. For a quick and conservative approach, turn a 35 mm camera on its side, as if shooting a vertical-format picture. The area seen from right to left in the viewfinder can be reasonably expected to be seen in the video image after you turn the camera back for the horizontally framed shot.
2. *Shoot only in horizontal format*: Vertical slides appear on TV with severe cutoff at top and bottom and with a black border on each edge.
3. *Keep contrast low*. Pictures taken in bright sunlight without additional fill light, or indoors with a single flash unit, are often too high in contrast to reproduce properly on

television (although they may look fine when projected on a screen). You should try to follow the same rules for lighting still photographs taken for television that you would in lighting for a video camera itself.

Film

It is not as easy to use film in television as it seems it ought to be. Two problems arise. First, film is usually shot without any regard for the television safe action and title areas. The outside 20 per cent or so of the film image is lost in the transfer process. Second, film is shot at 16, 18 or 24 frames per second. Broadcast film chains use special shutters in their projectors to repeat every fourth frame, bringing the frame rate up from twenty-four to the thirty frames per second required for television. Film shot at sixteen or eighteen frames per second cannot be synchronized to television without special projection equipment.

Not so long ago virtually every television station had a film chain, both for news film and for theatrical films. Now they are rare indeed. To use film in a video production you will almost certainly have to convert it to video at a photo store of duplicator that has the necessary equipment. The transfer should be made to digital video, such as miniDV or DVCAM if possible.

Computers

Computers can be used to generate television graphics in live productions if their output signals are adapted to the NTSC standard. Most often computer graphics are integrated into programmes during editing using nonlinear editing programmes.

Computer screen outputs differ from standard NTSC video in several ways. First, most are "non-interlace." That is, there is no division of the picture into alternating odd-line and even-line fields. Second, the rate at which frames are displayed is usually much faster than the nominal thirty frames per second used in television. And third, many computer graphics displays leave a fairly large border, or "safe area," around the active graphics area. The television video area fills the entire screen. Although a variety of add-on products might allow recording of computer images on videotape, conversion to actual broadcast television standards requires a special video card.

Even still images on computer take up a lot of space. Each true broadcast-quality image requires about one million bytes to display. To make transfer and storage of video images more practical, two basic compression techniques have been developed, with more on the way.

JPEG compression deals with discrete images, one at a time. Typical video frames can be compressed to one seventh of their original size with no discernable reduction in quality. It is usually possible in using JPEG compression to specify the degree of compression desired, so noticeable image degradation can be avoided.

MPEG compression works on the assumption that much of the image from one frame to the next in film or video remains the same. Except for key frames, no single MPEG frame is complete and each has meaning only with reference to the frame that preceded it.

Rights and Responsibilities

Television, more than any other medium, by nature can invade the privacy and trample on the rights of the people it uses. The television producer makes himself responsible to the people shown on camera and to the creators of materials he might use. He must also guarantee that he will use his medium responsibly and fairly. The ability to make and distribute television programmes depends largely on the continuing trust these people have for the producer and his crew.

Rights can be divided broadly into those involving people who actually appear on camera and those involving the acquisition and use of the creative works of others. The two sometimes overlap when musical or dramatic performances are involved. Both need to be given careful attention.

People on Camera

In certain kinds of programmes everyone who appears on camera does so by choice. This does not necessarily give the producer the free and clear right to use recordings made under these circumstances in any way he pleases. First, those appearing should be informed of the intended use of the recording and its potential distribution. Understanding the producer's intentions, they should then give the producer permission to carry out those intentions by signing a "release form" stating the intent of the producer and any compensation to be received by the performer.

In other programmes, people may be videotaped without permission. This may be done if the following conditions are met:

1. The taping is done in a public place.
2. No attempt is made to hide the fact that a recording is being made.

In any case, a person appearing on camera is in the hands of the producer, who has certain responsibilities toward him:

1. To respect any verbal promises or understandings made at the time the recording was make.
2. To refrain from using or editing the material in a way that alters the meaning of any statements made by the person appearing.
3. To refrain from editing the material in such a way as to misrepresent the circumstances of the recording in a way detrimental to the person appearing.
4. To refrain from distributing the material beyond the distribution agreed to and stated in the release form.

A talent release can be anything from the simple form below to a contract running hundreds of pages. It all depends on the complexity of the issues and the need to guard against unforeseen circumstances. This sample is a simple expression of good faith by both parties.

Sample Release Form

GENERAL RELEASE

In consideration of the payment to me of the sum of $___________, receipt whereof is hereby acknowledged, I hereby agree as follows:

1. I give and grant for a period of___________years (hereinafter referred to as the "Term") to MOVING PICTURES, its successors

and assigns, the right to use, publish, and copyright my name, picture, portrait and likeness in a television programme produced by MOVING PICTURES____________________and in all media and types of advertising and promotion of the above programme.

2. I agree that all videotape of me used and taken by MOVING PICTURES is owned by them and that they may copyright material containing same. If I should receive any copy thereof, I shall not authorize its use by anyone else.

3. I agree that no material need be submitted to me for any further approval and that MOVING PICTURES shall be without liability to me resulting from the publication of my likeness.

4. I warrant and represent that this license does not in any way conflict with any existing commitment on my part.

5. Nothing herein will constitute any obligation of MOVING PICTURES to make any use of any of the rights set forth herein.

____

(Signature) (Date)

____

(Printed Full Name)

____

____

(Address)

If releaser is not yet 21 years old, complete the following form:

I, the undersigned, hereby warrant that I am____________________*of____________________, a minor, and have full authority to authorize the above release which I have read and approved. I hereby release and agree to indemnify MOVING PICTURES and their successors and assigns, from and against any and all liability arising out of the exercise of the rights granted by the above release.

______________________________ __________

(Signature of Parent or Guardian) (Date)

* Insert the word "parent" or "guardian," as appropriate.

In addition, it is important to respect the wishes of people who appear on camera. It is possible, for example, that a person recorded during a traumatic event might later decide to ask that he not be used in your programme. Unless you can make a good case for the importance of that person's appearance, it would be wise to accede to his wishes. It is also a common courtesy to allow people appearing in your programmes to preview material before it is shown in public. While this does not suggest that they have any right to edit or control your product, they may be able to make suggestions for changes that would improve the accuracy or impact of a programme.

You also have an obligation to be fair in your treatment of issues. The composition of every shot, as well as its duration, is an editorial judgement. The process of selecting and rejecting sequences for inclusion, too, implies editorial judgements. If you have a bias or an axe to grind, get it out front both in dealing with those who appear in your programme and in presenting it to your audience. No one is free of all bias, but in the communications media you have a special responsibility to the public to deal honestly and fairly with facts and with issues, as well as with people.

Copyright

Copyright is the great two-edged sword everyone in the media must face sooner or later. In copyright, as in most areas of law, the more you know the more confusing it can become. Far from being legal advice, what follows is intended to let you know when to start asking the hard questions and not to lull you into a false sense of security.

Copyright is designed to foster the creation and publication of ideas by allowing the author to sell his ideas on the open market. It is thought that only if the creative process can provide economic rewards to creative people can the maximum flow of ideas be promoted. Thus, to deprive an author of his right to earn money by selling his product, whether a photograph, book, song, or videotape, harms us all by discouraging him from publishing his work.

Any use of a copyrighted work without the copyright holder's permission is an infringement of his rights. In certain cases, however, such use can be defended using the principles of "fair use." This basically means that the use will not cause financial injury to the author and that the need of the public to have use of the material can be demonstrated to be more important than the author's right to protect his creative work. Except in broadcast news and educational situations there is little point in considering "fair use" further.

The proliferation of home recorders (both video and audio) has created a right to record materials for personal, private use. You do not have the right to "distribute, duplicate, or perform (present to an audience)" your home recordings except under very limited fair use guidelines. There are limited exceptions for educational use, but whether you make a profit violating someone else's copyright is irrelevant. The mere fact that you are not making any money does not give you permission to break the law.

A perfect (and common) technical violation of copyright takes place when you videotape your child's performance in a school concert or play. As long as the recording is for personal use only this kind of taping is permissible. If the recording will be used by the participants as part of their training it is correct. Again, any public performance, distribution, or duplication of your private copy (outside your immediate family) creates a real copyright violation.

The number one copyright rule is not to step on someone else's toes. It must be assumed that anything printed or published or shown is protected by copyright. This is not literally true, but it is better to assume a work is protected until you can prove otherwise than to infringe on someone's copyright. Virtually everything in print is copyrighted. Most music, whether in sheet form or recorded is also protected. Broadcast radio and television stations pay a licensing fee to ASCAP and BMI for the right to use music on the air. Since you do not have a license to use copyrighted music, you will have to resort to one of three alternatives: write and perform your own, buy limited rights for a specific recording or song, or buy a record library which you can use without restriction.

Dramatic works are a problem in that there are two considerations beyond merely purchasing rights. Not only will the licensing agent make sure your "performance" of a work would not conflict with any theatrical production in the same region of the country, but the agent may feel that a videotape recording of a work might, by virtue of its amateurish performance, actually harm the reputation of the work and deny permission on that ground alone. This is also true of short stories and novels, where the author has a legitimate right to impose conditions on adaptations of his work. Regardless of the type of work involved, the best way to find out who has the rights and how to acquire them is to write to the publisher of the work.

On the brighter side, as a creator of television programmes, you are also protected from copyright infringement. In order to obtain protection, you should place a copyright notice prominently on your work. On a script or book it should appear on or near the title page. On a film or videotape the notice may appear at the beginning or end, as long as a viewer is likely to see it. Although an explicit copyright notice is no longer required by law, if you publish or distribute a work without a copyright notice you may give the impression you do not intend to protect your rights and are implicitly placing the work in the public domain.

Technically, you are required to register your copyright with the Register of Copyrights, Library of Congress, Washington, D.C. 20559, by sending in an application along with two copies of your work. In practice this is rarely done. You can file your copyright at any time. Usually actual applications are made only if the copyright holder intends to sue someone for infringement. Obviously, the copyright has to be registered before such a suit can be brought.

In summary, a reasonable respect for the rights of people you deal with in the production of television programmes is perhaps the most important single responsibility you have as a television producer. Respect for the rights of others will pave the way for your own work and the work of those who follow you. On the other hand, a disregard for the rights of others will make people reluctant to work with you, on or off camera, and close doors for everyone who depends on the good will of the public.

Taking it to the Next Level

If you intend to distribute your work commercially or have large quantities made by a commercial replicator you will want to take special care in documenting your rights. Many replicators are members of the International Recording Media Association. As one of the conditions of membership, these companies will require you to fill out a form supplied by the association (and available on their web site at http://www.recordingmedia.org/) and to provide documentation of the rights and permissions related to your project. If you are using pre-recorded music you must be able to produce proof that you have the right to use the music. This could take the form of a copy of your original contract with the music distributor, such as a "buy out" license or a letter from the distributor verifying your rights. If your audio is licensed separately you will need proof of audio/video synchronization licensing. For CD's containing special software to make them play back like DVD's you will need distribution licensing documentation for the software. You should be able to affirm that you have all of the releases necessary for your talent and permission to use any other copyrighted materials. Needless to say, it is much easier to keep track of all of your paperwork as you go along than it is to assemble it after the fact.

Getting the Word Out

Videotape

VHS videotape is still a viable distribution option preferred for audiences that are resistant to change.

CD

There are several ways to distribute video on CD's. They have been especially popular as a medium for motion pictures using the MPEG 1 standard. The quality of these "video CD's" is about the same as VHS. Some DVD authoring software can be used to make CD's that behave like DVD's. The total run time for these disks is about fifteen minutes. The special software needed to play back the CD content is included on the disk. These CD's are for computer CD/DVD drives only and are generally programmed to run the software automatically when the disk is inserted. While this is a viable way of distributing DVD-quality video to computer users, its usefulness diminishes as new computers are delivered with DVD drives as standard equipment.

It is also possible to make CD data disks that contain MPEG 2 or Windows Media Format files. Most computers now have the codecs needed to play MPEG 2 or WMF files. Again, at about four Mb/Sec a CD can hold about fifteen minutes of video. The increased compression of the WMF format allows more than sixty minutes on one CD. The WMF format fits the specifications for MPEG 4, the compression regimen designed to accommodate high definition television. Both Quicktime and Real Player also offer compressed video formats that can be included on data CD's. The appropriate players will have to be downloaded by your viewers.

Finally, there is software available for authoring data CD's, or CD-ROM's. These software packages allow the integration of files on the disk with files on the internet in addition to many of the navigation features common to DVD's.

DVD

One popular way to distribute video is the DVD. A DVD is an optical disk, actually a reflective film sandwiched between two protective acrylic layers, like a CD, but with some differences. The most important difference is that a typical DVD can hold up to 4.7 GB of data, including formatting information on a single layer disk and twice that on a dual layer disk. You have roughly four gigabytes of space available for project on a single layer disk.

There are two ways of using DVD technology to distribute video. The traditional method is to use DVD authoring software to create a DVD that can be played on a stand-alone DVD player, typically called a "set top" player. Set top players require a specific MPEG 2 format which makes it nearly impossible to reverse-engineer the video for editing. This DVD format is ideal for distribution. In small quantities you can make your own DVD's with relatively inexpensive software and hardware. Colour printers capable of printing directly on the DVD face are very affordable as well. It should be noted that from the beginning there have been problems with compatibility between DVD-R and DVD+R disks and some set top DVD players, especially models made before 2001.

For large quantities you will want to use a commercial disk replicator. Replication is a two step process. First a glass master disk is made. Then the master disk is used to press or stamp a reflective disk, which is then sandwiched between two acrylic layers for protection. The minimum cost for replication is usually the same as the cost of making 800 to 1000 copies. In other words, whether you ask for one hundred, two hundred, or a thousand copies of your masterpiece, the total cost of replication (not including album cases or other packaging) will be about the same.

Most commercial disk replicators will now accept a DVD-R as a master, although the preferred medium for mastering DVD's is DLT, or digital linear tape. DLT was developed to backup or archive computer networks and servers. If you want digital copy protection for your DVD's you will have to submit your masters on DLT.

When dealing with a commercial replicator, be prepared to be able to prove you have the right to use all of the audio and video on your disk. Replicators do not like to be sued.

Making a DVD

A DVD can be as straightforward as a videotape. Pop it in the player and the programme runs from start to finish with no embellishments. Or it can have a complex system of menus allowing the viewer to select various programmes or go to specific points within programmes. Menus can allow viewers to select different audio channels or call up subtitles.

The first step in making a DVD is to assemble all of your finished media as digital files. There are only limited opportunities to edit materials in DVD authoring software. It is best if all of your materials are in final form before you go any further. Audio files should be in the wav format. Your video files are probably either Quicktime or .avi files. They must be converted to MPEG 2. This option should be available in your video editing software. If you have optional audio tracks you can convert your video using your primary mix of audio tracks, then save your secondary mix of audio tracks separately as a .wav file. You can do this by turning the appropriate tracks on or off before exporting the file. In addition, you may have still images you want to use in your DVD, perhaps as menu backgrounds or buttons. Full frame stills should be 640x480 pixels for NTSC or 640x576 for PAL. Your DVD authoring programme will change these stills, which have square pixels, to 720x480 or 720x576 pixels where the width of each pixel is nine tenths of the height. The difference is pixel aspect between digital stills and digital video affects all of your still images, whether full frame or smaller.

Your authoring software will allow you to import video, audio, and still image files. The categories may be straightforward or have more imaginative names, such as "Media," "Backgrounds," and "Buttons."

At this point it may or may not tell you if your project will fit on a DVD. You have about four gigabytes available. If your project is too large you can go back to your video editing software and change the MPEG 2 conversion settings to increase the compression and decrease the file size of each MPEG 2 file. While the DV files you generally work with in your editing software are compressed to about four Megabytes per second, MPEG 2 files are generally compressed to from 3.5 to 8 Megabits per second. At the lowest compression you have a little over an hour of video on a DVD. At the highest compression you can get about two hours on a disk. As you increase the compression of your video files you also increase the chance that you will lose detail in your video during quick movements. The loss of detail will take the form of pixilation. Your video will be reduced to a jumble of blocks until the rate of video change returns to a more normal rate. You should probably keep your data rate at four megabits per second or higher.

There is actually more to the MPEG 2 format than the data rate. While in the DV format compression is achieved frame by frame, MPEG 2 is divided into groups of pictures (GOP's) usually twelve to fifteen frames long. The first frame (I) of each GOP has all of the information necessary to reconstruct the frame. The remaining eleven to fourteen frames (P and B frames) contain only enough information to reconstruct the video by combining information from previous frames (P frames) or by combining information from both previous and following frames (B frames).

The best consumer authoring programmes will allow you to import your video and use it to create all of your menus and buttons in a very straightforward and intuitive way. Typically, once you have imported your video clips you can select one of several menu styles. If you have more than one video clip, you can assign each clip to a button on the menu. You may even be able to create intermediate menus and use the time line of your video you can select chapter points and drag those points to menu buttons. In some cases the video from the clip will form a still image in the button automatically. When you are done you usually have at least two options: burn one or more DVD's using the current project settings, or create a file that is an exact image of the contents of the DVD. When you burn your DVD's from the current project your programme will create a temporary file on your hard drive in which all of your materials are converted into the required DVD format. Your disks are burned from the temporary file, which is deleted as soon as the disks are done. When you elect to create an image file, the file is created on your hard drive but no disks are burned. You can use the image file to burn your disks later as you need them.

Professional software will allow you to do anything you will see on a commercial DVD. Professional software is not, as a rule, either user-friendly or intuitive. It is more powerful and flexible.

The Internet

Using video on the internet creates a set of considerations and problems that should be part of the video planning process before any video is shot. The basic fact about the internet is that it was never designed to transmit video and audio at four megabytes per second or even four megabits per second. To send video over the internet more compression is necessary.

There are several compression schemes for internet video that rely on four ways of reducing picture information.

1. They generally reduce the frame size.
2. They reduce the frame rate.
3. They reduce the amount of information in each frame beyond the compression available in MPEG 2 by sacrificing picture quality when content in moving and maintaining higher resolution when images are relatively still.
4. They "buffer" the bit stream.

Reducing the frame size reduces the amount of picture detail available and should be an important consideration in shooting for the internet.

Loss of detail can turn excellent images into mud. Just as commercial motion pictures are often shot not for the resolution available with 35 mm film, but with the more limited resolution of

NTSC video in mind, you should shoot for resolutions much lower than standard video.

After decades of experimentation the film industry settled on a few frame rates. For silent consumer film either sixteen or eighteen frames per second was used. There was a noticeable flicker when films were projected at these rates. Commercial sound motion pictures are projected at twenty-four frames per second. The frame rate for NTSC television is thirty frames per second: Frame rates for streaming video are often below fifteen frames per second. The impact on motion is obvious. At fifteen frames per second, how many frames does it take to swing a baseball bat?

The third method of reducing the data rate, sacrificing detail during motion sequences, further "muddies" the picture. Motion and fine detail are mutually exclusive in the world of streaming video.

Buffering can be as simple as actually downloading the entire video at one rate in order to play it back on a computer at the designed normal rate. More commonly, playback is delayed until enough data has been downloaded to allow playback of a significant part of the video. When the playback catches up with the download (and runs out of data to play) the playback is paused until more data is downloaded. This process often causes awkward pauses during playback, but that is progress.

Streaming video should accommodate a range of users, from those with 56 Kbps dial-up modems to those with DSL and cable modems receiving in excess of one gigabit per second at the modem (but less than 54 Mbps over their wireless network). When you export video from your editing software you will have the option of two or three streaming formats. Pick the one you believe will offer your viewer the best picture quality, given the content of your video) with the least inconvenience and delay. Each of these will in turn allow you to choose either a single streaming rate or multiple rates dependent on the viewer's reception rate.

All that is left to be done is to move the finished streaming video file onto a web site for downloading.

Archiving your work

Most of the time most artists want their work to last at least as long as they live. Throughout recorded history we have been able to save some pieces of art or literature on cloth, paper, stone, or metal. Each of these has properties that cause the information to degrade, but all have one thing in common: It does not take any equipment beyond the human eye to recognize and read the information, although the eye may need a brain behind it trained in hieroglyphics or ancient Greek.

Times have changed. Your hardware may become obsolete or even incompatible with newer operating systems. Changes in the computer world have given an entirely new meaning to the word "legacy." Until recently the word referred to property inherited or traditions passed down from one generation to the next. In the computer world "legacy" has become an adjective referring to the data in any application that can no longer be used by readily available software or hardware. The 5 ¼ inch floppy disk is a legacy system in that no computers sold today can read those disks. The 3 ½ inch floppy disk is pretty close to legacy status itself. As you move from one operating system to the next or from one capture card to a different brand you risk rendering all of your .avi files unreadable. Keep the tape. And while you are at it, take very good care of your playback equipment, too.

So far we have gone through the following videotape formats: Two-inch quad, one inch helical of various formats up through type C, half-inch EIAJ reel to reel, U-Matic and U-Matic SP, Betamax, VHS, Betacam and Betacam SP, M2, S-VHS, 8 Millimeter, and Hi-8 analog formats; DV, Digital 8, DV Cam, DV Pro, Digital Betacam, a more. If your tape is stored properly at moderate temperature and humidity you are more likely to have trouble finding playback equipment than you are to have trouble with the videotape itself.

The best you can do is to make copies of your work in the highest quality digital format you believe has a user base large enough to keep it in use for a long period of time and that you can afford. While many are choosing to "archive" their work on DVD in MPEG 2, that medium is much more highly compressed than the DV format, which is in general use and slowing replacing both VHS and 8 mm as the recording format of choice, both by amateurs and many professionals. For works under fifteen minutes DV files can be stored as .avi or .mov files on DVD-R disks without further compression. A dual layer writable disk could hold up to thirty minutes. With the advent of high definition video there is no way to know how long the equipment to play back standard definition tapes will be generally available, while current DVD drives and both blue laser disk formats can play material on existing DVD-R disks. Properly stored DVD-R disks should last at least one hundred years, while rewritable disks can be expected to last at least twenty-five years. Considering the formats and equipment in common use twenty-five years ago, you should be prepared to re-record your work to new formats as it becomes advisable or necessary.

TELEVISION PRODUCTION PROCESS: A CASE STUDY

There are essentially two ways of doing television. Programmes are shot either in a specially designed television studio using several cameras which are fed into a control room and assembled in "real time," or they are shot using a single camera on location and assembled later in an editing room or on a computer. Obviously, almost all non-professional video is shot using a single camera. That makes it what the pros call "electronic field production," or EFP. In electronic field production, the director is like a composer of music, creating and assembling images and impressions, fitting them together carefully, weighing the quality and importance of each as he goes. He works much as a film director would, in a linear fashion from one shot to the next, one scene to the next. He is dealing with only one picture and one situation at a time. Since the programme will be edited later, he can shoot out of sequence, repeat shots, and record extra shots to be included later. Electronic field production allows for a richness of scene and artistic creativity born sometimes out of necessity and sometimes out of opportunities suggested by the location itself. Professionals spend most of their time planning, scripting, and organizing their productions. The amount of time spent actually recording the programme is surprisingly short compared to the time spent preparing for it. Each programme goes through several important stages, from development of the concept through planning and scripting, then on to set design or location scouting, acquisition of performers and rehearsal. Along the way, the producer schedules his equipment, finds a competent crew, and brings all of the necessary elements together for actual production of the programme. Television is an amalgam of many diverse disciplines. Professional productions often depend on the skill and cooperation of many people, as well as the ability of the producer and director to bring these people together in a cooperative effort. On the other hand, with digital technology, it is also possible to be a "one man band," performing all of the various functions yourself, and produce a "broadcast quality" programme. While this book will deal with many of the techniques of production, it doesn't pretend to tell you how to do anything. After all, rules are made to be broken. Or ignored. Still, picking the mind of a professional television producer will help you get better results every time you pick up a camera.

Understanding Shooting Video for Editing

Now that computer based editing is affordable, you don't have to shot video in sequence. It's much simpler to shot a series of scenes and then edit them together later. However, to do this you must preplan your shots. Think in terms of the type of shots you'll need to tell the story and what happens in the frame to show continuity. In other words, to shoot for editing you need to be aware of how the finished sequence will look before you take the camera out of the box.

(a) Each time you start and stop the videotape, you've created a shot. You edit shots together into sequences that tell a story.
(b) To produce really good edited video you need to start with a storyboard. Storyboards are a tool to help you think visually. Draw pictures of what you are going to see. Next to your pictures write down what you want the shot to look like and what audio will be heard. Here's a sample storyboard.
(c) Your shots need to link together to make your audience believe it is one continuous scene. People, hands, etc. should remain in the relative same place within a series of shots in order to have continuity in the sequence.
(d) A cutaway is a shot that allows you to cover up an edit. They are very useful when editing interviews. Always be thinking of cutaways you can get when on location.

Understanding the Lighting Process

The camera doesn't know what's important in the picture. It sets the iris in the lens according to the brightest light.

White Background with no Added Lighting

If your background is brighter than your subject the subject gets dark

Shadows are a big problem on the face.

Background Darker than Subject with no Added Lighting

The subject is lighter than the background in this picture. The camera adjusts the iris for the best light level on the subject.

Shadows are less but still there.

White Background with Lighting Added

In this picture we've added lights aimed at the subject and not on the background. This makes the subject brighter than the background.

The added lighting has reduced the shadows on the face, but the subject doesn't really stand out from the background very well.

Background Darker than Subject with Lighting Added

The lights are aimed at the subject and do not hit the background. This makes the subject brighter than the background.

The added lighting has reduced the shadows on the face and the subject stands out from the darker background.

Organizing TV Production Shots

There are four types of shots used in video production. All TV shows are just combinations of these four shots put in order to make sequences.

Long Shot (*LS*): A long shot allows your audience to see everything. It shows the big picture.

Medium Shot (*MS*): This shot gets rid of any distractions in the picture and starts the process of zeroing in on the action.

Close-up (*CU*): This shot cuts out extraneous visual material. Faces should fill up most of the screen.

Extreme Close-up (*ECU*): Use this shot to focus attention on what's important. It enlarges small objects to show details.

Taking into Account the Continuity Considerations

A good videographer and editor will look for movements within a sequence that tie the shots together.

- When changing to a different shot within a sequence, you should plan to have things in the same position. For example, when switching from a medium shot to a close-up of someone writing, their hand should be in the same place when the edit is made.
- Make sure movement in the frame goes in the same direction. For example, have your talent walk out of the frame to the left and into the next shot from the right.

Establishing Shot: Your audience is limited to what you show them so it's important to let them know where you are. Usually a long shot.

Continuity Considerations: Plan how you enter and exit the frame so the edited sequence looks like one continuous action.

Long Shot: A long shot allows your audience to see everything. It shows the big picture.

Continuity Considerations: This shot allows the editor to match the action in the previous shot. The edit should take place when the man is in approximately the same location in each shot.

Medium Shot: This shot gets rid of any distractions in the picture and starts the process of zeroing in on the action.

Continuity Considerations: The editor should allow the man to walk out of the previous shot then walk into this shot. This helps the audience get a sense of the size of the room.

Extreme Close-up: Use this shot to focus attention on what's important. It enlarges small objects to show details.

Continuity Considerations: The editor should match the hand location in the previous shot.

Close-up: This shot cuts out extraneous visual material. Faces should fill up the screen. Who wants to see a person's feet when they are saying something we need to hear?

Continuity Considerations: This close-up is used as a cutaway. A cutaway is any shot that covers an edit. It's most commonly used to shorten interviews.

Reestablishing Shot: This shot reminds people where you are.

Continuity Considerations: It's good to end with a shot that reminds people where you are. Exiting the frame is also a good closer.

Understanding the Storyboarding Process

When you draw pictures of what you are going to see it forces you think visually. Storyboards will also help you identify the shots you will need to construct a sequence. Listing the audio will help you decide what microphones, sound effects, music, or narration you'll need.

Storyboard Title: The Entrance

Shot 1: Long shot. Show the front of the building

For continuity, man enters the frame and goes into building from right to left.

Audio: Natural sounds

Shot 2: Long shot. Interior of the building as man enters.

For continuity, make sure man enters from right and exits to the left,

Audio: Natural sound

Shot 3: Medium shot. Man approaches front desk and signs in. For continuity, use right to left movement.

Audio: Typing in the background.

Shot 4: Extreme Close-up. Shot of hands signing paper.

For continuity, Have hand in same position as in MS of man approaching front desk. Make sure nothing but paper shows in this shot.

Audio: Typing in the background

Shot 5: Close-up. Receptionist turns to the camera and says good morning.

For continuity, use a high camera angle so it looks like the man is looking at her while standing.

Audio: Receptionist says a cheery "Good morning." Typing stops.

Shot 6: Medium shot. Man finishes signing in and moves out of the frame.

For continuity, this shot needs to be a continuation of the first medium shot.

Audio: Man Mumbles "Good morning."

The Ways of Using Cutaways in Interviews

Cutaways are shots the videographer gets that can be used to cover up edits. They are very helpful when editing an interview. The cutaway is usually something related to the location or what the person on camera is saying. The video "cuts away" from the person talking so the editor can cut out unnecessary audio.

This is the unedited interview. The man gives a good sound bite, but with a little bit of irrelevant material in the middle.

The edited interview. We have taken out the irrelevant material and placed a cutaway of a globe over the audio to hide the edit point.

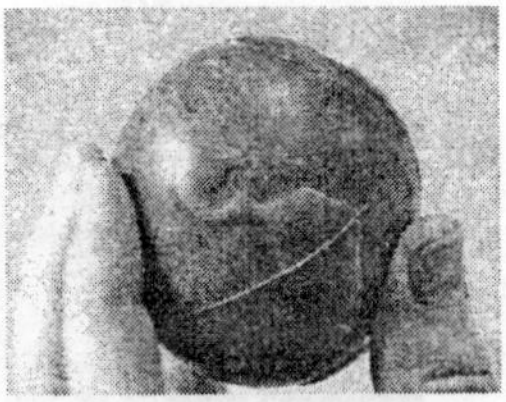

This brings up the issue of ethical editing. In the examples below you can see how an editor can make someone say something they didn't intend. This is why so many people argue they were quoted out of context or were simply misquoted. When editing, care must be taken so you don't change the intended meaning.

The unedited comment. You'd think it wouldn't be easy to change the intent of the speaker.

By rearranging what the speaker says, the meaning is totally changed. Of course, it's easy to spot this edit because the speaker jumps around in the frame.

Editors use cutaways to cover up the edit. In this example the meaning has been totally changed and a cutaway has been used to cover the edit.

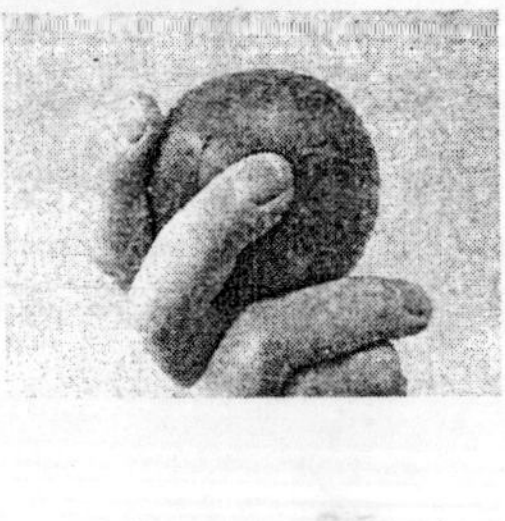

7

TV Broadcasting, Production and Scheduling Programmes: Special Focus on Indian Television

BROADCAST PROGRAMMING

Broadcast programming, or scheduling, is the practice of organizing television or radio programmes in a daily, weekly, or season-long schedule. Modern broadcasters regularly change the scheduling of their programmes to build an audience for a new show, retain that audience, or compete with other broadcasters' programmes.

Television scheduling strategies are employed to give programmes the best possible chance of attracting and retaining an audience. They are used to deliver programmes to audiences when they are most likely to want to watch them and deliver audiences to advertisers in the composition that makes their advertising most likely to be effective (Ellis 2000 p. 136).

At a micro level, scheduling is the minute planning of the transmission; what to broadcast and when, ensuring that every second of airtime is covered.

Scheduling Strategies

Dayparting

In broadcasting, dayparting is the practice of dividing the day into several parts, during each of which a different type of radio programming or television programming appropriate for that time is aired. Programmes are most often geared toward a particular demographic, and what the target audience typically engages in at that time.

Theming

Having a special theme-night.

Stripping

Running a syndicated television series every day of the week. It is commonly restricted to describing the airing of shows which were weekly in their first run; *The West Wing* could be stripped, but not *Jeopardy!*, as daily is the schedule for which it is intended.

Stacking

Stacking is a technique used to develop audience flow by grouping together programmes with similar appeals to "sweep" the viewer along from one programme to the next (Vane and Gross, 1994, p. 175).

Counter Programming

Counterprogramming is used when a time period is filled with a programme whose appeal is different from the opponent programme because it is a different genre or appeals to a different demographic.

Bridging

Bridging is being used when a station tries to prevent the audience from changing channels during a junction point—the main evening breaks where all channels stop programmes and shift gear (Ellis, 2000). This is achieved in a number of ways including: having a programme already underway and something compelling happening at a junction point, running a programme late so that people 'hang around' and miss the start of other programmes, or advertising the next programme during the credits of the previous.

Tentpoling

In tent pole programming the programmers bank on a well-known series having so much audience appeal that they can place two unknown series on either side, and it is the strength of the central programme that will bring the others along to victory.

Hammocking

A technique used by broadcasters whereby an unpopular programme is scheduled between two popular ones in the hope that viewers will watch it. Public-service broadcasters use this as a way of promoting serious but valuable content.

Cross Programming

Cross-programming involves the interconnection of two shows. This is achieved by dragging a storyline over two episodes of two different programmes.

SCHOOL OF BROADCASTING: A CASE STUDY

Brown's DNA is broadcasting. Richard and Helen Brown started the School of Broadcasting in 1946 to train young men and women for careers in the emerging field of Radio Broadcasting. In the 1950s, television changed communication forever. Brown responded with the addition of the Television Production Programme in 1954.

Today, technology—including the Internet, streaming audio, on-demand video, satellite radio and podcasts—is fueling a communications revolution. And this revolution is creating opportunities for people who can produce the audio and video messages to feed an information-hungry world.

The Twin Cities of Minneapolis and St. Paul comprise one of the nation's largest media markets. You will find Brown alumni on the air and behind the scenes at a number of radio and television station in both towns. In fact, Brown grads from our Television Production Programme are helping produce news and entertainment every day, for stations from New York to LA, from small-town radio shows to CNN.

The school of broadcasting offers three programmes:

1. *Communication Studies*: Bachelor of Science
2. *Radio Broadcasting*: Applied Associate of Science
3. *Television Broadcasting*: Applied Associate of Science

Associate of Applied Science in Television Production: The possibilities, responsibilities and rewards might amaze you

You might be surprised by the range of careers in television production and by the variety of employers in this field. Broadcast television stations, industrial video firms, cable companies and satellite operations head the list. Helping you prepare for an entry-level position as a production specialist at employers such as these, is the aim of the Associate of Applied Science Degree Programme in Television Production.

You will have an opportunity to learn all the positions behind the camera, and you can experience substantial hands-on training in a multi-camera studio and on location with this television production programme. Concepts of both linear and non-linear editors are also taught. The curriculum includes an internship or practicum project. The television production programme's General Education component can contribute to the shaping of a well-informed broadcast professional, and can help you develop the problem-solving and human relations skills sought by today's employers.

Career Opportunities for Television Production Graduates

- Camera operator
- Floor director
- Graphics operator
- Producer
- Production assistant
- Video editor

The Television Production Programme is available at the Mendota Heights campus.

"It does not feel like school. It feels like you are really producing news or commercials."

—*Bandon Rickert*, Graduate, Television Production

Associate of Applied Science Degree

18 months—6 quarters—90 quarter credits

Educational Philosophy

The Brown College philosophy is to provide quality programmes that are sound in concept, implemented by a competent and dedicated faculty, and geared to serve those seeking a solid foundation in knowledge and skills required to obtain employment in their chosen fields. The programmes offered emphasize hands-on training, are relevant to employers' needs, and focus on areas that offer strong, long-term employment opportunities.

To offer students the training and skills that can lead to successful employment, the college Will:

- Continually evaluate and update educational programmes
- Provide modern facilities and training equipment
- Select faculty with professional experience in the career areas in which they teach and with the ability to motivate students to develop to their greatest potential
- Promote self-discipline and motivation so that students may enjoy success on the job and in society

Campus Facilities

Brown College is located in Mendota Heights, Minnesota, with a branch campus in Brooklyn Center. Both campuses are conveniently located close to major highways and have access to public transportation. Parking is available to students.

The Mendota Heights campus occupies an 18-acre site. The campus buildings provide more than 122,000 square feet of classroom, labs, studios and office space. Centralized student services include a Learning Resource Center, cafeteria and lounge space. The Library/Learning Resource Center provides access to computers, study space, laptop tables and printers. Students in Brown College's technology programmes have access to networking equipment, computer labs and software.

The College laptop center enables students to work on multiple projects from both school and home. Students in Brown College's broadcasting programmes receive hands-on training on equipment and software that is similar to industry standards. In Scott Studio, Radio Broadcasting students use computerized screens to programme operations. Television Production students have the opportunity to experience both linear and non-linear editing using Avid software.

The facilities and equipment of Brown College and its branch campus comply with federal, state and local ordinances and regulations, including those related to fire safety, building safety and health.

Approvals and Memberships

The college voluntarily undergoes periodic accrediting evaluations by teams of qualified examiners. These examiners include subject matter experts, specialists in occupational education, and professionals in private college administration.

The college president can provide additional information upon request.

- Accredited by the Accrediting Commission of Career Schools and Colleges of Technology (ACCSCT).
- Licensed to operate by the Minnesota Office of Higher Education Services Office.
- Eligible institution under the Federal Stafford Loan Programme (FSL) and Federal Parent Loan for Undergraduate Students (FPLUS).
- Eligible institution for Federal Supplemental Educational Opportunity Grant (FSEOG), Federal Pell Grant and Federal Work-Study (FWS) programmes.
- Eligible institution for Minnesota student grants and Student Education Loan Fund programme (SELF).
- Authorized under federal law to enroll non-immigrant alien students.

- Approved for the training of veterans and eligible persons under the provisions of Title 38, United States Code.
- Provides training services for the State Department of Vocational Rehabilitation.

Testimonials

"I attended the Computer Programming course at Brown College and graduated with honours in 2005. The teachers were always there to teach me as much as I was willing to learn. They genuinely cared about me and my education. After college, with a few interviews and some strong effort I was able to find a great job where I can build on and utilize the skills I developed while pursuing my degree. Without the education I received at Brown, I would still be stuck in a dead-end job, missing weekends and holidays in a struggle to pay my bills."

—Shaunda Wiering, Graduate, Computer Programming

"The most beneficial aspect of attending Brown College was that I was learning from industry insiders, people who were working in the business. And while other people were still trying to pass GenEd courses at a four year university, I was already on the air, co-hosting mornings and working as a Programme Director."

—Ron Carleton, Graduate, Radio Broadcasting

"I would say my time at Brown was well worth my money and effort. Brown taught me everything that I would encounter in radio, and then some. They were very thorough and complete in their coverage of subjects, such as production, news, interviewing, music and technical. If you are thinking of radio broadcasting, Brown has all the basics covered in their curriculum, and I would highly recommend taking their courses, as they will teach what you need to know and prepare you for a career in the industry.

—Scott Thomsen, Graduate, Radio Broadcasting

"Brown College has prepared me well in the field of graphic design. The teachers are well versed in the applications used and have experience to back it up. I would recommend Brown

College to anyone that has a passion for what they do. With their help I was offered a job in the field even before I graduated!"—*Chris Jacobson, Graduate, Visual Communications*

TV PRODUCTION OVERVIEW: AN ILLUSTRATED MODEL

Although most who use these modules study in class situations, many people go through these modules on an individual basis—i.e., they work for government agencies, TV production facilities, or they just need a personal understanding of the concepts.

Thousands of students around the world are now using this award-winning course in television production to meet serious personal and professional goals.

Completing this course could mean an exciting career in broadcast television, Internet webcasting, institutional videography, satellite programming, mobile video, and other areas—including advertising and public relations aspects of any of these. And video production now includes feature films—the kind you see at your local theater.

Although the modules emphasize studio and field production for broadcast television, what is presented will be applicable to a wide variety of audio- and video-based media. It's all pretty much the same once you know the basics.

Of course, it is desirable to have audio and video equipment to work with—either personal equipment or equipment provided in a school or lab setting.

Some equipment may not be available to you. That is true; it is important to understand the equipment and techniques that are part of larger production facilities.

For one thing, you may suddenly be confronted with an internship or job opportunity where this knowledge is essential.

Camerapersons, writers, directors, producers, and even on-camera talent find that having a solid understanding of the tools and techniques of the entire process makes a major difference in the success of productions—not to mention their careers.

In television production, as in most of today's high-tech areas, *knowledge is power*.

A Bird's Eye View of the Production Process

Let is take a whirlwind tour of the production process. But unlike a whirlwind tour of Europe (if it is Tuesday, this must be Barcelona), we will come back to these people and places later. For now, let is take a quick look at the production process from the standpoint of the key people.

We will start by thinking big—big productions, that is—because many of these things can be scaled down, combined, or eliminated in smaller productions.

Who Does What and Why

This list is long, but have you noticed the lengthy credit lists for major films and TV programmes?

The person generally in charge of launching entire production is the producer.

He or she comes up with the programme concept, lays out the budget for the production, and makes the major decisions. This person is the team leader, the one who works with the writers, hires the director, decides on the key talent, and guides the general direction of the production.

In smaller productions, the producer may also take charge of the more mundane activities. And in small productions, the director may handle the producer's responsibilities. In this case, the combined job title becomes (want to guess?), producer-director.

Some productions may also have an associate producer who sets up schedules for the talent and crew and who generally assists the producer.

On a major production, one of the producer's first jobs is to hire a writer to write the script (the document that tells everyone what to do and say). The script is like a written plan or blueprint for the production.

The producer will next consider the key talent for the production. In general, the talent includes actors, reporters, hosts, guests, and off-camera narrators—anyone whose voice is heard or who appears on camera.

Sometimes talent is broken down into three sub-categories: actors (who portray other people in dramatic productions), performers (who appear on camera in non-dramatic roles), and announcers (who generally do not appear on camera).

In a large production, the producer will hire a director.

The director is in charge of working out pre-production (before the production) details, coordinating the activities of the production staff and on-camera talent, working out camera and talent positions on the set, selecting the camera shots during production, and supervising postproduction work.

In other words, once the producer sets things in motion, the director is in charge of taking the script from the beginning to the very end of the production process.

Assisting a director in the control room is typically a technical director who operates the video switcher.

The technical director, or TD, is also responsible for coordinating the technical aspects of the production.

One or more production assistants (PAs) may be hired to help the producer and director. Among other things, PAs keep notes on ongoing production needs and changes.

The lighting director (LD) designs the lighting plan, arranges for the lighting equipment, and sets up and checks the lighting.

As we will see, lighting is a key element in the overall look of a production.

Some productions have a set designer who, along with the producer and director, designs the set and supervises its construction, painting, and installation.

The makeup person, with the help of, for example, cosmetics and hair spray, sees that the talent look their best—or worst, if that is what the script calls for.

Makeup is just one of the areas where a link will take you to advanced information. (We will discuss the meaning of the colored squares below).

It should be emphasized that specific responsibilities of production personnel will vary widely, depending on the production facility. In Europe, and in particular at the BBC (British Broadcasting System) in London, these distinctions are made.

Before you move on to Part Two of this module, let me call your attention to some things:

First, you will notice the *Site Search/Key Terms* link at the end of each module. This link is useful in finding terms and phrases anywhere on the site.

Links will also take you to about 100 associated files intended to add to the basic information presented in these modules. (The makeup link above is an example.)

For important background information on the television medium, check out the series of modules.

After you visit any of these links, you can either close the window that pops up or click on the back arrow at the top of your browser to get back to the module you were reading.

These modules are available on independent Internet servers in the United States and Brazil. In case you get lost in cyberspace at some point, you might want to make a note of the following independent sites in the U.S. where these materials can be found:

- http://www.CyberCollege.com/tvp_ind.htm
- http://www.CyberCollege.org/tvp_ind.htm
- http://www.InternetCampus.com/tvp_ind.htm
- http://www.InternetCampus.org/tvp_ind.htm

If you find that one site bogs down—we have all known the Internet to do that on occasion—try another site. All these sites carry the same TV Production and Mass Media modules.

The "Quick Quiz" button at the end of each chapter takes you to a very short interactive matching game that acts as a review of some of the major concepts in the chapter (and checks to see if you really were awake while you were reading it!).

Green, Yellow, Blue, and Red Readings

And now to explain those little colored squares before most links.

A green square in front of a link indicates information that is *important to what is being discussed*. We cover this information in the interactive tests and puzzles.

A yellow square indicates helpful *background reading*. This material is not included on the interactive tests, but instructors may include the readings on their own tests.

A blue square indicates *technical information* designed for advanced classes and professionals; again, this material may or may not be required by an instructor (if you are in a classroom setting).

A red square indicates *external links* with related information not included on the interactive tests—but your instructor, of course, has the option of asking that you read this information. Please note that the links to these external sources should in no way be considered endorsements, and no compensation is received by Cyber College or the Internet Campus for including these links. Unlike the links which go to information on this site, we have no control over the content of these external links.

Note: If you find that some of the interactive features on this site do not work, you are probably using an old browser or you have JavaScript disabled. Note that the wavy underline here indicates the mouse over option of more information.

TELEVISION IN INDIA

A huge industry by itself, the Indian silver screen has thousands of programmes in all the states of India. The small screen has produced numerous celebrities of their own kind some even attaining national fame. TV soaps are extremely popular with housewives as well as working women. Some small time actors have made it big in Bollywood.

History

Post-independence Television

Television first came to India (named as Doordarshan or DD) as the National Television Network of India. The first telecast started on September 15, 1959 in New Delhi. After a gap of about 13 years, second television station was established in Mumbai (Maharashtra) in 1972 and by 1975 there were five more television stations at Srinagar (Kashmir), Amritsar (Punjab), Kolkata (West Bengal), Chennai (Tamil Nadu) and Lucknow (Uttar Pradesh). For many years the transmission was mainly in black and white. Television industry got the necessary boost in the eighties when Doordarshan introduced colour TV during the 1982 Asian Games.

1980s

Indian small screen programming started off in the early 1980s. At that time there was only one national channel Doordarshan, which was government owned. The Ramayana and Mahabharat was the first major television series produced. This serial notched up the world record in viewership numbers for a single programme. By the late 1980s more and more people started to own television sets. Though there was a single channel, television programming had reached saturation. Hence the government opened up another channel which had part national programming and part regional. This channel was known as DD 2 later DD Metro. Both channels were broadcast terrestrially.

Post Liberalization Television

The central government launched a series of economic and social reforms in 1991 under Prime Minister Narasimha Rao. Under the new policies the government allowed private and foreign broadcasters to engage in limited operations in India. This process has been pursued consistently by all subsequent federal administrations. Foreign channels like CNN, Star TV and domestic channels such as Zee TV and Sun TV started satellite broadcasts. Starting with 41 sets in 1962 and one channel (Audience Research unit, 1991) at present TV in India covers more than 70 million homes giving a viewing population more than 400 million individuals through more than 100 channels. A large relatively untapped market, easy accessibility of relevant technology and a variety of programmes are the main reasons for rapid expansion of television in India.

Cable Television

In 1992, the government liberated its markets, opening them up to cable television. Five new channels belonging to the Hong Kong based STAR TV gave Indians a fresh breath of life. MTV, STAR Plus, BBC, Prime Sports and STAR Chinese Channel were the five channels. Zee TV was the first private owned Indian channel to broadcast over cable. A few years later CNN, Discovery Channel, National Geographic Channel made its foray into India. Star expanded its bouquet introducing STAR World, STAR Sports, ESPN and STAR Gold. Regional channels flourished along with a multitude of Hindi channels and a few English channels. By 2001 HBO and History Channel were the other international channels to enter India. By 2001-2003, other international channels such as Nickelodeon, Cartoon Network, VH1, Disney and Toon Disney came into foray. In 2003 news channels started to boom.

8

Radio Programming and Production: An Overview

RADIO PROGRAMMING

Radio programming is the content that is broadcast by radio stations.

In the early radio age, content typically included a balance of comedy, drama, news, music and sports reporting. U.S. radio programmes included the most famous Hollywood talent of the day. Radio soap operas began in the U.S. in 1930 with *Painted Dreams*. Despite radio's majority use being spoken entertainment, the *Grand Ole Opry*, as of 2006 being the longest-running radio programme, has been focused on broadcasting country music since it began in 1925.

In the late 1940s and early 1950s, television eroded the popularity of radio comedy, drama and variety shows. By the late 1950s, radio broadcasting took on much the form it has today—strongly focused on music, news and sports, though drama can still be heard, especially on the BBC.

In Britain during the 1950s, radio broadcasting was dominated entirely by the BBC. Rock and pop music fans, dissatisfied with the BBC's output, often listened to Radio Luxembourg. During the post-1964 period, western Europe offshore radio (such as Radio Caroline broadcasting from ships at anchor or abandoned forts) helped to supply the demand for the pop and rock music. The BBC launched their own pop music station, BBC Radio 1 in 1967.

In South Asia, Radio Ceylon (the oldest radio station in the region) was the King of the Airwaves from the 1950s and 1960s. Broadcasting in Ceylon was launched by British Engineer, Edward

Harper in 1925. Radio Ceylon became a public corporation in 1967 and was known as the Sri Lanka Broadcasting Corporation when the island turned into a republic in 1972.

There has been a recent resurgence of interest in what is now called old-time radio with surviving shows being traded and collected in reel-to-reel, cassette, CD and MP3 formats.

BROADCASTING PROGRAMME: A CASE STUDY

Students in the Broadcasting programme study digital audio and video production techniques, including nonlinear editing, post-production, animation, web and multimedia graphics, and sports. WIUS-FM gives students the opportunity to put into practice learned skills.

They also examine the impact of history, law, and programming on broadcasting, cable, and satellite operations. Graduates of the programme enter various careers in television, radio, cable, satellite, and post-production operations including directing, producing, reporting, on-air talent programming, sales, advertising, sports, and post-production.

All students taking a broadcasting class that requires writing or a lab of any sort must adhere to our attendance policy.

Bachelor of Arts—Broadcasting

*CORE (15)—**All students must take these core courses***

BC 100	Intro to Broadcasting
BC 101	Intro to Broadcast Production
BC 102	Intro to Broadcast Research and Writing
BC 323	Broadcasting and Society
BC 425 WID	Broadcast/Cable Law and Ethics

There are two sequences to choose from. Students may choose News and Performance or Production. Classes from the sequence not chosen may be taken as elective credit.

News and Performance Sequence (19)

BC 200	Broadcast Reporting I

BC 222	Broadcast Performance
BC 310 or	Advanced Broadcast Performance
BC 312	Broadcast Sports Performance
BC 315	Broadcast News I
BC 415	Broadcast News II
BC 419 or	Online Writing, Design and Production
BC 431	Special News/Sports Projects
BC 385 or	Production Practicum I
BC 386 or	Production Practicum II
BC 485 or	Production Practicum III
BC 486 or	Production Practicum IV

Production Sequence (19)

BC 250 or	Audio Production I
BC 260	Video Production I
BC 302	Broadcast Research and Writing II
BC 350 or	Audio Production II
BC 361	Video Production II
BC 402	Advanced Broadcast Writing
BC 385	Production Practicum I
BC 386	Production Practicum II
BC 485	Production Practicum III
BC 486	Production Practicum IV
BC 490	Senior Workshop in Production

Broadcast Electives (6)

BC 325	Comparative Broadcast Systems
BC 328W	Mass Media and Minorities
BC 400	Senior Honours Thesis Research
BC 401	Honours Thesis
BC 418	Independent Research
BC 420	Television Graphics
BC 426	Sports Broadcasting
BC 430	Multimedia Design for Mass Media

RADIO BROADCASTING PROGRAMME: A CASE STUDY

Associate of Applied Science Degree

For over 60 years, Brown has been educating successful radio broadcasters and producers. In fact, 17 of our grads have found their way into the Minnesota Radio Broadcasting Hall of Fame.

But broadcasting's best days lie ahead. Streaming audio, podcasts, and satellite radio are just a few of the emerging technologies that will demand skilled broadcasters and producers for years to come.

The Associate of Applied Science degree in Radio Broadcasting is designed to help you develop an on-air presence and the technical skills needed for positions in this growing industry. Business aspects of broadcasting are illuminated, including station management and sales. The programme also explores the relationship between broadcasting and the Internet, and includes an internship or practicum project.

Career Opportunities for Radio Broadcasting Graduates

- Audio production director
- Newscaster
- On-air talent
- Producer
- Radio newscaster
- Media sales account executive
- Sports play-by-play announcer and reporter

Listen Live to "The VBC" The Voice of Brown College
Available at the Mendota Heights campus.

"The instructors guide and mentor you throughout the programme."

—Siobhan Kierans, *Graduate, School of Broadcasting*

Associate of Applied Science Degree

18 months—6 quarters—90 quarter credits

RADIO FORMAT

A radio format or programming format describes the overall content broadcast on a radio station. Radio formats are frequently employed as a marketing tool, and constantly evolve. Music radio; All-news radio; Sports radio; Talk radio and Weather radio describe the operation of different genres of radio format and each format can often be sub-divided into many speciality formats.

RADIO SOFTWARE

Almost all radio stations today use some form of broadcast automation. Although some only use small scripts in audio players, a more robust solution is using a full Radio Automation Suite. There are many commercial and free radio automation packages available.

Free and Open-source Developments

- Soma Suite
- Campcaster
- Rivendell
- IKRA

Commercial Products

- Raduga
- Pulsar Multimídia
- Backbone Networks

RADIO COMMERCIAL

A radio commercial (often called an advert in the United Kingdom, or a spot to people in the business) is a form of advertising in which goods, services, organizations, ideas, etc. are promoted via the medium of radio. Many commercials are produced by an outside ad agency or radio production company and, airtime is purchased from a station or network in exchange for sponsorship of its programming.

Radio commercials are sold in 10, 20, 30, 40, 50, 60 or 120 second increments. While a :60 radio commercial is twice as long as a :30 radio commercial, it is rarely sold at twice the price. While practices vary, most radio stations only charge 20-30 per cent more for the longer spot.

While many commercials are professionally produced, radio is not out of reach for the small retail business owner. Most local radio stations have the ability to produce radio commercials in house using their own announcers. Often local radio stations will write and even produce the radio commercials for local retail advertisers at no additional cost when the merchant purchases a schedule of "spots" on the station.

Radio commercials can be delivered to a network of radio stations directly from the recording studio on a DAT cassette or transmitted via satellite or ISDN.

The first radio commercial is credited to WEAF, New York on August 28, 1922 for the Queensboro real estate corporation. The ten-minute live commercial was voiced by H.M. Blackwell, a representative of Queensboro.

RADIO DOCUMENTARY

A radio documentary or feature is a radio documentary programme devoted to covering a particular topic in some depth, usually with a mixture of commentary and sound pictures. Some radio features, especially those including specially composed music or other pieces of audio art, resemble radio drama in many ways, though non-fictional in subject matter, while others consist principally of more straightforward, journalistic-type reporting—but at much greater length than found in an ordinary news report.

Quotes

> "At its best, radio combines the power and immediacy of great documentary films with the intimacy and poetry of a *New Yorker*-style magazine piece."
>
> (*Columbia Graduate School of Journalism*)

"Staring red-eyed at the mirror in front of me, having spent another day and half of the night with my computer, I ask myself fundamental questions: Why radio? Why documentary? Answer: No other medium can provide me with more freedom of creation and investigation. It meets my urgent interest in reality and the desire for a 'musical' expression. The material (*der Werkstoff*) is sound. And sound always surrounds us. And: I'm not so much interested in the description of stable situations, but in processes. Our medium is not space, but time; our stories are not glued to the ground, but have motion, life... . That's why!"

(*Helmut Kopetzky, German author*)

Notable Radio Documentary and Feature Makers

- American RadioWorks
- John Biewen
- Kyla Brettle
- Ira Glass
- Berit Hedemann (Prix Europa Yleisradio 1997 and 1998)
- David Isay
- Bill Lichtenstein
- Ewan MacColl
- Charles Parker
- Joe Richman
- Steve Rowland

PRODUCING RADIO PROGRAMMES: A CASE STUDY

Most Popular

- 30 People Who Shaped Sound
- Videos From AES 2007
- Tracking Paul McCartney's *Memory*
- Read—Watch—Listen—Play!
- SONAR 7 Videos

Classics

- Alicia Keys Opens Recording Studio

- Making Tool's *10,000 Days*
- Behind the Scenes at Pink Martini's 2006 tour
- Meet Daft Punk
- Phil Collins' "In the Air Tonight"

Remix Hotel News

RHLA Ramps Up November 8-10

Participating artists and producers include 9th Wonder, Aloe Blacc, Carmen Rizzo and Freq Nasty. Click here for complete details about RHLA and to register.

Apple Logic Pro 8 Classes at Remix Hotel L.A.

Apple Computer will host daily classes and demos on its flagship DAW, Logic Pro 8. For dates, times and locations, go to remixmag.com/remixhotel.

Looking for new revenue possibilities for your studio? Producing radio programmes can provide income that does not come with clients who have fist fights during recording sessions or want the monitors turned up to 11. In fact, in the best cases, the client comes in, records the voice tracks and splits, leaving you the flexibility to put the show together as it suits you.

Radio programme production might seem as simple as sequencing recorded elements-sort of like sequencing music tracks on a CD. Unlike CD sequencing, however, producing a music radio programme often combines widely divergent audio elements that challenge a producer's ability to make the show hang together. Jazz musicologist Jim Murphy's "Journey Into Jazz," a one-hour weekly programme that covers 50 years of music, provided just that sort of challenge.

When you have recordings from Sinatra, Tito Puente, the Four Freshmen, The Rippingtons, The Hi-Los, Max Roach, MJQ, Oscar Peterson, Spyro Gyra and Sonny Rollins, you have got a very listenable but very wide hour of music.

The show, with 13 weeks of programming already in the can, was produced on an Orban Audicy workstation, with the music loaded in a cut at a time. Under direction not to "mess with the music" (which I interpreted as no EQ or compression), I found the loudest passage of each cut and set record levels accordingly. Against my gut instincts, all of the voice and music elements of the first two shows were mixed without processing.

After listening to the mixed programmes, Murphy was not happy. The first problem was that the intros to some of the pieces started at rather low levels, which became more apparent when sequenced with the voice tracks. I explained that raising the level would be changing the dynamic properties of the music, and that is what he said he did not want. He cleared things up by saying he wanted the audio to sound like it did on the radio.

That changed everything and made my gut feel better. Almost everything on the radio is EQ'd, compressed and limited. Part of running a "tight board" (radio lingo for no dead air and consistent levels) is raising the level of soft intros and backing them off as the song builds. After that, you let the station's compressor, limiter and clipper do the work. If the song fades at the end, it is not unusual to increase its level until the subjectively "best" musical moment for either a segue to the next tune or the back announce. That part of the recipe was working.

The other part is the appropriate use of compression and limiting on both the voice and music. I know some people think music should not be messed with—it is a complete art form and the degree of compression and limiting is part of the art form. I also know that in the 17 years I spent working at radio stations, every single one compressed, limited and clipped at the transmitter. (So, no flame mail!) In the 1960s and early 1970s, stations were using the CBS Audimax and Volumax. They were crude by today's standards, but they increased the average modulation level. In AM (amplitude-modulated) signals, a good portion of the signal strength and coverage area is produced by the modulation in the side bands. The harder you bang it, the bigger it gets. Bigger coverage area means more listeners.

In the late 1970s, Bob Orban's multiband Optimod 8000 revolutionized the sound of FM radio by reducing the amount of artifacts produced by massive amounts of gain reduction. Multibanding was part of the solution; using a small amount of delay to prepare the gain reduction circuits for what was about to hit them was another. Other manufacturers contributed boxes with their own "secret sauce," resulting in some truly hideous audio when too many radio stations tried to turn it up to 11.

(And that is the last time I am going to use that phrase in this article.)

The point is, you never know if the programming you are producing is going to end up being aired on a station where management has decided that louder is better. If you give them the full, unadulterated stuff, with no...er...preprocessing, it will sound a lot worse on the air than if you do some of the gain reduction work with relatively transparent gear beforehand. That way, their equipment does not have to work as hard, which generally means fewer artifacts and better sound.

Preprocessing also falls right into line when loading said audio into a workstation. The more bits you use, the better the sound, but digital "overs" suck. Striking the right balance of compressor and limiter settings took some time because the production styles and mix techniques within 50 years of jazz vary wildly. In the end, I found that an Aphex Compellor followed by a Studio Dominator set at light but fast settings contributed a consistency. The Compellor is a very transparent device, and the tri-band stereo limiting of the Studio Dominator kept the lid on without pumping. Compression ran at a fairly constant 2 to 4 dB. The Studio Dominator was set to catch the occasional peaks, most of which required 1 to 3 dB of gain reduction. A few of the selections, some with bongo accents and drum and vibe solos, had extremely high peaks, requiring the Dominator release times to be set faster to avoid pumping. From there, the input level to the Compellor/Dominator stage was varied as needed to account for level differences on the LPs and CDs. In most cases, the newer tunes were produced with more overall compression than some of the earlier ones. The more gain reduction I heard in the original recording, the less I used.

After testing several mics on Murphy's voice, I settled on a Gefell UM 70 through a GML mic preamp with no EQ. The voice tracks were recorded through the Compellor/Studio Dominator chain using the same settings as for the music tracks. The Audicy was used to cut the center out of Murphy's breaths, leaving enough to imply natural breathing.

A good turntable, stylus, cartridge and preamp all make a difference. You cannot "get by" with bad stuff. I used a Stanton 981 HZ-Mk II-S cartridge with a II D98S stylus in a Techniques SL-D1 direct drive turntable and a Stanton Model 210 phone preamp. Murphy's LP collection is in very good condition, requiring only that a standard, moistened Discwasher be used to remove the usual dust buildup. Some of the older, more frequently played discs had developed some crackles and pops. The Audicy got rid of the pops with no problem, but the budget was not there for more extensive noise removal.

The show was mixed to a Panasonic SV-3900 DAT in quarter-hour segments. It is very easy to let the level of a sequenced show creep away from you. The tendency is to make each segment just a little louder than the last. I used the -6dB peak hold indicator on the DAT meters as a guide, with rare excursions to -4 dB and -2 dB.

After making high-speed DAT backup copies of each programme with a Tascam DA-302 dual-well DAT, the DATs were sent off for CD replication. The house with the best price is not always the best deal. Of the first ten shows sent out, 1 to 7 came back in mono, and 8 and 9 came back in stereo with the channels reversed, but that is another story.

Modern Recording and Mixing

This 2-DVD set will show you how the best in the music industry set up a studio to make world-class records. Regardless of what gear you are using, the information you will find here will allow you to take advantage of decades of expert knowledge.

Mastering Cubase 4

Electronic Musician Magazine and Thomson Course Technology PTR have joined forces again to create the second volume in their Personal Studio Series, Mastering Steinberg's Cubase(tm). Edited and produced by the staff of Electronic Musician, this special issue is not only a must-read for users of Cubase(tm) software, but it also delivers essential information for anyone recording/ producing music in a personal-studio.

Delivered straight to your inbox every other week, MixLine Live takes you on the road with today's hottest tours, new sound reinforcement professional products, recent installs, industry news and much more. to read the latest edition; sign up.

Read, Watch, Listen, Play

- Blog
- Video
- Photos
- TalkBack
- Events
- Podcasts: Updated!
- eNews
- Remix Hotel
- Mix Guides
- Music/DVD Reviews

Mixbooks

- Modern Recording and Mixing
- Classic Tracks
- Critical Listening for Audio Pros
- Pro Tools DVD: Volume I
- Ruthless Self-Promotion in Music Industry
- Networking Strategies for the New Music Business
- The S.M.A.R.T. Guide to Producing and Engineering Music

Directories

- AES
- NAB
- Winter NAMM
- Summer NAMM
- Education
- NSCA
- Musikmesse

Enews

- MixLine
- MixLine Live
- eDeals
- AudioBytes
- eClassifieds
- Archives
- Sign Up Now

Resources

- Site Index
- About Mix
- Contact Mix
- Advertising Information
- Subscribe Now
- Customer Service
- JobZone
- Reprints

Industry Orgs

- AES
- NAB
- NAMM
- NARAS P&E Wing
- SPARS
- Women's Audio Mission
- Hearnet
- House Ear Institute

Mixguides

- Consoles
- Studio Monitors
- Microphones
- Audio Education
- Studio Design

Related Sites

- Electronic Musician
- Remix
- TEC Awards
- Sound and Video Contractor
- Music Education Technology
- Live Design
- Broadway Sound Master Class
- Digital Content Producer

- Broadcast Engineering
- Penton Media

RADIO PRODUCTION: A CASE STUDY

Students interested in radio use a radio production facility encompassing five studios. All studios contain state-of-the-art radio production equipment.

Our Facilities

- 24 channel Teac mixing console
- 10 channel on-air board
- Digital audio cassette recorders
- Digital Minidisk recorders and players
- The latest digital signal processing equipment
- Digital computerized editing suites
- Adobe audition sound editing software

Radio Station WIUS

- Radio station WIUS is a licensed operation that broadcasts live in the Macomb area.
- The station is completely run by WIU students and plays a variety of formats including urban contemporary and alternative rock.
- WIUS is an excellent opportunity for broadcast majors and other students interested in radio to get professional air time.
- Listen Live to WIUS-FM.

Advanced Radio Production

- If you are looking for more challenging radio production work, the advanced radio production classes have what you are looking for.
- Students complete more intricate technical and dramatic projects using state-of-the-art digital equipment.

- You will learn to master the "big board" with all the latest in signal processors, digital players and recorders, and multi-track recording.

RADIO PRODUCTION COURSES:
SELECT ANALYTICAL STUDY

Certificate: Industrial Technology
Credit Requirements: 24 Semester Credit Hours

This certificate is designed for students who wish to pursue a career in Radio Production primarily as board operators and production assistants but also in some cases as on-the-air talent.

Admission into the programme requires proof of high school graduation (or GED) and qualifying scores on SAT, ACT, or the TTC placement test.

Recommended Sequence of Courses

First Semester—Fall

RTV 101	Audio Techniques	3
RTV 109	Writing for Electronic Media	3
RTV 111	Radio Studio Techniques I	3
		Total 9

Second Semester—Spring

RTV 112	Radio Studio Techniques II	3
RTV 121	Introduction to Broadcasting	3
RTV 231	SCWE in Broadcasting I	3
		Total 9

Third Semester—Summer

RTV 211	Radio Studio Techniques III	3
RTV 232	SCWE in Broadcasting II	3
		Total 6

Acronym and Glossary of Terms

A

AC. Alternating Current. Electrical current that changes polarity regularly and continually.

Access Channel. One of the three cable channels designed for use by the public, government, or education.

AGC. Automatic Gain Control.

Ambient Sound. Unintelligible background noise found in and generally unique to an audio environment.

Amp. Ampere. Unit of electrical measure equal to one volt sent through a resistance of one ohm. Also one watt divided by one volt.

Amphenol Connector. A threaded connector sometimes used for unbalanced microphone lines.

Amplified. Any electronic device used to increase the level or power of signals applied to it.

Aperture (1). Any electronic device used to increase the level or power of signals applied to it.

Aperture (2). Opening in camera lens controlling and allowing light to pass through.

ASA. American Standards Association. A unit measuring the sensitivity of photographic emulsions. The higher the ASA number, the more sensitive the emulsion.

ASCAP. American Society of Composers, Authors and Publishers.

Assemble Edit. A video editing procedure which records new video, audio, and control track information simultaneously without reference to any signal already on the tape.

Attack Time (1). The response time of an automatic gain control circuit to rapidly increasing signals.

Attack Time (2). The time the rotating video head actually contacts the videotape and begins to write or read video information.

Audio. Sound.

Automatic Gain Control. Electronic circuit designed to keep signals at an acceptable level by amplifying signals that are too low and attenuating or reducing signals that are too high.

Available Light. Light from a natural source or commonly used lamp, as opposed to light added to a scene by using special photographic or television lights.

AWG. American Wire Gauge. A unit of measure of the cross sectional diameter of wire. The higher the number, the thinner the wire. Ordinary lamp wire is 18 AWG.

B

Back Focus. The distance from the rear element of a lens to the image plane.

Background Light. Any light used to illuminate the background of a set or scene, but not intended to illuminate the subject.

Backlight. Light striking a subject from the direction opposite to the camera. Generally used to highlight the subject and set it apart from the background.

Balanced Line. A cable carrying two equal signals of opposite polarity on separate conductors, both surrounded by a grounded shield.

Bandwidth. The amount of audio or radio spectrum required or used by a signal or waveform.

Barn Door. A metal flap or group of metal flaps attached to the front of a lamp housing to prevent light from spilling outside a desired area.

Base Light. An even, diffuse, light filling a setting with sufficient light to keep shadows from key or back lights from being too dark.

Base Video. A video signal that is not combined with a carrier to place it in the radio frequency spectrum. Normally has an amplitude of one volt peak to peak across an impedance of 75 ohms.

Bayonet Mount. A lens mount, or electrical connector which engages by means of interlocking fingers and cams and permits attachment with only a relatively small amount of twisting action.

Beta Format. A group of videotape formats similar to U-matic used with half inch colour videocassette recorders and players.

Betacam. A component broadcast system using half-inch tape and cases similar to those for the Beta format.

Bi-directional Microphone. A microphone designed to pick up sound on two sides of the microphone along the same axis, but reject sound from any other direction.

Bloom. A loss of picture detail and increase in size of bright portions of a video picture seen when too much light is allowed to strike a pickup tube or when the signals controlling a tube allow it to be overdriven.

BMI. Broadcast Music, Incorporated. A music licensing service.

BNC Connector. A connector with a bayonet lock used with coaxial video cable.

Boom Microphone. Any microphone, but usually a unidirectional or shotgun microphone, attached to a pole or boom to keep the microphone near an audio source but outside of the field of view.

Broad. A light with a long bulb perpendicular to the direction in which the light is aimed, designed to throw an even light with an indistinct shadow.

Brightness Control. A control used to adjust the illumination of viewfinders, monitors, and receivers, but not affecting signal levels from cameras or other picture sources.

Burn. Part of a pickup tubes that has a depletion of charge evidence by a negative image of the picture source causing the depletion. This condition is temporary unless the tube is turned off and allowed to cool before the problem is corrected.

Burst. A gated 3.58 megahertz signal immediately following horizontal sync and used as a reference in controlling the hue, or phase, of colour signals.

C

Cable (1). The electrical cords used to interconnect pieces of audio and video equipment.

Cable (2). A term generally referring to a broadband distribution system using wire rather than over-the-air broadcast.

Camera Cap. A cap screwed or mounted onto the front of a camera in place of the lens to protect the camera pickup tube from light or dirt when the lens is not in place.

Cannon. A three-pin connector used with balanced audio lines for line and mic level audio signals. Also known as an XL or XLR connector.

Capacitor. An electrical device which stores energy as an electrostatic charge. Often used as a component in filter circuits.

Capstan. The spindle that actually drives tape across head assemblies.

Cardioid Microphone. A somewhat unidirectional microphone with a heart-shaped pickup pattern.

Carrier. The RF signal which is modulated by a video or audio signal for broadcast transmission.

CATV. Community Antenna Television. Broadband distribution system using coaxial cable rather than over-the-air broadcast.

CCD. Charge-coupled device. In television, the device that senses light coming through the lens and translates it into electrical impulses (replacing the pickup tube).

CCU. Camera control unit.

CD. Compact disk. Laser disk with five inch diameter, which may contain video, audio, or data in digital format.

CD ROM. Compact disk with digital data used with a computer as "read-only memory".

Character Generator (CG). A small computer used to generate titles and other text electronically without the use of a camera.

Characteristic Impedance. The apparent resistance to an alternating current shown by a wire or electronic device.

Chroma. The characteristic of a colour which refers to its saturation or intensity. Also the colour pattern of the television signal.

Chroma Key. A key based on the chroma saturation and hue of portions of a picture, rather than on the luminance, or brightness. A specific hue is replaced by one picture source, while the rest of the picture is replaced by another picture source. A chroma key is an external key.

Chrominance. The colour portion of the television signal.

C-mount Lens. A lens with a standard one-inch threaded mount assembly that is screwed into the camera body, as opposed to a bayonet or "m" mount.

Close-up. A shot emphasizing detailed elements in a scene, as opposed to the more panoramic wide view.

Coaxial Cable. A cable having a center conductor surrounded by insulation and a grounded shield.

Colour Killer. A circuit designed to detect the presence of burst in a television signal and deactivate the colour circuits if the burst signal is low or absent.

Compatible. Meeting all of the electronic requirements for signals and levels necessary to interface devices to achieve desired results.

Condenser Microphone. A microphone using a power supply (usually a battery) to maintain a charge across two plates which modulate a voltage when the distance between them changes.

Confidence Head. A video head separate from the normal record/ play head found on some videotape recorders and used to monitor the actual recorded signal on the videotape during recording.

Contrast. The difference in illumination between the brightest and darkest parts of a scene or picture.

Contrast Control. A control used to change the amplitude of the video signal in viewfinders receivers, and monitors, but not affecting the output of cameras or other video sources.

Control Track. A reference signal recorded on videotape and used to control the path of the video heads across the tape on playback.

Credits. Listings of all those involved in making a programme, usually appearing at the end of a television programme or film.

Critical Focus. The plane in front of a focused lens in which the image will be precisely in focus on the film or pickup tube.

CU. Close-up.

Cume. The total audience size (number of viewers) for a programme or series of programmes over several showings. Repeat viewers are not counted.

Cut. The instantaneous transition from one picture or audio source to another.

Cutaway. A shot interposed at an edit point to prevent the appearance of a jump cut at the edit point.

Cyclorama. A seamless background, blending into the floor and usually lit from behind. Used to eliminate any background detail from a set.

D

DA. Distribution Amplifier.

dB. Decibel. A unit used to compare the relative levels of electrical signals on a logarithmic scale. The formula for the calculation is db=10(log(P2/P1)), or db=20(log(E2/E1)).

Demodulation. The process of separating a signal from its carrier frequency.

Depth of Field. The range of distances in front of the lens in which objects appear to be in acceptable focus.

Depth of Focus. The range of distances from the rear of the lens to the face of the pickup tube in which acceptable focus can be achieved.

DIN (1). A type of multi-pin connector.

DIN (2). A standard for film sensitivity similar to ASA. Not Direct Current. An electrical current that does not change polarity.

Dissolve. The gradual change from one picture to another, allowing the pictures to be superimposed during the transition.

Distribution Amplifier. An amplifier with essentially unity gain used to distribute control and picture signals to equipment in a television system.

Distortion. Any undesirable alteration in an audio or video signal.

Dolly (1). A wheeled device attached to a tripod to allow smooth movement of a camera.

Dolly (2). A camera movement toward or away from the subject (dolly forward, dolly back).

Dub. To copy by playing back on one machine and recording on another.

Duct Tape. A shiny adhesive tape designed for holding metal heating and cooling ducts, but also commonly used as a substitute for gaffers tape, a general purpose tape used in television and film.

Dynamic Microphone. A microphone which uses a magnet moving in a coil of wire to generate an electrical signal.

E

Edit. In television, to record from any programme source altering the duration or temporal sequence of events using a recorder specifically designed to do this efficiently and cleanly, maintaining continuity of sync and proper timing relationships between signals at edit points.

EIA. Electrical Industries Association.

EIAJ. Electrical Industries Association of Japan. Universal standard for video recording in black and white on half inch reel-to-reel videotape recorders. The standard involves a tape speed of 7½ inches per second with a sixty-minute capacity using a seven inch reel. There is only one audio channel.

Eight-pin. A common rectangular connector generally used between television monitors and videotape recorders combining all of the cable connections necessary for record and playback functions into a single connector.

EFP. Electronic Field Production.

Electret. A type of condenser microphone.

Electronic Field Production. (EFP) Production of a television programme or programme segment by recording material on location with a single camera and editing this material to make the finished product.

E to E. Electronics to Electronics. Refers to the normal record mode in a videotape recorder in which the recorder output is connected to the recorder input and cannot show the actual signal recorded on tape. Some videotape recorders have special confidence heads which allow direct tape monitoring during recording. Most do not.

Equalization. Changing the relative balance of frequencies in an audio or video signal.

Equalizing Pulses. A series of sync pulses within the horizontal interval which determine the starting point for the first scan line of each field of video.

Establishing Shot. A shot used to introduce a scene, including a relatively wide angle of view and showing the relationships between objects, settings, and people in the scene.

F

Fade. The gradual change from one picture or sound source to another. Usually to or from black (video) or silence (audio).

F Connector. A small threaded connector used with coaxial cable in the RF distribution of television signals.

Fidelity. A subjective appraisal of the amount of distortion in the reproduction and transmission of signals.

Field. One scan from the top to the bottom of the television frame, tracing alternate horizontal lines and taking one sixtieth of a second to complete.

Fill Light. Light used to fill in shadows left by key light and keep the contrast range of a scene within the capabilities of the recording medium.

Film Chain. An equipment grouping including a dedicated camera, super 8 mm and 16 mm projectors, dual dissolving 35 mm slide projectors, and a special rotating mirror assembly (multiplexer) which transmits the images from one of the projectors to the dedicated camera.

Filter (1). A flat piece of glass or gelatin with no optical properties other than to control the colour or intensity of light.

Filter (2). An electrical device used to reduce the transmission of signals in some frequency ranges and allow transmission of signals in other frequency ranges.

Flag. Temporary persistence of a bright spot on the pickup tube as the image causing the spot is moved across the face of the tube.

Flag. The horizontal shift observed at the top of the screen when a timing error occurs due either to skew and tension problems on playback or to slight timing errors at an edit point created in the editing process.

Flag. A metal flap used near a lens to keep lights from shining directly into the lens and causing lens flare.

Flare. An undesired image, or overall haziness of an image caused by undesired reflections of light from surfaces within the lens itself.

Flat. A framed upright panel, usually 4 × 8 feet or larger, used to simulate a wall or wall section in a television set.

Flat Response. The reproduction or transmission of a signal with very little deviation from the original amplitude of the signal over its entire frequency range. Deviations in amplitude are expressed in db, plus or minus.

Flood Light. Any light throwing a broad, even illumination in a circular pattern with diffused shadows.

Flutter. A form of signal distortion caused by rapid fluctuations in the speed of a tape crossing a head assembly.

Flying Erase Head. An erase head mounted on the rotating video head drum in advance of the record/playback head.

Focal Length. The distance from the optical centre of a lens to the focal plane.

Focal Plane. The plane perpendicular to the lens axis at which parallel rays striking the lens are converged to a point.

Focus. To cause a sharp image from a lens to be projected onto the focal plane (in the case of a camera) or onto a screen (in the case of a projector). Also to adjust the electron beam converging circuits in a television monitor for maximum sharpness as they strike the surface of the picture tube.

Foot Candle. The amount of light produced by a standard candle at a distance of one foot. The most common unit of measure for incident light used in film and television work.

Frame. A complete television picture consisting of two interlaced fields of video. The frame rate for NTSC television is thirty frames per second.

Freeze Frame. The continuous repetition of a single frame of video. It is technically not possible for helical videotape recorders to display freeze frames, since they read only one field of video on each pass across the videotape.

Frequency. The rate of repetition of an electrical or audio signal, expressed in Hertz (cycles per second).

Fresnel. A special light-weight lens used in focusing beams of light. Originally used in lighthouses, now also used in high-quality studio and theatrical lights.

f-stop. The size of the aperture in a lens, given in f-numbers. The lower the f-number, the more light passes through the lens. It is the ratio of the lens focal length to the actual diameter of the aperture opening.

Fuse. A device designed to interrupt an electrical circuit in the event of an overload of that circuit.

G

Gaffer. The crew member principally responsible for transporting, maintaining, and setting up lighting equipment.

Gaffer's Tape. A strong adhesive tape used in film and television production.

Gain. Degree of amplification. The difference between the signal level at the input of a device and the level at the output, usually expressed in dB.

Generation. The number of duplication processes by which a videotape is removed from the live source. The original recording is first generation, while a copy of an original recording is second generation, and so on.

Genloc. To reference a signal generator to a signal normally external to and separate from the system controlled by the signal generator. The purpose is to bring a system, such as a studio, into proper timing with an external source, such as a live remote camera, so that special effects as wipes, keys, and dissolves can be done using the external source in combination with internal sources.

Grip. The crew member principally responsible for the transportation, maintenance and mounting of the camera.

Ground. A connection to the chassis or a common return path, or an actual connection to the earth in an electrical device.

H

Head (1). The camera without lens or viewfinder.

Head (2). The uppermost portion of a tripod or pedestal which provides for the ability to pan and tilt the camera.

Head (3). A small electromagnet with a very small air gap between the poles used to record and play back magnetic pulses on audio or video tape.

Head Gap. The space between the poles of a head. Good frequency response is dependent on proper width of the head gap. Dirt or oxide particles clogging a head can cause reduced signal level and distortion of the signal.

Head Room. The space between the top of a subject's head and the top of the video frame.

Helical. Like a helix. Specifically, the geometric pattern formed by a rotating video head in relation to videotape moving across the rotating head assembly. Thus, referring to any videotape recorder using a rotating head assembly that reads a complete field of video on each pass across the tape. These include all EIAJ, U-matic, Beta, and VHS formats as well as one-inch SMPTE types A, B, and C.

Hertz. Cycle per second.

Heterodyne. A system used for recording colour video signals at a reduced frequency.

High Level. Audio signal intended to attain a maximum, or peak, level of zero db, or one volt at six hundred ohms impedance. (0.775 volts rms.)

Hiss. The background noise generated in an audio system which is internally generated by microphones, amplifiers, and tape.

Horizontal Hold. An adjustment on viewfinders, monitors, and receivers to make the frequency of the horizontal sweep circuits to the horizontal sync pulse from an incoming signal.

Horizontal Sync. That portion of the sync signal that controls the horizontal timing (and therefore horizontal location) of each line of picture.

Hue. Shade of colour, determined in television by the phase angle between a colour and the colour sub-carrier or colour burst reference signal.

Hum. Unwanted low frequency audio noise caused by improperly shielded or improperly grounded audio cables and circuits.

I

Impedance. The apparent resistance to an alternating current shown by a wire or electronic device.

Impedance Matching. The use of a transformer or other device to alter the impedance of a device to equal the impedance of another device. Minimum distortion and loss of signal can be achieved only where the output transmitting a signal, the cable carrying the signal, and the input receiving the signal all have the same impedance.

Incident Light. Light striking a subject, as opposed to light reflected by a subject. Usually measured in film and television by light meters calibrated in foot candles.

Insert. A shot or sequence inserted into a television programme used to illustrated a subject.

Insert Edit. A video or audio edit made with reference to pre-recorded control track so synchronization is maintained and the insert can be ended without visible disruption of the picture.

Interlace. The process of combining the two video fields into frames by writing only even-numbered lines in one field and only odd-numbered lines in the other.

Internal Sync. Synchronizing signals generated by a camera, recorder, or other picture source without reference to or need of external synchronizing signals.

IRE. Institute of radio engineers. Now IEEE. Also a unit of measure of video amplitude. One IRE unit is equal to 1/140 volt, peak to peak. The composite video signal is composed of sync, from – 40 to 0 IRE and video, from 0 to 100 IRE. Black is normally set at between 7.5 IRE and 10 IRE.

J

Jump Cut. An edit made without regard to the thirty degree rule, which results in a visual discontinuity as subjects appear to "jump" on screen.

K

Key. A video special effect in which the level of a video signal is used as a switch which allows selective substitution of picture information from one source with picture information from a different source. Luminance keyers use the amplitude of the monochrome portion of the signal, while chroma keyers use the amplitude of a specific colour or hue. Most printed material is inserted into video using luminance keys, while picture information is inserted using chroma keys.

Key Light. The primary illumination for a scene, generally giving the impression of a natural light source and throwing the darkest and most defined shadows in a scene.

Keystone. The effect of projecting an image onto a surface that is not perpendicular to the axis of the projecting lens. Parallel lines tend to converge in the direction where the surface is closer to the lens.

L

Lag. The tendency in some camera pickup tubes to retain an image after it is no longer presented to the tube. This effect is most evident when a relatively bright image is replaced by a darker field of view and is aggravated when a bright image is stationary in the field of view for an extended period of time before it is replaced.

Latent Image. The image retained by a pickup tube after the source of that image is removed. If a latent image is present on a pickup tube when a camera is turned off, the image may be permanently fixed on the tube.

Lavalier. A microphone worn on the body and held in place either with a lanyard worn around the neck or a clip fastened to clothing. The frequency response of a lavalier microphone is skewed toward the higher frequencies to compensate for the low frequency sound transmitted directly to the microphone by contact with the body.

Lens Hood. Also lens shade. A cone fastened to the front end of a lens to keep incident light from striking the lens elements and causing lens flare.

Limiter. An amplifier designed to limit or compress signals over a desired level, thus reducing the chances of distortion and keeping the range of signal levels within the range that can be recorded. Unlike an automatic gain control, a limiter does not augment or boost low levels.

Line Level. In audio, a signal with a peak power of about one milliwatt at an impedance of 600 ohms, or zero dBm. This is equivalent to a voltage of .775 volts rms. Also know as "high level" or "auxiliary level."

Live. Not prerecorded. Occurring at the same instant as it is seen or recorded.

Live Card. A card, usually about 11 × 14, used in television to display text or graphics to a camera.

Live on Tape. Unedited. Recorded exactly as occurring with no compression of time or alteration of any sequence of events.

Long Shot. A shot including a relatively wide view of an overall scene, often used as an establishing shot.

Low Level. Microphone Level. An audio signal with a maximum level of about minus fifty dB, relative to line level, or 2.45 millivolts at 600 ohms impedance.

Lux. The amount of light produced by a standard candle at a distance of one meter.

M

Master. A control uniformly governing the outputs of a number of other controls.

Master. Sometimes in editing, the source, or playback, machine.

Master. The finished copy of a programme from which copies are made for distribution.

Matching Transformer. A transformer used to alter the impedance of a signal source to match the input impedance of another device. A common use of matching transformers is to change the characteristic impedance of a 75 ohm coaxial antenna cable to 300 ohms to match the antenna input of a television set.

Medium Shot (MS). A shot showing a single subject, rather than an overall scene, but not in detail. For example, a shot of a person including the body from the waist to slightly above the top of the head.

Mic Mouse. A soft foam pad or holder for a microphone which is placed on a stage or studio floor. The mic mouse holds the microphone very near the floor without allowing it to touch. The purpose is to eliminate the effect of sound waves bouncing off the floor and interfering with sound waves transmitted directly to the microphone.

Mixer. An electronic device for combining the outputs of several sound sources, with separate control over the volume or quality of each.

Modulation. The process of varying the instantaneous amplitude, frequency, or phase of a carrier signal in response to the waveform of an information-bearing signal.

Multiplexer. A device which uses a movable mirror to select images from one of several optical sources for transmission to the dedicated camera in a film chain.

N

Neutral Density Filter. A filter having no effect on colour and no optical effect on the lens to which it is attached, but which reduces the overall amount of light reaching the lens. A one power filter reduces transmission by half, or by one f-number. A two power filter reduces transmission by two f-numbers.

Noise. Any unwanted signal interfering with the clarity and intelligibility of desired signals. The background of static inherent in any recording or amplifying device, generally forty to sixty db below the peak output level of the device.

Nose Room. The space between the nose of a subject's head in profile and the edge of the video frame the subject is facing.

NTSC (National Television Systems Committee). Referring to any standard for signals devised by that body, such as NTSC colour bars or NTSC sync. The television system used in the United States, Canada, Japan, Central America, and a number of other countries. The NTSC system has 525 interlaced horizontal lines and 30 frames per second. Look for countries using NTSC.

Nuvicon. A type of video pickup tube used in inexpensive colour television cameras.

O

Octave. A doubling of frequency. Almost all audio devices have a sound frequency range of from four to ten octaves. A piano, with 88 keys, has a range of seven and a third octaves. A video signal has a range of almost twenty octaves.

Omnidirectional Microphone. A microphone which picks up sound equally well from all directions.

Optical Viewfinder. A camera viewfinder which has no electronics and therefore cannot reflect the actual picture being transmitted from the camera. Optical viewfinders for inexpensive television cameras are rangefinder viewfinders which are separate from the camera lens system and show a picture slightly different from that seen by the camera. The difference is most troublesome for subjects close to the camera where the angle of difference, or parallax, is greatest.

Original. Usually first generation audio or videotape from which a master is made.

One-hundred Eighty Degree Rule. A rule of visual continuity which states that when dealing with two or more subjects, shots may only be cut together if they are taken from the same side of a line drawn through the subjects. Used to maintain proper direction on the screen.

P

PAL (Phase Alternating Line). The television system used in western Europe, China, and most of the rest of the world. The PAL system has 625 interlaced lines and 25 frames per second. Look for countries using PAL.

Pan. A camera movement in which the camera is rotated in the horizontal axis. The proper commands are "pan right" and "pan left."

Parabola. A parabolic dish used to reflect sound waves, concentrating them on a microphone, allowing sound to be picked up from greater distances than with even a normal unidirectional or shotgun microphone.

Parallax. The difference in view caused by looking at a scene from two slightly different locations.

Patch Bay. Patch panel. A control panel where all the video and audio lines used in a studio are brought together and terminated in connectors allowing any combination of lines to be wired together as desired by patching in short lengths of cable.

Patch Cord. A short cable with connectors used to interconnect lines in a patch panel. Any audio or video cable used for temporary connections.

Peak to Peak. Literally, encompassing the entire waveform from the most negative part to the most positive. One of two ways to measure signal amplitude, the other being rms (root mean square). Peak to peak measurements are usually more meaningful in video, while rms is more meaningful in audio.

Pedestal (1). A camera support generally restricted to studio use having a single elevator column mounted on a tricycle base.

Pedestal (2). Also called setup. The black level in a television picture, 7.5 to 10 IRE units above sync. Per cent modulation. The amount of amplitude of a signal in terms of the maximum amplitude that signal can be allowed to achieve.

Phase (1). The difference, expressed in degrees, in the instantaneous amplitude of two signals of the same frequency.

Phase (2). The difference, expressed in degrees, between two signals. In colour television, the angle between the burst reference signal and any colour or hue.

Phone Jack. An audio connector generally used with unbalanced lines and intercom systems. Phone jacks may have a single conductor with ground (unbalanced lines) or two conductors with shield (intercom systems and stereo headphones).

Photoflood. Any of a number of lamps designed for still photography that throw an even, diffuse light. They may be designed to fit into a dish reflector or have internal reflectors. Since they are ordinary tungsten bulbs, they tend to lose output power and change colour temperature with age, making them unsuitable for colour television.

Pickup Tube. A light-sensitive electron tube which is scanned by an electron beam to convert an image focused on the face of the tube into an electronic signal.

Pixel. The smallest indivisible area of a computer display that can be addressed.

Plumbicon. A pickup tube used in almost all tube-type broadcast colour cameras.

Pop. Microphone distortion caused by speaking certain consonants (especially "p") into a microphone placed too close to the mouth.

Portapak. A brand name for a battery-operated portable video camera and recorder combination.

Pot. Potentiometer. A variable resistor used to control the level of a signal.

Preamp. An amplifier used to increase signal levels prior to additional processing.

Presence. The ambient sound found in and unique to a recording location.

Proc amp. Processing amplifier. Separates the video signal into sync and picture components to allow limited adjustment of pedestal, gain, and some other aspects of the picture and recombination with internally generated sync signals.

Profile. Side view, especially of a person.

Proximity Effect. An overemphasis of low-frequency tones caused by speaking too close to a unidirectional microphone.

Q

Quad. Broadcast videotape recorder having four rotating video heads, each of which reads only 17 horizontal lines of picture per pass over the tape. Quad recorders use two-inch videotape.

Quartz-halogen. The light of choice in colour television, designed to maintain correct colour temperature and uniform output throughout its life. Provides much higher output than conventional tungsten light of the same power consumption and has a life up to one hundred times that of common tungsten photographic lights. These lamps are sensitive to shock and handling and should never be touched with bare hands.

R

Radio Frequency (RF). That part of the frequency spectrum in which it is possible to radiate (transmit) electromagnetic waves. Any part of the broadcast band, including radio and television.

Radio mic. Transmitter mic or wireless mic. A microphone connected to a small radio transmitter, used in situations where cables would be cumbersome or impossible to use. FCC regulations are stringent in the use of transmitter microphones.

Rating. The percentage of the total potential television homes tuned to a specific programme. Because the rating is based on total television homes, including those that are not watching any television, the totaling one sixtieth of a second to complete.

RCA Pin Plug. A small connector used with unbalanced single conductor shielded audio cables to interconnect home entertainment audio products. Also used as high level inputs and outputs on some video recorders and audio mixers. Also called a phone plug.

Receiver. Any device capable of demodulating an RF signal, such as a radio, tuner, or television set.

Recorder. Any device that converts an electronic signal to a magnetic pattern in the oxide coating of a magnetic tape.

Recorder. In editing, the videotape recorder or machine on which the edited tape is compiled.

Reel-to-reel. Any audio or videotape format which uses tape packaged on open reels which must be threaded manually, rather than enclosed in a cassette or cartridge.

Reflected Light. Light reaching the camera after being reflected by a subject. Measured in candles per square foot.

Reflector Flood. A sealed floodlight with a self-contained reflector.

Reflector Spot. A sealed spotlight with a self-contained reflector.

Release Time. The response time of an automatic gain control circuit to rapidly decreasing signal levels.

Remote. A production at a location other than a television studio using a special effects generator and other equipment associated with multiple-camera studio facilities.

Resolution. The degree to which fine detail can be recorded or displayed. In film, measured in pairs of light and dark lines per millimeter. In television, measured in lines per scan. Thus, the horizontal resolution of a television camera would be measured by the number of discernible vertical lines that could be displayed across the width of the screen.

RF. Radio frequency.

RF Modulator. A device used to convert a signal to a form similar to that transmitted by an over-the-air broadcast so the output can be used by standard receivers.

RF Splitter. A passive device used to distribute radio frequency signals to two or more receivers.

Riser. A platform on which talent sit or stand, used to raise the talent to a level more suited to coverage by the television camera.

rms. Root mean square. A measure of the effective level of an audio signal or alternating current.

Roll-off. The gradual reduction of frequencies above or below a certain point. Filters which roll off the bass frequencies are often included in unidirectional microphones to compensate for proximity effect.

ROM. Read only memory. Computer memory that can be read, but cannot be overwritten by the host computer.

Rover. A brand name for a battery-operated portable video camera and recorder combination.

rpm. Revolutions per minute.

S

Safe Area. In television graphics or film shot for television, the area which is almost certain to be displayed on any television set. About 80 per cent of the scanned area.

Saticon. A television pickup tube used mostly in industrial television and electronic news gathering.

Scanned Area. In television graphics, the area on a slide or live card which is to be scanned by the television camera. This area is about 25 per cent larger than the safe area.

Scrim. A wire mesh used to reduce and soften the light from a light.

SECAM (Sequential Colour with Memory). The colour television system developed in France using 25 frames per second and 625 horizontal lines. Look for countries using SECAM.

SEG (Special Effects Generator). The device in television used to switch between and combine various picture sources. Also called a switcher.

Sensitivity. The ability of a device, such as a camera or microphone, to sense intelligible information and convert it into a usable electronic signal.

Servo. An electronic circuit used to control the speed of a motor which drives a videotape recorder head assembly drum, which must be controlled with great precision.

Share. The percentage of the total television sets in use that are tuned to a specific programme.

Shield. The outer metal portion of a shielded or coaxial cable, normally grounded, to protect conductors from interference.

Shock Mount. A support for a microphone which used rubber of foam supports to isolate the mic from vibrations which can appear as low frequency rumble in the audio.

Shotgun Microphone. A unidirectional microphone with a narrow pickup pattern.

Sibilance. An undesired hissing sound resulting from over emphasis of high-frequency sound in the reproduction of "s" and "z" sounds in speech. Reduced by equalization or use of a windscreen.

Signal Generator. A device used to generate electronic test signals and, in television, the drive and synchronizing signals used to control and time components in a television system.

Signal to Noise Ratio. The difference in amplitude between unintelligible noise and the maximum signal output of a device.

Skew. In television, the tendency of a picture to hook at the top of the television screen and the control found on some videotape recorders which adjusts tape tension in order to correct this picture problem.

Slave. In some editing systems, the record machine, or the machine on which the edited tape is compiled.

Slow Motion. Playback of a film or videotape at a speed slower than the speed at which it was recorded. This is impossible to do in all but a few specialized videotape recorders without sacrificing picture stability.

SMPTE (Society of Motion Picture and Television Engineers). An organization devoted to the standardization of equipment and practices.

SMPTE Leader. The leader with the eight second count-down commonly used in film.

SMPTE Type A, B, or C. The standards for one inch videotape recorders. Type C is the preferred standard for broadcast one inch videotape.

Source. Any piece of equipment which transmits information to another piece of equipment. Usually referring to devices attached to the input ports of audio mixing consoles, special effects generators, or recorders.

Special Effects Generator (SEG). The device in television used to switch between and combine various picture sources.

Splitter. A passive device used to distribute RF signals. Spotlight. A light having a narrow beam that casts well-defined shadows.

Subcarrier. The 3.58 megahertz signal used in generating and controlling the hue of NTSC colour television signals.

Superimposition. The adding or mixing of two video signals to produce and image with two or more pictures visible simultaneously. Used when a keyer is not available to add graphics to video. Sometimes used to refer to a key.

Switcher. Also special effects generator or SEG. The device in television used to switch between and combine various picture sources.

Sync. Any of the signals used to generate and control a television picture, but, specifically, the portion of the composite video signal from zero to minus forty IRE units consisting of vertical and horizontal timing pulses and equalizing signals to maintain the proper relationship of the two fields of video making up each frame.

Sync Defeat. A switch on videotape recorders that use the composite video signal at the video input to control the internal timing of the recorder which interrupts that control function, allowing the recorder to control timing functions without reference to the incoming video signal.

Synthesizer. A device used to generate video signals without a camera, used in the production of graphics.

T

Take. The instantaneous transition from one picture source to another. A cut.

Target Voltage. The voltage applied to the pickup tube which determines the sensitivity of the tube to light.

TBC. Time base corrector.

Telephoto Lens. Any lens with a focal length significantly greater than the standard focal length for the format in which it is to be used. The standard length for 35 mm still cameras and one inch television cameras is 50 mm.

Thirty-degree Rule. A principle of visual continuity which states that the relative angle of view of any two similarly framed shots of the same subject which are to be cut together should vary by at least thirty degrees.

Tilt. A camera movement in which the camera is rotated in the vertical axis. The commands are "tilt up" and "tilt down."

Time Base Corrector. A highly specialized device with the primary function of making the unstable video output of a videotape recorder conform to the rigid timing of a signal generator, allowing videotape to be used as a picture source in combination with other sources driven by the signal generator.

Titles. Graphic information appearing at the beginning of a programme, generally including the title, author, producer, writer, director, and major personalities.

Tracking Control. The control used to maintain alignment of the video head with the tracks of video information on a tape.

Tracking Head. The magnetic head that writes and reads a sixty hertz pulse on videotape. During playback this pulse is used to maintain proper alignment of the video heads with the tracks of video information on a tape.

T-stop. Similar to an f-stop, this is a number which indicates the effective aperture opening of a lens after compensation is made for the amount of light lost due to internal absorption and reflection. The T-number is always larger than the corresponding f-number.

Tuner. The demodulator section of a radio, television set, or videotape recorder.

U

UHF (Ultra High Frequency). Radio frequencies from 300 to 3,000 megahertz.

UHF. A television broadcast band consisting of channels 14 through 83.

UHF Connector. A threaded video connector used with coaxial cable.

U-matic. The standard format for 3/4 inch videocassette recorders. This format has a maximum record/play time of one hour and two discrete audio channels.

Unbalanced Line. A cable with a single signal-carrying conductor and a grounded shield.

V

Vectorscope. A special type of oscilloscope designed to display the saturation and hue of chroma signals in a polar pattern.

This device is essential in the evaluation of colour signals when aligning colour picture sources or matching and timing colour sources in a television system.

Vertical Hold. A control on television monitors, viewfinders, and receivers used to control the frequency of the vertical oscillator and allow the vertical sweep circuits to lock to the vertical sync component of an incoming video signal.

Vertical Interval. The period of time between the last line of a field and the first line of the next field.

Vertical Interval Switching. Switching based on circuits that delay switching from one picture source to another until the picture source being switched to is between fields, or in the vertical interval.

Vertical Interval Editing. Use of a videotape recorder which is capable of recording and erasing video field by field (has a "flying" erase head) and employs vertical interval switching at the edit point.

VHF (Very High Frequency). Radio frequencies from 30 to 300 megahertz.

VHF. The television broadcast band having television channels 2 through 13.

VHS. A half inch videocassette format using the "M" wrap tape path. Not compatible with the BETA format.

Video. The picture portion of a television signal, sometimes referred to as "composite video" when both picture and sync signals are present.

Videocassette. A container holding both the feed and take-up reels which is inserted into a videotape recorder and threaded automatically.

Vidicon. A type of television pickup tube common in inexpensive cameras and still used to some extent in broadcast cameras.

Volt. The standard unit for measuring the difference of potential between two points in an electronic circuit.

VTR. Videotape recorder.

VU (Volume Unit). Unit of measure of complex waveforms such as audio signals.

W

Watt. Unit of electrical power equal to one volt across a resistance of one ohm, or one volt at a current of one ampere.

Waveform Monitor. A specialized oscilloscope designed to display the video waveform with great stability and high resolution. Essential in determining and setting correct levels for the luminance (monochrome) and sync portions of the composite video signal and useful in evaluating critical timing relationships.

Wide Angle. Any lens with a focal length significantly less than the standard length for the format in which it is used. For 35 mm still cameras and one inch television cameras, the standard length is 50 mm.

Wide Shot (WS). A picture showing a subject in the context of the surroundings to establish the relationship between the subject and the surroundings.

Wind Screen. A thin soft foam cover for microphones which reduces the noise made by wind striking the microphone.

Wipe. The transition between television picture sources in which each picture source is displayed on only a portion of the screen, that portion being determined by an electronically generated pattern which can be sized and positioned using a special effects generator.

Wow. The slow fluctuation in speed of a transport mechanism which results in low frequency instability and distortion in playback of an audio or video tape.

X

XL. Also **XLR** or cannon. A three-pin audio connector used with balanced lines in microphone and line level audio applications.

Z

Zoom. To change the focal length of a zoom lens.

Zoom Lens. A lens with a variable focal length.

Zoom Ratio. The ratio of the longest focal length to the shortest focal length of a zoom lens.

Bibliography and Links

Bibliography

A.L. Zambrano. *Dickens and Film*. New York: Gordon, 1976.

Abel, Richard. *The Cine Goes to Town: French Cinema 1896-1914*. University of California Press, 1998.

Acker, Ally (1991). *Reel Women: Pioneers of the Cinema, 1896 to the Present*. New York: Continuum. ISBN 0826404995.

Acker, Ally. *Reel Women: Pioneers of the Cinema, 1896 to the Present*. London: B.T. Batsford, 1991.

Alan Goble. *The Complete Index to Literary Sources in Film*. New Providence, NJ: Bowker-Sauer, 1999.

Alan Williams. *Republic of Images: A History of French Filmmaking*. Cambridge: Harvard University Press, 1992.

Alex Barris. *Stop the Presses! The Newspaperman in American Films*. Cranbury, NJ: A.S. Barnes, 1976.

Alexander Walker. *The Shattered Silent: How the Talkies Came to Stay*. New York: Morrow, 1979.

Alice Bach (ed.) *Biblical Glamour and Hollywood Glitz*. Atlanta, GA: Scholars Press, 1996. (Semeia; 74).

Alistair Whyte. *New Cinema in Eastern Europe*. London: Dutton, Studio Vista, 1966.

Allan L. Woll. *The Hollywood Musical Goes to War*. Chicago: Nelson-Hall, 1983.

Allen Eyles. *The Western*. South Brunswick, NJ: A.S. Barnes, 1975.

Allen J. Scott (2005). *On Hollywood: The Place the Industry*. Princeton University Press.

Allen L. Woll. *The Latin Image in American Film*. Los Angeles: UCLA Latin American Center, 1977.

American Cinema Editors—"2004 Oscar Nominees Discuss their Craft at the Egyptian Theater."

Amy L. Unterburger (ed.) *Women Filmmakers and Their Films*. Detroit: St. James Press, 1998.

Andre Bazin. *"The Evolution of the Western"*.

Andre Bazin. *"The Western, or the American Film Par Excellence"*.

Andre Pierre Colombat. *The Holocaust in French Film*. Metuchen, NJ: Scarecrow, 1993.

Andrea Walsh. *Women's Film and Female Experience, 1940-1950*. New York: Praeger, 1984.

Andrew Bergman. *We're in the Money: Depression America and its Films*. New York: Columbia University, 1971.

Andrew Dowdy. *The Films of the Fifties: The American State of Mind*. New York: Morrow, 1973.

Andrew Horton and Joan Magretta (eds.) *Modern European Filmmakers and the Art of Adaptation*. New York: Ungar, 1981.

Andrew Sarris. *"You Ain't Heard Nothin' Yet": The American Talking Film, History and Memory, 1927-1949*. New York: Oxford University Press, 1998.

Andrew Sarris. *Politics and Cinema*. New York: Columbia University Press, 1978.

Andrew Sarris. *The American Cinema: Directors and Directions, 1929-1968*. New York: Dutton, 1968.

Ann Fienup-Riordan. *Freeze Frame: Alaska Eskimos in the Movies*. Seattle: University of Washington Press, 2003 [1995].

Ann Powers. *Blacks in American Movies: A Select Bibliography*. Metuchen, NJ: Scarecrow, 1974.

Anna Everett. *Returning the Gaze: A Genealogy of Black Film Criticism, 1909-1949*. Durham, NC: Duke University Press, 2001.

Annette Insdorf. *Indelible Shadows: Film and the Holocaust*. New York: Random House, 1983.

Annette Kuhn (ed.) *The Woman's Companion to International Film*. London: Virago, 1990.

Annette Kuhn. *Women's Pictures: Feminism and Cinema*. London: Verso, 1993 [1982].

Anthony Davies and Stanley Wells (eds.) *Shakespeare and the Moving Image: The Plays on Film and Television*. Cambridge University Press, 1994.

Anthony Schillaci. *Movies and Morals*. Notre Dame: Fides, 1970.

Anthony Slide. *Aspects of American Film Before 1920*. Metuchen, NJ: Scarecrow, 1978.

Anthony Slide. *Early American Cinema*. New York: A.S. Barnes, 1970.

Anthony Slide. *Early Women Directors*. New York: A.S. Barnes, 1977.

Anthony Slide. *The New Historical Dictionary of the American Film Industry*. Lanham, MD: Scarecrow, 1998.

Antonia Lant. *Blackout: Reinventing Women for Wartime British Cinema*. Princeton University Press, 1991.

Antonia Levi. *Samurai from Outer Space: Understanding Japanese Animation*. Chicago: Open Court, 1996.

Antonin J. Liehm. *Closely Watched Films: The Czechoslovakian Experience*. White Plains, NY: International Arts and Sciences, 1974.

Arthur Nolleti and David Desser (eds.) *Reframing Japanese Cinema: Authorship, Genre, History*. Bloomington: Indiana University Press, 1992.

Ashish Rajadhyaskha and Paul Willemen. *Encyclopedia of Indian Cinema*. London: BFI, 1994.

Audie Bock. *Japanese Film Directors*. New York: Kodansha, 1985.

Axel Madsen. *The New Hollywood: American Movies in the 1970s*. New York: Crowell, 1975.

B. Babington and P.W. Evans. *Biblical Epics: Sacred Narrative in the Hollywood Cinema*. Manchester: University Press, 1993.

Barbara Tepa Lupack (ed.) *Take Two: Adapting the Contemporary American Novel to Film*. Bowling Green, OH: Bowling Green State University, 1994.

Barbara Tepa Lupack (ed.) *Vision/Re-vision: Adapting Contemporary American Fiction by Women to Film*. Bowling Green, OH: Bowling Green State University, 1996.

Barbara Tepa Lupack. *Literary Adaptations in Black American Cinema: From Micheaux to Morrison*. Rochester, NY: University of Rochester Press, 2002.

Barnes, John. *The Cinema in England: 1894-1901 (5 Volumes)*. University of Exeter Press, 1997.

Barry Grant (ed.) *Film Genre Reader II*. Austin: University of Texas Press, 1995.

Barry Grant (ed.) *Film Genre Reader*. Austin: University of Texas Press, 1986.

Barry Grant (ed.) *Film Genre: Theory and Criticism*. Metuchen, NJ: Scarecrow, 1977.

Basten, Fred E. (1980). *Glorious Technicolor: The Movies' Magic Rainbow*. Cranbury, NJ: AS Barnes & Company. ISBN 0498023176.

Basten, Fred E. (writer); Peter Jones (director and writer); Angela Lansbury (narrator). (1998). Glorious Technicolor [Documentary]. *Turner Classic Movies.*

Basten, Fred E. *Glorious Technicolor: The Movies' Magic Rainbow.* AS Barnes & Company, 1980.

Benjamin B. Hampton. *A History of the Movies.* New York: Covici, Friede, 1931. [later reprinted as: History of the American Film Industry from its Beginnings to 1931].

Berenice Reynaud. "Chinese Cinema" *OGFS* (543-549).

Bernard B. Scott. *Hollywood Dreams and Biblical Stories.* Minneapolis: Fortress, 1994.

Bernard F. Dick. *The Star-Spangled Screen: The American World War II Film.* Lexington: University of Kentucky Press, 1985.

Bertil O. Osterberg. *Colonial America on Film and Television.* Jefferson, NC: McFarland, 2001.

Beth Olton. *Arthurian Legends on Film and Television.* Jefferson, NC: McFarland, 2000.

Bey Logan. *Hong Kong Action Cinema.* NY, 1996.

Bill Marshall. *Quebec National Cinema.* Montreal: McGill-Queens University Press, 2001.

Bowser, Eileen. *The Transformation of Cinema 1907-1915 (History of the American Cinema, Vol. 2).* Charles Scribner's Sons, 1990.

Brandon French. *On the Verge of Revolt: Women in American Film of the Fifties.* New York: Ungar, 1978.

Brian Garfield. *Western Films: A Complete Guide.* New York: Da Capo, 1982.

Brian McFarlane. *Australian Cinema.* New York: Columbia University, 1988.

Brian McIlroy. *Shooting to Kill: Filmmaking and the 'Troubles' in Northern Ireland.* Trowbridge, Eng.: Flick Books, 1998.

Brian Neve. *Film and Politics in America: A Social Tradition.* New York: Routledge, 1992.

Bruce Kawin. *Faulkner and Film.* New York: Ungar, 1977.

Bryan P. Stone. *Faith and Film: Theological Themes at the Cinema.* St. Louis, MO: Chalice Press, 2000.

Buck Rainey. *The Reel Cowboy: Essays on the Myth in Movies and Literature.* Jefferson, NC: McFarland, 1996.

C.D. Peavy. "The Secularized Christ in Contemporary Cinema" *Journal of Popular Film and Television.* 3/2, p. 137-155.

Carl J. Mora. *Mexican Cinema: Reflections of a Society, 1896-1988*. Revised ed. Berkeley: University of California Press, 1989.

Casetti, Francesco (1999). *Theories of Cinema, 1945-1995*. Austin, TX: University of Texas Press. ISBN 0292712073.

Charles Higham and Joel Greenberg. *Hollywood in the Forties*. New York: A.S. Barnes, 1968.

Charles Higham. *Hollywood Cameramen: Sources of Light*. Bloomington: Indiana University Press, 1970.

Charles Higham. *The Art of the American Film*. Garden City, NJ: Doubleday, 1973.

Charles Musser. *The Emergence of Cinema: The American Screen to 1907*. New York: Scribner's, 1990 (History of the American Cinema; 1).

Charles Ramirez Berg. *Cinema of Solitude: A Critical Study of Mexican Film, 1967-1983*. Austin: University of Texas Press, 1992.

Charles Ramirez Berg. *Latino Images in Film: Stereotypes, Subversion, Resistance*. Austin: University of Texas Press, 2002.

Charles W. Eckert (ed.) *Focus on Shakespearean Films*. Englewood Cliffs, NJ: Prentice-Hall, 1972.

Charlie Keil. *Early American Cinema in Transition: Story, Style, and Filmmaking, 1907-1913*. Madison: University of Wisconsin Press, 2001.

Charlotte Brunsdon (ed.) *Films for Women*. London: BFI, 1986.

Chon A. Noriega (ed.) *Visible Nations: Latin American Cinema and Video*. Minneapolis: University of Minnesota Press, 2000.

Chon Noriega (ed.) *Chicanos and Film: Representation and Resistance*. Minneapolis, MN: University of Minnesota, 1992.

Chris Berry (ed.) *Perspectives on Chinese Cinema*. London: BFI, 1991.

Chris Berry. "China Before 1949" *OHWC* (409-413).

Christopher Deacy. *Screen Christologies: Redemption and the Medium of Film*. Cardiff: University of Wales, 2001.

Christopher E. Gittings. *Canadian National Cinema: Ideology, Difference and Representation*. London: Routledge, 2002.

Clayton R. Koppes and Gregory D. Black. *Hollywood Goes to War: How Politics, Profits and Propaganda Shaped World War II Movies*. New York: Free Press, 1987.

Clive Hirschhorn. *The Warner Brothers Story*. New York: Crown, 1979.

Clive Hirschorn. *The Columbia Story*. New York: Crown, 1989.

Clive Hirschorn. *The Universal Story*. New York: Crown, 1983.

Clive Marsh, *et al.* (eds.) *Explorations in Theology and Film: Movies and Meaning*. Blackwell, 1998.

Coco Fusco (ed.) *Reviewing Histories: Selections from New Latin American Cinema*. Buffalo: Hallwalls, 1987.

Colin Crisp. *The Classic French Cinema, 1930-1960*. Bloomington: Indiana University, 1993.

Colin Shindler. *Hollywood in Crisis: Cinema and the American Society, 1929-1939*. Routledge, 1996.

Cook, David A., *A History of Narrative Film*, 2nd edition. New York: W.W. Norton, 1990.

Craig W. Campbell. *Reel America and World War I: A Comprehensive Filmography and History of Motion Pictures in the United States, 1914 to 1920*. Jefferson, NC: McFarland, 1985.

D. Graham. "Images of Christ in Recent Film" in *Images of Christ: Ancient and Modern*. Sheffield: Academic Press, 1997.

D.B. Jones. *Movies and Memoranda: An Interpretive History of the National Film Board of Cananda*. Ottawa: Canadian Film Institute, 1981.

Dana Polan. *Power and Paranoia: History, Narrative and the American Cinema, 1940-1950*. New York: Columbia University Press, 1986.

Daniel Curran. *Guide to American Cinema, 1965-1995*. Greenwood, 1998.

Daniel J. Goulding. *Five Filmmakers: Tarkovsky, Forman, Polanski, Szabo, Makavejev*. Bloomington: Indiana University Press, 1994.

Daniel J. Goulding. *Post New Wave Cinema in the Soviet Union and Eastern Europe*. Bloomington: Indiana University Press, 1989.

Daniel J. Leab. *From Sambo to Superspade: The Black Experience in Motion Pictures*. Boston: Houghton Mifflin, 1975.

Daniel Lopez. *Films by Genre: 775 Categories, Styles, Trends and Movements. Defined with a Filmography for Each*. Jefferson, NC: McFarland, 1993.

David A. Black. *Law in Film: Resonance and Representation*. Urbana: University of Illinois Press, 1999.

David A. Cook. *Lost Illusions: American Cinema in the Shadow of Watergate and Vietnam, 1970-1979*. New York: Scribner's, 2000. (History of the American Cinema; 9).

David Austin. *"Continental Westerns" Films and Filming*. 17 (July 1971), 36-44.

David Boardwell, Janet Saiger and Kristin Thompson. *The Classical Hollywood Cinema: Film Style and Mode of Production to 1960*. New York: Columbia University, 1985.

David Bordwell. *Planet Hong Kong: Popular Cinema and the Art of Entertainment*. Cambridge, MA: Harvard, 2000.

David Desser. *Eros Plus Massacre: An Introduction to the Japanese New Wave Cinema*.

David E. James. *Allegories of Cinema: American Film in the Sixties*. Princeton, NJ: Princeton University, 1989.

David H. Mould. *American Newsfilm, 1914-1919: The Underexposed War*. New York: Garland, 1983.

David L. Parker and Esther Siegel. *Guide to Dance in Film*. Detroit: Gale, 1978.

David Meeker. *Jazz in the Movies: A Guide to Jazz Musicians 1917-1977*. New Rochelle, NY: Arlington House, 1977.

David Overbey (ed.) *Springtime in Italy: A Reader on Neorealism*. London: Talisman, 1978.

David Robinson. *Hollywood in the Twenties*. New York: A.S. Barnes, 1968.

David Trottier (1998). *The Screenwriter's Bible: A Complete Guide to Writing, Formatting, and Selling Your Script*. Silman-James Press. ISBN 1-879505-44-4. Paperback.

Dawn B. Sova. *Women in Hollywood: From Vamp to Studio Head*. NY: Fromm International, 1998.

Denis Gifford. *Books and Plays in Films, 1896-1915: Literary, Theatrical and Artistic Sources of the First Twenty Years of Motion Pictures*. Jefferson, NC: McFarland, 1991.

Dennis Washburn and Carole Cavanaugh (eds.) *Word and Image in Japanese Cinema*. Cambridge University Press, 2001.

Derek Elley. *The Epic Film: Myth and History*. London: Routledge and Kegan Paul, 1984.

Diane Jacobs. *Hollywood Renaissance*. New York: A.S. Barnes, 1977.

Dmytryk, Edward. *On Film Editing: An Introduction to the Art of Film Construction*, Boston: Focal Press, 1984.

Donald Bogle. *Toms, Coons, Mulatoes, Mammies and Blacks: An Interpretive History of Blacks in American Films*. New Expanded ed. New York: Continuum, 1989 [1973].

Donald Crafton. *The Talkies: American Cinema's Transition to Sound, 1926-1931*. New York: Scribner's, 1997. (History of the American Cinema; 4).

Donald Richie. *A Hundred Years of Japanese Film*. Tokyo: Kodansha, 2001.

Donald Stewart Hull. *Film in the Third Reich*. Berkeley: University of California, 1969.

Donald W. McCaffrey and Christopher P. Jacobs. *Guide to the Silent Years of American Cinema*. Greenwood, 1999.

Dorothy B. Jones. "Hollywood Goes to War" *Nation* (January 27, 1945), 93-95.

Douglad Brode. *The Films of the Fiftes: Sunset Boulevard to on the Beach*. Secaucus, NJ: Citadel, 1976.

Douglas Brode. *The Films of the Sixties*. Secaucus, NJ: Citadel, 1980.

Douglas Brodie. *The Films of the Eighties*. New York: Citadel, 1991.

Douglas Gomery. *Shared Pleasures: A History of Movie Presentation in the United States*. Madison: University of Wisconsin Press, 1992.

Douglas Gomery. *The Hollywood Studio System*. New York: St. Martin's, 1986.

E. Ann Kaplan (ed.) *Women in Film Noir*. New ed. London: BFI, 1998.

E. Ann Kaplan. *Women and Film: Both Sides of the Camera*. New York: Methuen, 1983.

Early Cinema—Primitives and Pioneers. BFI Video 2005 (Compilation of early films up to 1908).

Eastman, S.T., and Ferguson, D.A. (2006). Media Programming: Strategies and Practices (7th ed.), Belmont, CA: Wadsworth.

Ed Guerrero. Framing Blackness: *The African American Image in Film*. Philadelphia: Temple University Press, 1993.

Ed Sikov. *Laughing Hysterically: American Screen Comedy of the 1950's*. New York: Columbia University Press.

Eddie Sammons. *Shakespeare: A Hundred Years on Film*. London: Shepheard-Walwyn, 2000.

Edward Buscombe (ed.) *The BFI Companion to the Western*. New York: Atheneum, 1988.

Edward Mapp. *Blacks in American Films: Today and Yesterday*. Metuchen, NJ: Scarecrow, 1972.

Eileen Bowser. *The Transformation of Cinema: 1907-1915*. New York: Scribner's, 1990 (History of the American Cinema; 2).

Elissa J. Rashkin. *Women Filmmakers in Mexico: The Country in Which We Dream*. Austin: University of Texas Press, 2001.

Ellen Baskin and Andrew G.S. Mayes (eds.) *Enser's Filmed Books and Plays: A List of Books and Plays from Which Films have been Made, 1928-2001*. Ashgate, 2003.

Ellen Summerfield and Sandra Lee. *Seeing the Big Picture: Exploring American Cultures on Film*. Yarmouth, ME: Intercultural Press, 2001.

Ellen Summerfield. *Crossing Cultures Through Film*. Yarmouth, ME: Intercultural Press, 1993.

Ellis, J. (2000). Seeing Things: Television in the Age of Uncertainty, London: I.B. Tauris.

Emanuel Levy. *Cinema of Outsiders: The Rise of American Independent Film*. New York University Press, 1999.

Eric Barnouw and S. Krishnaswany. *Indian Film*. Revised edition. New York: Columbia University Press, 1980.

Eric Rentschler (ed.) *German Literature and Film: Adaptations and Transformations*. New York: Methuen, 1986.

Erich Leon Harris. *African-American Screen-writers Now: Conversations with Hollywood 's B!ack Pack*. Los Angeles: Silman-James Press, 1996.

Erwin Leiser. *Nazi Cinema*. New York: Macmillan, 1968.

Esther Yau. "China After the Revolution" *OHWC* (693-704).

Ethan Mordden. *Medium Cool: The Movies of the 1960's*. New York: Knopf, 1990.

Evan William Cameron (ed.) *Sound and the Cinema: The Coming of Sound to American Film*. New York: Redgrave, 1980.

Faber, Liz and Walters, Helen (2003). *Animation Unlimited: Innovative Short Films Since 1940*. London: Laurence King, in association with Harper Design International. ISBN 1856693465.

Flashback: Films and History. Special issue of: *Cultures* 2:1 (1974).

Frank M. Lawrence. *Hemmingway at the Movies*. Jackson: University of Mississippi, 1981.

Frank Manchel. *Cameras West*. Englewood Cliffs, NJ: Prentice-Hall, 1971.

Frederic Dannen and Barry Long. *Hong Kong Babylon: An Insider's Guide to the Hollywood of the East*. NY: Miramax/Hyperion, 1997.

Frederic Jameson. *The Geopolitical Aesthetic: Cinema and Space in the World System*. London: BFI, 1992.

G. Ortiz. "Jesus at the Movies: Cinematic Representation of the Christ-Figure" *The Month* (Dec. 1994), p. 491-497.

G. William Jones. *Sunday Night at the Movies*. Richmond, VA: John Knox, 1967.

Garth Jowett. *Film, the Democratic Art: A Social History of American Film*. Boston: Little, Brown, 1976.

Gary A. Smith. *Epic Films: Cast, Credits and Commentary on Over 250 Historical Spectacle Movies*. Jefferson, NC: McFarland, 1991.

Gary Crowdus. "The Screening of Irish History" *Cineaste* 22:4 (1997), 14-19.

Gary D. Keller. *A Biographical Handbook of Hispanics and United States Film*. Tempe, AZ: Bilingual Press, 1997.

Gary Null. *Black Hollywood: The Negro in Motion Pictures*. Secaucus, NJ: Citadel, 1975.

Gary Solomon. *The Motion Picture Prescription: Watch This Movie and Call Me in the Morning*. Santa Rosa, CA: Aslan Publishing, 1995. ["200 movies to help you heal life's problems"].

Gene Brown. *Movie Time: A Chronology of Hollywood and the Movie Industry from its Beginnings to the Present*. New York: Macmillan, 1995.

Gene D. Philips. *Conrad and the Cinema: The Art of Adaptation*. New York: P. Lang, 1997.

Gene Fernett. *American Film Studios: An Historical Encyclopedia*. Jefferson, NC: McFarland, 1988.

Gene M. Moore. *Conrad on Film*. New York: Cambridge University Press, 1997.

Geoff Andrew. *Stranger Than Paradise: Maverick Film-makers in Recent American Cinema*. New York: Limelight Editions, 1999.

George Aichele and Richard Walsh (eds.) *Screening Scripture: Intertextual Connections Between Scripture and Film*. Harrisburg, PA: Trinity Press International. 2002.

George N. Fenin and William K. Everson. "The European Western" *Film Culture* 20 (1959), 59-72.

George N. Fenin and William K. Everson. *The Western: From Silents to the Seventies*. NY: Grossman, 1973.

George Sempsel (ed.) *Chinese Film: The State of the Art in the People's Republic*. NY: Praeger, 1987

George Sempsel, Hou Jianpin, Xia Hong (eds.) *Chinese Film Theory: A Guide to the New Era*. NY: Praeger, 1987.

Gerald E. Forshey. *American Religious and Biblical Spectacular Films*. Westport, CT: Praeger, 1992.

Gerald Weales. *Canned Goods as Caviar: American Film Comedies of the 1930s*. Chicago: University of Chicago Press, 1985.

Gilles Poitras. *The Anime Companion: What's Japanese in Japanese Animation*. Berkeley, CA: Stone Bridge, 1998.

Ginette Vincendeau (ed.) *The Encyclopedia of European Cinema*. London: Cassell, 1995.

Giuliana Bruno and Maria Nadotti (eds.) *Off Screen: Women and Film in Italy*. London: Routledge, 1988.

Giuliana Muscio. *Hollywood's New Deal*. Philadelphia: Temple University Press, 1997.

Glen Man. *Radical Visions: American Film Renaissance, 1967-1976*. Westport, CT: Greenwood, 1994.

Glen O. and Krin Gabbard. *Psychiatry and the Cinema*. 2nd ed. Washington, DC: American Psychiatric Press, 1999. *Glorious Technicolor*; directed by Peter Jones. Based on the book (above); written by Basten & Jones. Documentary, (1998).

Gordon Gow. *Hollywood in the Fifties*. New York: A.S. Barnes, 1971.

Gordon Hendricks. *Beginnings of the Biograph: the Story of the Invention of the Mutoscope and the Biograph and Their Supplying Cameras*. 1964.

Gordon Hendricks. *The Kinetoscope: America 's First Commercially Successful Motion Picture Exhibitor*. 1966.

Gorham Kindem (ed.) *The American Movie Industry: The Business of Motion Pictures*. Carbondale: University of Illinois Press, 1982.

Greg Merritt. *Celluloid Mavericks: A History of American Independent Film*. New York: Thunder's Mouth, 2000.

Gregory Battcock (ed.) *The New American Cinema*. New York: Dutton, 1967.

Gregory D. Black. "The Production Code and the Hollywood Film Industry, 1930-1940", *Film History* 3:2 (1989), 167-189.

Gretchen Bataille and Charles L.P. Silet (eds.). *The Pretend Indians: Images of Native Americans in the Movies*. Ames: Iowa State University, 1980.

Gretchen Bataille and Charles L.P. Silet. *Images of American Indians on Film: An Annotated Bibliography*. New York: Garland, 1985.

Grzegorz Balski. *Directory of Eastern European Filmmakers and Films 1945-1991*. Trwobridge: Flicks Books, 1992.

Guy Austin. *Contemporary French Cinema*. Manchester: Manchester University Press, 1996.

Hagener, Malte and Töteberg, Michael (2002). *Film: An International Bibliography*. Stuttgart: Metzler. ISBN 3476015238.

Hamid Dabashi. *Close Up: Iranian Cinema, Past, Present and Future*. New York: Verso, 2001.

Hanns Zischler. *Kafka Goes to the Movies*. Chicago: University of Chicago, 2003.

Harris Ross. *Film as Literature, Literature as Film: An Introduction to and Bibliography of Film's Relationship to Literature*. New York: Greenwood, 1987.

Harry M. Geduld. *The Birth of the Talkies: From Edison to Jolson*. Bloomington: Indiana University Press, 1975.

Henry T. Sampson. *Blacks in Black and White: A Source Book on Black Films*. Metuchen, NJ: Scarecrow, 1977.

Hill, John and Gibson, Pamela Church (1998). *The Oxford Guide to Film Studies*. Oxford; New York: Oxford University Press. ISBN 0198711247.

Howard Good and Michael J. Dillon. *Media Ethics Goes to the Movies*. Westport, CT: Praeger, 2002.

Howard Good. *Girl Reporter: Gender, Journalism, and the Movies*. Lanham, MD: Scarecrow, 1998.

Howard Good. *Outcasts: The Image of Journalists in Contemporary Film*. Metuchen, NJ: Scarecrow, 1989.

Howard Good. *The Drunken Journalist: The Biography of a Stereotype*. Lanham, MD: Scarecrow, 2000.

I.C. Jarvie. "*Case Study: Films About Marriage*" *Movies as Social Criticism*. Metuchen, NJ: Scarecrow, 1978 (45-81).

I.C. Jarvie. *Movies and Society*. New York: Basic Books, 1970.

I.C. Jarvie. *Movies as Social Criticism*. Metuchen, NJ: Scarecrow, 1978.

Ian Jarvie. *Hollywood's Overseas Campaign: The North Atlantic Movie Trade, 1920-1950*. New York: Cambridge University Press, 1992.

Irving Schneider. "Images on the Mind: Psychiatry in the Commercial Film." *The American Journal of Psychiatry*, 134 (1977) 613-620.

Istvan Nemeskurty. *Word and Image: History of the Hungarian Cinema*. 2nd ed. Corvina, 1974.

Ivan Butler. *Religion in the Cinema*. New York: A.S. Barnes, 1969.

Ivan Butler. *The War Film*. New York: A.S. Barnes, 1974.

J.C. Bulman and H.R. Coursen (eds.) *Shakespeare on Television: An Anthology of Essays and Reviews*. University Press of New England, 1988.

Jacinda Read. *The New Avengers: Feminism, Femininity and the Rape Revenge Cycle*. Manchester University Press, 2000.

Jack Boozer. *Career Movies: American Business and the Success Mystique*. Austin: University of Texas Press, 2002.

Jack G. Shaheen (ed.) *Nuclear War Films*. Carbondale: Southern Illinois University Press, 1978.

Jack G. Shaheen (ed.) *Nuclear War Films*. Carbondale: Southern Illinois University Press, 1978.

Jack J. Jorgens. *Shakespeare on Film*. Bloomington: University of Indiana Press, 1977.

Jack Nachbar (ed.) *Focus on the Western*. Englewood Cliffs, NJ: Prentice-Hall, 1974.

Jack Nachbar. *Western Films: An Annotated Critical Bibliography*. New York: Garland, 1975.

Jack Spears. *"The Indian on the Screen" Hollywood: The Golden Era*. New York: A.S. Barnes, 1971 (361-396).

Jack Spears. *The Civil War on the Screen and Other Essays*. New York: A.S. Barnes, 1977.

Jack Temple Kirby. *Media Made Dixie: The South in American Imagination*. Baton Rouge, LA: Louisiana State University Press, 1978.

Jack, G. Shaheen. *Reel Bad Arabs: How Hollywood Vilifies a People*. New York: Olive Branch Press, 2001.

Jackie Stacy. *Star Gazing: Hollywood Cinema and Female Spectatorship*. London: Routledge, 1994.

Jacquelyn Kilpatrick. *Celluloid Indians: Native Americans and Films*. Lincoln: University of Nebraska, 1999.

James A. Wall. *Church and Cinema: A Way of Viewing Films*. Grand Rapids, MI: Eerdmans, 1971.

James Bernardoni. *The New Hollywood: What the Movies Did with the New Freedoms of the Seventies*. Jefferson, NC: McFarland, 1991.

James Monaco. *American Film Now*. New York: New American Library, 1979.

James Monaco. *The New Wave; Truffaut, Godard, Chabrol, Rohmer, Rivette*. New York: Oxford, 1976.

James P. Murray. *To Find an Image: Black Films from Uncle Tom to Super Fly*. Indianapolis: Bobbs-Merrill, 1973.

James Robert Parish and Micahel Pitts. *The Great Western Pictures*. Metuchen, NJ: Scarecrow, 1976.

Jami Bernard (1995). *Quentin Tarantino: The Man and His Movies.* HarperCollins Publishers. ISBN 0-002556-44-8. Paperback.

Jams MacKillop (ed.) *Contemporary Irish Cinema: From The Quiet Man to Dancing at Lughnasa.* Syracuse University Press, 1999.

Jan-Christopher Horak (ed.) *Lovers of Cinema: The First American Film Avant-garde, 1919-1945.* Madison: University of Wisconsin Press, 1995.

Jane Austin at the Movies. Washington, PA: Washington and Jefferson College, 1997.

Janet Staiger (ed.) *The Studio System.* New Brunswick, NJ: Rutgers University Press, 1995.

Janet Todd (ed.) *Women and Film.* New York: Holmes and Meier, 1988.

Janice R. Welch. *Film Archetypes: Sisters, Mistresses, Mothers and Daughters.* New York: Arno, 1978.

Jay Leyda. *Dianying: An Account of Films and the Film Audience in China.* Cambridge, MA: MIT Press, 1972.

Jay Leyda. *Kino: A History of the Russian and Soviet Film.* 3rd ed. Princeton, NJ: Princeton University, 1983.

Jeanine Basinger. *The World War II Combat Film: Anatomy of a Genre.* New York: Columbia University Press, 1986.

Jeanne Belancourt. *Women in Focus.* Dayton, Ohio: Pflaum, 1974.

Jeffrey Eagan Welch. *Literature and Film: An Annotated Bibliography, 1900-1977.* New York: Garland, 1981.

Jeffrey Egan Welch. *Literature and Film: An Annotated Bibliography, 1978-1988.* New York: Garland, 1993.

Jenni Calder. *There Must be a Lone Ranger: The American West in Film and in Reality.* London: Hamish Hamilton, 1974.

Jenny Lion (ed.) *Magnetic North* [*Canadian Experimental Video*]. Minneapolis: University of Minnesota Press, 2000 [Catalog of an exhibition of 40 videos shown at Walker Art Center (Minneapolis) 10/00 and Plug In (Winnipeg, Manitoba) 11/00].

Jeremy M. Devine. *Vietnam at 24 Frames per Second: A Critical and Thematic Analysis of Over 400 Films about the Vietnam War.* Austin: University of Texas Press, 1999.

Jerome F. Shapiro. *Atomic Bomb Cinema: The Apocalyptic Imagination on Film.* New York: Routledge, 2002.

Jerry Vermilye. *The Films of the Thirties.* Secaucus, NJ: Citadel, 1982.

Jerry Vermilye. *The Films of the Twenties.* Secaucus, NJ: Citadel, 1985.

Jill Forbes. *The Cinema in France after the New Wave.* Bloomington, IN: Indiana University, 1992.

Jill Rubenson Fenton (ed.) *Women Writers From Page to Screen*. New York: Garland, 1990.

Jim Hiller (ed.) *American Independent Cinema: A Sight and Sound Reader*. London: BFI, 2001.

Jim Kitses. *Horizons West: Anthony Mann, Budd Boetticher, Sam Peckinpah: Studies of Authorship within the Western*. Bloomington: Indiana University Press, 1970. (Cinema One; 12)

Jim Pines. *Blacks in Film: A Survey of Racial Themes and Images in the American Film*. London: Studio Vista, 1975.

Jo Fox. *Filming Women in the Third Reich*. Oxford: Berg, 2000.

Joan Mellen. *Voices from the Japanese Cinema*. New York: Liveright, 1975.

Joan Mellen. *Women and Their Sexuality in the New Film*. New York: Horizon Press, 1973.

Joe Morella, Edward Z. Epstein and John Griggs. *The Films of World War II*. Secaucus, NJ: Citadel, 1973.

Joe Saltzman. *Frank Capra and the Image of the Journalist in American Film*. Los Angeles: Norman Lear Center, The Annenberg School for Communication, 2002.

Joel W. Martin and Conrad E. Ostwalt (eds.). *Screening the Sacred: Religion, Myth and Ideology in Popular American Film*. Boulder, CO: Westview, 1995.

John A. Lent. *The Asian Film Industry*. Austin: University of Texas Press, 1990.

John Baxter. *Hollywood in the Sixties*. New York: A.S. Barnes, 1972.

John Baxter. *Hollywood in the Thirties*. New York: A.S. Barnes, 1968.

John C. Tibberts and James M. Welsh. *Novels into Film: The Encyclopedia of Movies Adapted from Books*. New York: Facts on File, 1998.

John Cooper and Carl Skade (eds.) *Celluloid and Symbols*. Philadelphia: Fortress, 1970.

John D.H. Downing (ed.) *Film and Politics in the Third World*. Brooklyn, NY: Autonomedia, 1987.

John Denvir (ed.) *Legal Reelism: Movies as Legal Texts*. Urbana: University of Illinois Press, 1996.

John Douglas Eames. *The MGM Story*. New York: Crown, 1976.

John Douglas Eames. *The Paramount Story*. New York: Crown, 1985.

John Dowling. *War/Peace: Film Guide*. Chicago: World Without War Publications, 1980.

John E. O'Connor and Martin A. Jackson (eds.) *American History/ American Film: Interpreting the Hollywood Image*. New York: Unger, 1979.

John G. Cawelti. *The Six-Gun Mystique*. Bowling Green: Bowling Green University Popular Press, 1971.

John H. Lenihan. *Showdown: Confronting Modern America in the Western Film*. Urbana: University of Illinois, 1980.

John Hofsess. *InnerViews: Ten Canadian Film-makers*. Toronto: McGraw-Hill Ryerson, 1975.

John Hora, *The American Cinematographer Manual*, 9th Edition.

John King. *Magical Reels: A History of Cinema in Latin America*. London: Verso, 1990.

John L. Mason. *The Identity Crisis Theme in American Feature Films, 1960-1969*. New York: Arno, 1977.

John Mueller. *Dance Film Directory*. Princeton, NJ: Princeton Book Co., 1979.

John Pierson. *Spike, Mike, Slackers and Dykes: A Guided Tour Across a Decade of American Independent Cinema*. New York: Miramax/ Hyperion, 1997.

John R. May (ed.) *Image and Likeness: Religious Visions in American Film Classics*. Paulist, 1992.

John R. May (ed.) *New Image of Religious Film*. Sheed and Ward, 1996.

John R. May and Michael Bird (eds.) *Religion in Film*. Knoxville: University of Tennessee, 1982.

John Sandford. *The New German Cinema*. Totowa, NJ: Barnes and Noble, 1980.

John W. Nelson. *Your God is Alive and Well and Appearing in Popular Culture*. Philadelphia: Westminster, 1976.

Jon Lewis (ed.) *The End of Cinema As We Know It: American Films in the Nineties*. New York University Press, 2002.

Jon Lewis (ed.) *The New American Cinema*. Durham: Duke University Press, 1998.

Jon Solomon. *The Ancient World in Cinema*. Rev. and expanded ed. New Haven: Yale, 2001.

Jon Tuska. *The American West in Films: Critical Approaches to the Western*. Westport, CT: Greenwood Press, 1985.

Jon Tuska. *The Filming of the West*. Garden City, NY: Doubleday, 1976.

Jonathan Clements and Helen McCarthy. *The Anime Encyclopedia: A Guide to Japanese Animation Since 1917*. Berkeley, CA: Stone Bridge Press, 2001.

Jonathan Rosenbaum. *Movies as Politics*. Berkeley: University of California Press, 1997.

Joseph L. Anderson and Donald Richie. *The Japanese Film*. Expanded ed. Princeton, NJ: Princeton University Press, 1982.

Joseph Skvorecky. *All the Bright Young Men and Women: A Personal History of the Czech Cinema*. Toronto: Peter Martin, 1971.

Juan A. Suarez. *Bike Boys, Drag Queens and Superstars: Avant-garde, Mass Culture and Gay Identities in the 1960s Underground Cinema*. Bloomington: Indiana University Press, 1996.

Judith H. Haag and Hillis, R. Cole (1980). *The Complete Guide to Standard Script Formats: The Screenplay*. CMC Publishing. ISBN 0-929583-00-0. Paperback.

Julian Smith. *Looking Away: Hollywood and Vietnam*. New York: Scribner's, 1975.

Julianne Burton (ed.) *Cinema and Social Change in Latin America: Conversations with Filmmakers*. Austin: University of Texas, 1986.

June Yip. "Taiwanese New Cinema" *OHWC* (711-713).

Karyn Kay and Gerald Peary (eds.) *Women and the Cinema: A Critical Anthology*. New York: Dutton, 1977.

Katherine Monk. *Weird Sex and Snowshoes, and Other Canadian Film Phenomena*. Vancouver, BC: Raincoast Books, 2001.

Kathryn Bernheimer. *The 50 Greatest Jewish Movies: A Critics Ranking of the Very Best*. Seacaucus, NJ: Birch Lane, 1998.

Kathy M. Howlett. *Framing Shakespeare on Film*. Athens: Ohio University Press, 2000.

Kay Sloan. *The Loud Silents: Origins of the Social Problem Film*. Chicago: University of Illinois Press, 1988.

Kaye Sullivan. *Films For, By and About Women*. Metuchen, NJ: Scarecrow, 1980.

Keiko I. McDonald. *From Book to Screen: Modern Japanese Literature in Films*. Armonk, NY: Sharpe, 2000.

Keiko McDonald. *Japanese Classical Theater in Films*. Farleigh Dickinson University Press, 1994.

Ken D. Jones and Arthur F. McClure. *Hollywood at War: The American Motion Picture and World War II*. New York: A.S. Barnes, 1973.

Ken Jones and Arthur McClure. *Hollywood at War: The American Motion Picture and World War II*. New York: Castle, 1973.

Ken Wlaschin. *Opera on Screen: A Guide to 100 Years of Films and Videos*. Beechwood, 1997.

Kenneth M. Cameron. *America on Film: Hollywood and American History*. New York: Continuum, 1997.

Kenneth MacGowan. *Behind the Screen: The History and Techniques of the Motion Picture*. New York: Delacorte, 1965.

Kenneth R.M. Short (ed.) *Feature Films as History*. Knoxville: University of Tennessee Press, 1981.

Kenneth Rothwell and Annabelle Henkin Melzer. *Shakespeare on Film: An International Filmography and Videography*. Neal-Shuman, 1990.

Kenneth Rothwell. *A History of Shakespeare on Screen: A Century of Film and Television*. New York: Cambridge University Press, 1999.

Kerry Segrave. *American Films Abroad: Hollywood's Domination of the World's Movie Screens from the 1890s to the Present*. Jefferson, NC: McFarland, 1997.

Kevin Brownlow. *The Parade's Gone By*. New York: Ballantine, 1968.

Kevin Rockett, Luke Gibbons and John Hill (eds.) *Cinema and Ireland*. Syracuse University Press, 1988.

King, Geoff (2002). *New Hollywood Cinema: An Introduction*. New York: Columbia University Press. ISBN 0231127596.

Klaus Kreimeier. *The UFA Story: A History of Germany's Greatest Film Company, 1918-1945*. New York: Hill and Wang, 1996.

Klaus Phillips (ed.) *New German Filmmakers, From Oberhausen Through the 1970's*. New York: Ungar, 1984.

Kristin Thompson. *Exporting Entertainment: America in the World Film Market, 1907-1934*. London: BFI, 1985.

Kuan-hsiang Chen. "Taiwanese New Cinema" *OGFS* (557-561).

Kwok-kan Tam and Wimal Dissanayake. *New Chinese Cinema*. NY: Oxford University, 1998. [Chen Kaige, Zhang Yimou, Tian Zhuangzhuang, Hou Hsiao-hsien, Edward Yang, Stanley Kwan].

Lalit Mohn Joshi (ed.) *Bollywood: Popular Indian Cinema*. London: Dakini, 2001.

Lance Pettitt. *Screening Ireland: Film and Television Representation*. New York: St. Martin's Press, 2000.

Larry Ceplair and Steven Englund. *The Inquisition in Hollywood: Politics in the Film Community, 1930-1960*. Garden City: Anchor Press, 1980.

Larry Langman. *A Guide to Silent Westerns*. New York: Greenwood Press, 1992.

Larry Langman. *American Film Cycles: The Silent Era*. Westport, CT: Greenwood, 1998.

Larry Langman. *The Media in the Movies: A Catalog of American Journalism Films, 1900-1996*. Jefferson, NC: McFarland, 1998. [annotated list of 1025 films, arranged alphabetically by title, with a personal name index].

Larry Langman. *Writers of the American Screen: A Guide to Film Adaptations of American and Foreign Literary Works*. New York: Garland, 1986.

Larry W. Ward. *The Motion Picture Goes to War: The U.S. Government Film Effort During World War I*. Ann Arbor, MI: UMI, 1985.

Lea Jacobs. *The Wages of Sin: Censorship and the Fallen Woman Film, 1928-1942*. Berkeley: University of California Press, 1997.

Ledoux, Trish & Ranney, Doug & Patten, Fred (1997). *Complete Anime Guide: Japanese Animation Film Directory and Resource Guide*. Issaquah, WA: Tiger Mountain Press. ISBN 0964954257.

Lee Server. *Asian Pop Cinema: Bombay to Tokyo*. San Francisco: Chronicle Books, 1999.

Leif Furhammer and Folke Isaksson. *Politics and Film*. New York: Praeger, 1971 [1968].

Leonard J. Leff and Jerrold L. Simmons. *The Dame in the Kimono: Hollywood, Censorship and the Production Code from the 1920s to the 1960s*. New York: Grove Wiedenfeld, 1990.

Les Adams and Buck Rainey. *Shoot-em Ups: The Complete Reference Guide to Westerns of the Sound Era*. New Rochelle, NY: Arlington House, 1978.

Les and Barbara Keyser. *Hollywood and the Catholic Church: The Image of Roman Catholicism in American Movies*. Chicago: Loyola University Press, 1984.

Les Keyser. *Hollywood in the Seventies*. San Diego: A.S. Barnes, 1981.

Leslie Midkift DeBauche. *Reel Patriotism: The Movies and World War I*. Madison: University of Wisconsin Press, 1997.

Lester D. Friedman. *The Jewish Image in American Film*. Seacaucus, NJ: Citadel, 1987.

Lester Friedman (ed.) *Unspeakable Images: Ethnicity and the American Cinema*. Urbana: University of Illinois Press, 1991.

Lewis Jacob. *The Rise of American Film: A Critical History*. With an Essay Experimental Cinema in America, 1921-1947. New York: Teachers College Press, 1968. [main text covers up to 1939].

Lewis Jacobs. "World War II and the American Film" *Cinema Journal* 7 (Winter 1967-8) 1-21.

Li Cheuk-to. "Popular Cinema in Hong Kong" *OHWC* (704-711).

Linda Dittmar and Gene Michaud (eds.) *From Hanoi to Hollywood: The Vietnam War in American Film*. New Brunswick, NJ: Rutgers University Press, 1990.

Linda Troost and Sayre Greenfield (eds.) *Jane Austin in Hollywood*. 2nd ed. Lexington: University Press of Kentucky, 2001.

Lindsay Patterson (ed.) *Black Films and Film-makers: A Comprehensive Anthology From Stereotype to Superhero*. New York: Dodd, Mead, 1975.

Lisa Odham Stokes and Michael Hoover. *City on Fire: Hong Kong Cinema*. London, 1999.

Lloyd Baugh. *Imaging the Divine: Jesus and Christ-Figures in Film*. Kansas City: Sheed and Ward, 1997.

Lorne M. Buchman. *Still in Movement: Shakespeare on Screen*. Oxford University Press, 1991.

Lotte Eisner. *The Haunted Screen; Expressionism in the German Cinema*. Berkeley: University of California, 1969.

Louis K. Greiff and D.H. *Lawrence: Fifty Years on Film*. Carbondale: Southern Illinois University Press, 2001.

Louis Spain. *Dance on Camera: A Guide to Dance Films and Videos*. Scarecrow, 1998.

Luda Schnitzer and Jean, and Marcel Martin (ed.) *Cinema in Revolution: The Heroic Era of Soviet Film*. New York: Hill and Wang, 1973.

Lynda E. Boose and Richard Burt (eds.) *Shakespeare, the Movie: Popularizing the Plays on Film, TV and Video*. London: Routledge, 1997.

Lynne Arany, Tom Dyja, Gary Goldsmith. *The Reel List: A Categorical Companion to Over 2,000 Memorable Films*. New York: Delta, 1995.

M. Joyce Baker. *Images of Women in Film: The War Years, 1941-1945*. Ann Arbor, MI: UMI, 1980.

M. Singer. "Cinema Savior: Portrayals of Christ on Film" *Film Comment* 24/5 (1988), p. 44-49.

Manny Farber. "*Movies in Wartime*" *New Republic* (January 3, 1944), 16-20.

Manthia Diawara (ed.) *Black American Cinema*. London: Routledge, 1993.

Manthia Diawara. African Cinema: Politics and Culture. Bloomington: Indiana University Press, 1992.

Marc Ferro (1988). *Cinema and History*. Detroit: Wayne State University.

Marc Sigoloff. *The Films of the Seventies: A Filmography of American, British and Canadian Films, 1970-1979.*

Marcia J. Citron. *Opera on Screen*. Yale University Press, 2000.

Margaret R. Miles. *Seeing is Believing: Religion and Values in the Movies*. Boston: Beacon, 1996.

Maria Wyke. *Projecting the Past: Ancient Rome, Cinema and History*. New York: Routledge, 1997.

Marilyn Singer and John G. Hanhardt. *A History of the American Avant-garde Cinema*. New York: American Federation of the Arts, 1976.

Mark A. Viera. *Sin in Soft Focus: Pre-Code Hollywood*. New York: Abrams, 1999.

Mark Schilling. *Contemporary Japanese Film*. New York: Weatherhill, 1999.

Mark, C. Carnes (1995). (ed.) *Past Imperfect: History According to the Movies*. New York: Henry Holt.

Marsha Kinder (ed.) *Refiguring Spain: Cinema, Media, Representation*. Durham, NC: Duke University Press, 1997.

Marsha Kinder. *Blood Cinema: The Reconstruction of National Identity in Spain*. Berkeley: University of California, 1993.

Martha McCaughey and Neal King (eds.) *Reel Knockouts: Violent Women in the Movies*. Austin: University of Texas Press, 2001.

Martin M. Winkler (ed.) *Classical Myth and Culture in the Cinema*. New York: Oxford, 2001.

Mary Lea Bandy (ed.) *Rediscovering French Film*. New York: Museum of Modern Art, 1983.

Matthew Stevens. *Jewish Film directory: A Guide to More Than 1200 Films of Jewish Interest from 32 Countries Over 85 Years*. Westport, CT: Greenwood, 1992.

Maxwell Taylor Courson. *The Newspaper Movies: An Analysis of the Rise and Decline of the News Gatherer as a Hero in American*

Motion Pictures, 1900-1974. [Ph.D. University of Hawaii, 1976].

Mbye Chan and Claire Andra de-Watkins (eds.) *Critical Perspectives on Black Independent Cinema.* Cambridge, MA: MIT Press, 1988.

Melissa Biggs. *French Films, 1945-1993: A Critical Filmography of the 400 Most Important Releases.* McFarland, 1996.

Merritt, Greg (2000). *Celluloid Mavericks: A History of American Independent Film.* New York: Thunder's Mouth Press. ISBN 1560252324.

Merritt, Greg. *Celluloid Mavericks: A History of American Independent Film.* Thunder's Mouth Press, 2001.

Micahel Skovmand (ed.) *Screen Shakespeare.* Aarhus University Press, 1994.

Michael Anderegg (ed.) *Inventing Vietnam: The War in Film and Television.* Philadelphia: Temple University Press, 1991.

Michael Fleming and Roger Manvell. *Images of Madness.* London: Associated University Press, 1985.

Michael Gray. *Stills, Reels and Rushes: Ireland and the Irish in 20th Century Cinema.* Dublin: Ashfield Press, 1999.

Michael Hilger. *From Savage to Nobleman: Images of Native Americans in Film.* Lanham, MD: Scarecrow, 1995.

Michael Hilger. *The American Indian in Film.* Metuchen, NJ: Scarecrow Press, 1986.

Michael J. Shapiro. *Cinematic Political Thought: Narrating Race, Nation and Gender.* New York University Press, 1999.

Michael Klein and Gillian Parker (eds.) *The English Novel and the Movies.* New York: Ungar, 1981.

Michael Renov. *Hollywood's Wartime Women: Representation and Ideology.* Anne Arbor, MI: UMI, 1988.

Michael Rogin. Blackface, *White Noise: Jewish Immigrants in the Hollywood Melting Pot.* Berkeley: University of California Press, 1996.

Michael Ryan and Douglas Kellner. *Camera Politica: The Politics and Ideology of Contemporary Hollywood Film.* Bloomington: Indiana University Press, 1988.

Michael Ryan and Douglas Kellner. *Camera Politica: The Politics and Ideology of Contemporary Hollywood Film.* Bloomington: Indiana University Press, 1990.

Michael S. Shull and David E. Witt. *Doing Their Bit: Wartime*

American Animated Short Films, 1939-1945. Jefferson, NC: McFarland, 1987.

Michael S. Shull and David E. Witt. *Hollywood War Films, 1937-1945: An Exhaustive Filmography of American Feature-length Motion Pictures Relating to World War II*. Jefferson, NC: McFarland, 1996.

Michel Esteve (ed.) "La Passionada Christ comme Theme Cinematographique" *Etudes Cinematographiques* 2. nos. 10-11 (Autumn 1961).

Mick LaSalle. *Complicated Women: Sex and Power in Pre-Code Hollywood*. St. Martin's Press, 2000.

Mick LaSalle. *Dangerous Men: Pre-Code Hollywood and the Birth of the Modern Man*. Thomas Dunne, 2002.

Mikel J. Koven. *Blaxploitation Films*. Pocket Essentials, 2001.

Millicent Marcus. *Filmmaking by the Book: Italian Cinema and Literary Adaptation*. Baltimore: Johns Hopkins University Press, 1993.

Millicent Marcus. *Italian Film in the Light of Neo-Realism*. Princeton: Princeton University Press, 1986.

Mira and Antonin J. Liehm. *The Most Important Art: East European Film After 1945*. Berkeley: University of California Press, 1977.

Mira Liehm. *Passion and Defiance: Film in Italy from 1942 to the Present*. Berkeley: University of California, 1984.

Molly Haskell. *From Reverence to Rape: The Treatment of Women in the Movies*. New York: Holt, Rinehart and Winston, 1974.

Murch, Walter. *In the Blink of an Eye: A Perspective on Film Editing*, Silman-James Press, 2d rev. ed., 2001. ISBN 1-879505-62-2.

Musser, Charles. *The Emergence of Cinema: The American Screen to 1907 (History of the American Cinema, Vol. 1)* Charles Scribner's Sons, 1990.

N. Frank Ukadike. *Black African Cinema*. Berkeley: University of California Press, 1994.

Neil P. Hurley. *Theology Through Film*. New York: Harper and Row, 1970.

Neil Rattigan. *Images of Australia: 100 Films of the New Australian Cinema*. Dallas: Southern Methodist University, 1991.

Neya Zorkaya. *The Illustrated History of the Soviet Cinema*. New York: Hippocrene, 1989.

Nicholas Galichenko. *Glasnost: Soviet Cinema Responds*. Austin: University of Texas, 1991.

Nick Browne (ed.) *Refiguring American Film Genres: History and Theory*. Berkeley: University of California Press, 1998.

Nick Browne, Paul G. Pickowicz, Vivian Sobchack and Esther Yau (eds.) *New Chinese Cinemas: Forms, Identities, Politics*. NY: Cambridge University, 1994.

Nick Roddick. *A New Deal in Entertainment: Warner Brothers in the 1930s*. London: BFI, 1983.

Noel Carroll. *The Future of Allusion: Hollywood in the Seventies (and Beyond)*. October 20 (1982), 51-81.

Norman Kagan. *The War Film*. New York: Pyramid, 1974.

Nowell-Smith, Geoffrey (1999). *The Oxford History of World Cinema*. Oxford; New York: Oxford University Press. ISBN 0198742428.

P. Adams Sitney. "Cinema and Religion" in *Encyclopedia of Religion* (1986).

P. Adams Sitney. *Visionary Cinema: The American Avant-garde, 1943-1978*. 2nd ed. New York: Oxford University Press, 1979.

P. Malone. *Movie Christs and Antichrists*. Crossroads, 1988.

Pam Cook and Philip Dodd (eds.) *Women and Film: A Sight and Sound Reader*. Philadelphia: Temple University Press, 1993.

Parker Tyler. *A Pictorial History of Sex in Films*. Secaucus, NJ: Citadel, 1974.

Parker Tyler. *Screening the Sexes: Homosexuality in the Movies*. New York: Doubleday, 1973.

Parker Tyler. *Sex, Psyche, Etcetera in the Film*. New York: Horizon, 1969.

Parkinson, David. *History of Film*. New York: Thames & Hudson, 1995. ISBN 0-500-20277-X.

Pat Billings and Allen Eyles. *Hollywood Today*. New York: A.S. Barnes, 1971.

Patricia Erens. *The Jew in American Cinema*. Bloomington: Indiana University, 1984.

Patrick Macias. *Tokyoscope: The Japanese Cult Film Companion*. San Francisco: Cadence, 2001.

Paul Bergman and Michael Asimov. *Reel Justice: The Courtroom Goes to the Movies*. Kansas City: Andrews and McMeel, 1996.

Paul Clark. *Chinese Cinema: Culture and Politics Since 1949*. Cambridge, MA: Cambridge University, 1987.

Paul Monaco. *The Sixties: 1960-1969. New York: Scribner's, 2001.* (History of the American Cinema; 8).

Paul O'Dell. *Griffith and the Rise of Hollywood*. Cranbury, NJ: Barnes, 1970.

Paul Smith (ed.) *The Historian and Film*. New York: Cambridge University Press, 1976.

Paula Marantz Cohen. *Silent Films and the Triumph of the American Myth*. New York: Oxford, 2001.

Peter Biskind. *Seeing is Believing: How Hollywood Taught Us to Stop Worrying and Love the Fifties*. New York: Pantheon, 1983.

Peter Bondanella. *Italian Cinema; From Neorealism to the Present*. New York: Continuum, 1990.

Peter C. Rollins and John E. O'Conner (eds.) *Hollywood's Indian: The Portrayal of the Native American in Film*. Lexington: University of Kentucky Press, 1998.

Peter C. Rollins and John E. O'Connor (eds.) *Hollywood's World War I: Motion Picture Images*. Bowling Green State University, 1997.

Peter Cowie. *Scandinavian Cinema: A Survey of Film and Filmmakers in Denmark, Finland, Iceland, Norway and Sweden*. London: Tantivy Press, 1992.

Peter Fraser. *Images of the Passion: The Sacramental Mode in Film*. Westport, CT: Praeger, 1998.

Peter Hames. *The Czechoslovak New Wave*. Berkeley: University of California Press, 1985.

Peter Harcourt. *Movies and Mythologies: Towards a National Cinema*. Toronto: CBC, 1977.

Peter Kenedy. *Films on Traditional Music and Dance*. Paris: UNESCO, 1970.

Peter Lev. *American Films of the 70's: Conflicting Visions*. Austin: University of Texas, 2000.

Peter Lev. *The Euro-American Cinema*. Austin: University of Texas, 1993.

Peter Noble. *The Negro in Films*. New York: Arno, 1970.

Peter Roffman and Jim Purdy. *The Hollywood Social Problem Film: Madness, Despair and Politics from the Depression to the Fifties*. Bloomington: Indiana University, 1981.

Peter Stanfield. *Hollywood, Westerns and the 1930's: The Lost Trail*. University of Exeter, 2001.

Peter Steven (ed.) *Jump Cut: Hollywood, Politics and Counter Cinema*. Toronto: Between the Lines, 1985.

Peter William Evans. *Spanish Cinema: The Auteurist Tradition*. Oxford University Press, 1999.

Phil Hardy. *Overlook Encyclopedia of Film: Western*. Woodstock, NY: Overlook, 1994.

Philip French. *Westerns: Aspects of a Movie Genre*. Revised edition. NY: Oxford University Press, 1977. (Cinema One; 25)

Philip John Davies and Paul Wells (eds.) *American Film and Politics from Reagan to Bush*, Jr. Manchester University Press, 2002.

Philip Rosen (2001). *Change Mummified: Cinema, Historicity, Theory*. Minneapolis: University of Minnesota Press.

Phyllis Klotman and Janet Cutler (eds.) *Struggles for Representation: African American Documentary Film and Video*. Bloomington: Indiana University Press, 1999.

Pierre Sorlin. *Italian National Cinema, 1896-1996*. London: Routledge.

Pierre Sorlin. *The Film in History: Restaging the Past*. Totowa, NJ: Barnes and Noble, 1980.

Poshek Fu and David Desser (eds.) *The Cinema of Hong Kong: History, Arts, Identity*. Cambridge: Cambridge University, 2000.

R.T. Witcombe. *The New Italian Cinema*. New York: Oxford, 1982.

Ralph E. and Natasha A. Friar. *The Only Good Indian... The Hollywood Gospel*. New York: Drama Book Specialists, 1972.

Randall Clark. *At a Theater or Drive-in Near You: The History, Culture an Politics of the American Exploitation Film*. New York: Garland, 1995.

Randall Johnson and Robert Stam (ed.) *Brazilian Cinema*. Austin: University of Texas, 1988.

Randall Johnson. *Cinema Novo x 5: Masters of Contemporary Brazilian Film*. Austin: University of Texas, 1984.

Rani Burra (ed.) *Film India: Looking Back, 1896-1960*. New Delhi: The Directorate of Film Festivals, 1981.

Rey Chow. *Primitive Passions: Visuality, Sexuality, Ethnography and Contemporary Chinese Cinema*. NY: Columbia University, 1995.

Richard A. Blake. Afterimage: The Indelible Catholic Imagination of Six American Filmmakers. Chicago: Loyola Press, 2000. [Scorsese, Hitchcock, Capra, Ford, Coppola, De Palma].

Richard A. Maynard (ed.) *Africa on Film: Myth and Reality*. Rochelle Park, NJ: Hayden, 1974.

Richard A. Maynard (ed.) *The Biack Man on Film*. Rochelle Park, NJ: Hayden, 1974.

Richard Abel. *French Cinema: The First Wave 1915-1929*. Princeton: Princeton University Press, 1984.

Richard B. and Mary Willems Armstrong. *Encyclopedia of Film Themes, Settings and Series*. Jefferson, NC: McFarland, 2001.

Richard B. Jewell. *The RKO Story*. New York: Arlington House, 1982.
Richard Barrios. *Screened Out: Playing Gay in Hollywood from Edison to Stonewall*. New York: Routledge, 2003.
Richard C. and Marie E. Helt. *West German Cinema 1985-1990: A Reference Handbook*. Scarecrow Press, 1992.
Richard C. and Marie E. Helt. *West German Cinema Since 1945: A Reference Handbook*. Scarecrow Press, 1987.
Richard Dyer (ed.) *Gays in Film*. London: British Film Institute, 1977.
Richard Dyer MacCann (ed.) *Film and Society*. New York: Scribner's, 1964.
Richard Dyer. *Now You See It: Studies on Lesbian and Gay Film*. London: Routledge, 1990.
Richard Fine. *Hollywood and the Profession of Authorship, 1928-1940*. Ann Arbor: UMI Research Press, 1979.
Richard H. Campbell and Michael R. Pitts. *The Bible on Film: A Checklist, 1897-1980*. Metuchen, NJ: Scarecrow, 1981.
Richard Koszarski. *An Evening's Entertainment: The Age of the Silent Feature Picture, 1915-1928*. New York: Scribner's, 1990. (History of the American Cinema; 3).
Richard Kozarski (ed.) *Hollywood Directors, 1914-1940*. New York: Oxford University Press, 1976.
Richard Maynard. *The American West on Film: Myth and Reality*. Rochelle Park, NJ: Hayden, 1974.
Richard R. Lingeman. "Will This Picture Help Win the War?" Don't You Know There's a War On? The American Home Front, 1941-1945. New York: Putnam's, 1970. (168- 223).
Richard R. Ness. *From Headline Hunter to Superman: A Journalism Filmography*. Lanham, MD: Scarecrow, 1997. [annotated list of 2166 films, grouped by year of release and then alphabetically within year by title, with a title index at the end].
Richard Stern, Clayton Jefford, Gueric Debona. *Savior on the Silver Screen*. New York: Paulist Press, 1999.
Richard Tapper (ed.) *The New Iranian Cinema: Politics, Representation and Identity*. London: I.B. Tauris, 2002.
Richard Taylor and Ian Christie (ed.) *The Film Factory: Russian and Soviet Cinema in Documents 1896-1939*. London: Routledge, 1988.
Richard Wortley. *Erotic Movies*. London: Studio Vista, 1975.
Rick Altman. Film/Genre. London: BFI, 1999.
Robert A. and Gwendolyn Wright Nowlan. *The Films of the Eighties:*

A Complete, Qualitative Filmography to Over 3400 Feature-Length English Language Films. Jefferson, NC: McFarland, 1991.

Robert Bookbinder. *The Films of the Seventies.* Secaucus, NJ: Citadel, 1982.

Robert Detweiler. "Christ and the Christ Figure in American Fiction" *The Christian Scholar* 47 (Summer 1964) p. 111-124.

Robert F. Willson. *Shakespeare in Hollywood,* 1929-1956. Madison, NJ: Farleigh Dickinson University Press, 2000.

Robert Frye. *The Hollywood Propaganda of World War II.* Metuchen, NJ: Scarecrow, 1994.

Robert G. Konzelman. *Marquee Ministry: The Movie Theatre as Church and Community Forum.* New York: Harper and Row, 1972.

Robert Henderson. *D.W. Griffith: The Years at Biograph.* New York: Farrar Strauss Giroux, 1970.

Robert Jewett. *Saint Paul at the Movies: The Apostle's Dialogue with American Culture.* Westminster/John Knox, 1993.

Robert Jewett. *Saint Paul Returns to the Movies: Triumph Over Shame.* Eerdmans, 1998.

Robert K. Johnson. *Reel Spirituality: Theology and Film in Dialogue.* Grand Rapids, MI: Baker, 2000.

Robert Lang. *Masculine Interests: Homoerotics in Hollywood Films.* New York: Columbia University Press, 2002.

Robert Mayer. *Eighteenth Century Fiction on Screen.* New York: Cambridge University Press, 2002.

Robert R.S. Chen. *The Historical and Cultural Experiences of the Taiwan New Cinema.* Taipei: Wuang-Hsiong, 1993.

Robert Shaughnessy (ed.) *Shakespeare on Film.* New York: Macmillan, 1998.

Robert Sklar. *Movie-made America: A Cultural History of American Movies.* Rev. ed. New York: Random House, 1994.

Robert, A. Rosenstone (1995). (Ed.) *Revisioning History: Film and the Construction of a New Past.* Princeton University Press.

Rocchio, Vincent F. (2000). *Reel Racism: Confronting Hollywood's Construction of Afro-American Culture.* Boulder, CO: Westview Press. ISBN 0813367107.

Rocchio, Vincent F., *Reel Racism. Confronting Hollywood's Construction of Afro-American Culture.* Westview Press, 2000.

Roger Dooley. *From Scarface to Scarlett: American Films in the 1930s.* New York: Harcourt Brace Jovanovich, 1979.

Roger Kahle and Robert E. Lee. *Popcorn and Parables: A New Look at the Movies*. Minneapolis: Augsburg, 1971.

Roger Manvell and Heinrich Fraenkel. *The German Cinema*. New York: Praeger, 1971.

Roger Manvell. *New Cinema in Europe*. London: Dutton, Studio Vista, 1966.

Roger Manvell. *Shakespeare and Film*. Revised and updated ed. South Brunswick, NJ: A.S. Barnes, 1979.

Ronald Bergan. *The United Artists Story*. New York: Crown, 1986.

Ronald Holloway. *Beyond the Image: Approaches to the Religious Dimension in the Cinema*. Geneva: Oikoumene, 1977.

Ronald Schwartz. *Latin American Films, 1932-1994: A Critical Filmography*. Jefferson, NC: McFarland, 1997.

Ronald Schwartz. *Spanish Film Directors (1950-1985): 21 Profiles*. Scarecrow Press, 1986.

Rosemary Ribich Kowalski. *Women and Film: A Bibliography*. Metuchen, NJ: Scarecrow, 1976.

Roy Armes. *A Critical History of British Cinema*. London: Secker and Warburg, 1978.

Roy Armes. *French Cinema*. New York: Oxford, 1985.

Roy Armes. *Patterns of Realism: A Study of Italian Neo-Realist Cinema*. A.S. Barnes, 1971.

Roy Armes. *Third World Film Making and the West*. Berkeley: University of California, 1987.

Roy Hoopes. *When the Stars Went to War: Hollywood and World War II*. New York: Random House, 1994.

Roy Kinnard and Anthony Davis. *Divine Images: A History of Jesus on the Screen*. New York: Citadel, 1992.

Russell Campbell. *Cinema Strikes Back: Radical Filmmaking in the United States, 1930-1942*. Ann Arbor: UMI Research Press, 1982.

Russell Earl Shain. *An Analysis of Motion Pictures About the War Released by the American Film Industry, 1939-1970*. New York: Arno, 1976.

Russell Jackson (ed.) *The Cambridge Companion to Shakespeare on Film*. 2000.

Ryan Gilbey. *It Don't Worry Me: The Revolutionary American Films of the Seventies*. Faber and Faber, 2003.

S. Craig Watkins. *Representing: Hip op Culture and the Production of Black Cinema*. Chicago: University of Chicago Press, 1998.

Salt, Barry. *Film Style and Technology: History and Analysis 2nd Ed.* Starword, 1992.

Salt, Barry. *Moving Into Pictures* Starword, 2006.

Sam Kashner and Jennifer Macnair. *The Bad and the Beautiful: Hollywood in the Fifties*. New York: Norton, 2002.

Sarah Street. *British National Cinema*. London: Routledge

Schrader, Paul (Spring 1972). "Notes on Film Noir." *Film Comment* Vol. 8 (Issue 1): pp. 8-13. ISSN 0015-119X.

Schrader, Paul. "Notes on Film Noir." *Film Comment*, 1984.

Schultz, John (writer and director); James Earl Jones (narrator). (1995). *The Making of 'Jurassic Park'* [Documentary]. Amblin Entertainment.

Scott Eyman. *The Speed of Sound: Hollywood and the Talkie Revolution*. New York: Simon and Schuster, 1997.

Screening Mystery: Light and Darkness at the Movies. [Special issue of *Catholic International* 10:9 (November 1999)]

Seth Cagin and Philip Dray. *Hollywood Films of the Seventies: Sex, Drugs, Violence, Rock n Roll and Politics*. New York: Harper and Row, 1984. [reprinted as: Born to Be Wild: Hollywood and the Sixties Generation (1994)].

Seth Feldman (ed.) *Take Two: A Tribute to Film in Canada*. Toronto: Irwin, 1984.

Seth Feldman and Joyce Nelson (eds.) *Canadian Film Reader*. Toronto: Peter Martin, 1977.

Shari Denise Hodges. *Theoretical Approaches to Dickens on Film: The Cinematic Interpretation of Charles Dickens Novels*. Dissertation (Ph.D.) University of Mississippi, 2000.

Sharon Smith. *Women Who Make Movies*. New York: Hopkins and Blake, 1975.

Sheldon Renan. *An Introduction to the American Underground Film*. New York: Dutton, 1967.

Siegfried Kracauer. *From Caligari to Hitler: A Psychological History of the German Film*. Princeton, NJ: Princeton University, 1947.

Stefan Hammond and Mike Wilkins. *Sex and Zen and A Bullet in the Head: The Essential Guide to Hong Kong's Mind-Bending Films*. NY: Fireside, 1996.

Stephen Prince. *A New Pot of Gold: Hollywood Under the Electronic Rainbow, 1980-1989*. New York: Scribner's, 2000. (History of the American Cinema; 10).

Stephen Teo and N. K Leung. "Hong Kong Cinema" *OGFS* (550-556).
Stephen Teo. *Hong Kong Cinema: The Extra Dimension*. London: BFI Publishing, 1997.
Steve Neale and Murray Smith (eds.) *Contemporary Hollywood Cinema*. London: Routledge, 1998.
Steve Neale. *Genre and Hollywood*. London: Routledge, 2000.
Steven J. Ross. *Working-Class Hollywood: Silent Film and the Shaping of Class in America*. Princeton University Press, 1998.
Stuart Fox. *Jewish Films in the United States: A Comprehensive Survey and Descriptive Filmography*. Boston: G.K. Hall, 1976.
Stuart Kaminsky. *American Film Genres: Approaches to a Critical Theory of Popular Film*. New York: Dell, 1974.
Study of the Film: God and Man. Chicago: Catholic Adult Education Center, 1967.
Sue Matthews. *35mm Dreams: Conversations with Five Directors about the Australian Film Revival*. Penguin, 1984.
Sumita S. Chakravarty. *National Identity in Indian Popular Cinema 1947-1987*. Austin: University of Texas Press, 1993.
Susan Hayward. *French National Cinema*. London: Routledge, 1993.
Susan J. Napier. *Anime: From Akira to Princess Mononoke*. New York: Palgrave, 2000.
Susan M. Griffin. *Henry James Goes to the Movies*. Lexington: University Press of Kentucky, 2002.
T. Weisser and Y.M. Weisser. *Japanese Cinema Encyclopedia: Horror, Fantasy, Science Fiction*. Miami: Vital Books, 1997.
T.J. Ross. *"Fantasy and Form in the Western: From Hart to Peckinpah"*. December 12:1 (Fall 1970) 158-69.
Tadao Sato. *Currents in Japanese Cinema*. Tokyo: Kodansha International, 1982.
Terry Ramsaye. *A Million and One Nights: A History of the Motion Picture Through 1925*. New York: Simon and Schuster, 1926.
Teshome K. Gabriel. *Third Cinema in the Third World: The Aesthetics of Liberation*. Ann Arbor, MI: UMI Research Press, 1982.
Thackway, Melissa (2003). *Africa Shoots Back: Alternative Perspectives in Sub-Saharan Francophone African Film*. Bloomington, IL: Indiana University Press. ISBN 0852555768.
The American Film Institute Catalog of Motion Pictures Produced in the United States. Berkeley: University of California Press,

1971. Contents: A. Film Beginnings, 1893-1910.—F1. Feature Films, 1911-1920.—F2. Feature Films, 1921-1930.—F3. Feature Films, 1931-1940.—F4. Feature Films, 1941-1950.—F5. Feature Films, 1951-1960.—F6. Feature Films, 1961-1970.—F7. Feature Films, 1971-1980.—F8. Feature Films, 1981-1990.—N1. Newsreels, 1908-1920.—N2. Newsreels, 1921-1930.—N3. Newsreels, 1931-1940.—N4. Newsreels, 1941-1950.—N5. Newsreels, 1951-1960.—N6. Newsreels, 1961-1970.—S1. Short Films, 1911-1920.—S2. Short Films, 1921-1930.—S3. Short Films, 1931-1940.—S4. Short Films, 1941-1950.—S5. Short Films,1951-1960.—S6. Short Films, 1961-1970.—S7. Short Films, 1971-1980.—S8. Short Films, 1981-1990.

The Cinema in Arab Countries. Beirut: Interarab Centre of Cinema and Television, 1966.

Theodore Ziolkowski. *Fictional Transfigurations of Jesus*. Princeton: Princeton University Press, 1972.

Thomas Cripps. *Black Film as Genre*. Bloomington: Indiana University Press, 1978.

Thomas Cripps. *Slow Fade to Black: The Negro in American Film, 1900-1942*. New York: Oxford University Press, 1977.

Thomas Doherty. *Pre-Code Hollywood: Sex, Immorality and Insurrection in American Cinema, 1930-1934*. New York: Columbia University Press, 1999.

Thomas Doherty. *Projections of War: Hollywood, American Culture and World War II*. New York: Columbia University Press, 1993.

Thomas Doherty. *Teenagers and Teen-pics: The Juvenilization of American Movies in the 1950's*. Boston: Unwin Hyman, 1988.

Thomas Elsaesser (ed.) *The BFI Companion to German Cinema*. London: BFI, 1999.

Thomas Elsaesser. *New German Cinema: A History*. New York: Macmillan, 1989.

Thomas G. Deveny. *Contemporary Spanish Film from Fiction*. Lanham, MD: Scraecrow, 1999.

Thomas Gunning. *D.W. Griffith and the Origins of American Narrative Film: The Early Years at Biograph*. Urbana: University of Illinois Press,

Thomas J. Harris. *Courtroom's Finest Hour in American Cinema*. Metuchen, NJ: Scarecrow, 1987.

Thomas M. Martin. *Images and the Imageless: A Study in Religious Consciousness and Film*. 2nd edition. Lewisburg, PA: Bucknell University, 1991.

Thomas R. Atkins (ed.) *Sexuality in the Movies*. Bloomington: Indiana University Press, 1975.

Thomas R. Whiston. *Guide to American Cinema, 1930-1965*. Greenwood, 1998.

Thomas Schatz. *Boom and Bust: The American Cinema in the 1940s*. New York Scribner's, 1997. (History of the American Cinema; 6).

Thomas Schatz. *Hollywood Genres: Formulas, Filmmaking and the Studio System*. Philadelphia: Temple University Press, 1981.

Thomas Schatz. *The Genius of the System: Hollywood Filmmaking in the Studio Era*. New York: Pantheon, 1988.

Thomas Wartenberg. *Unlikely Couples: Movie Romance as Social Criticism*. Boulder, CO: Westview.

Thomas Weisser. *Asian Cult Cinema*. New York: Boulevard Books, 1997.

Tim Barnard (ed.) *Argentine Cinema*. Toronto: Nightwood Editions, 1986.

Timothy Barnard and Peter Rist (eds.) *South American Cinema: A Critical Filmography 1915-1994*. New York: Garland, 1996.

Tino Balio (ed.) *The American Film Industry*. Rev. ed. Madison: University of Wisconsin Press, 1985.

Tino Balio. "Adjusting to the New Global Economy: Hollywood in the 1990s" in *Film Policy: International, National and Regional Perspectives* ed. Albert Moran. London: Routledge, 1996.

Tino Balio. *Grand Design: Hollywood as a Modern Business Enterprise, 1930-1939*. New York: Scribner's, 1993. (History of the American Cinema; 5).

Todd McCarthy and Charles Flynn (eds.) *Kings of the B's: Working Within the Hollywood System: An Anthology of Film History and Criticism*. New York: Dutton, 1975.

Tom Costello. *International Guide to Literature on Film*. London: Bowker-Sauer, 1994.

Tom Henighan. *The Maclean's Companion to Canadian Arts and Culture*. Vancouver, BC: Raincoast Books.

Tom O'Regan. *Australian National Cinema*. London: Routledge.

Tom Stempel. *Framework: A History of Screenwriting in the American Film*. New York: Continuum, 1988.

Tom Zaniello. *Working Stiffs, Union Maids, Reds and Riffraff: An Expanded Guide to Films About Labor*. Ithaca: Cornell University Press, 2003.

Tony Rayns and Scott Meek (ed.) *Electric Shadows: Forty-five Years of Chinese Cinema*. London: BFI, 1980.

Tony Rayns. *More Electric Shadows: Chinese Cinema 1922-1984*. London: BFI, 1985.

Tony Rayns. *The New Chinese Cinema: An Introduction*. London: Faber and Faber, 1989.

Tony Thomas. *The Films of the Forties*. Secaucus, NJ: Citadel, 1975.

Trish Ledoux (*et al.*, ed.) *Anime Interviews: The First Five Years of Animerica Anime and Manga Monthly*. San Francisco: Cadence Books, 1997.

Trish Ledoux and Doug Ranney (ed.). *The Complete Anime Guide: Japanese Animation Video Directory and Resource Guide*. Washington: Tiger Mountain Press, 1996.

Tsivian, Yuri. *Silent Witnesses: Russian Films 1908-1919*. British Film Institute, 1989.

Tytti Soila, *Astrid Soderbergh Widding, Gunnar Iversen*. Nordic National Cinemas. London: Rouledge, 1998.

Uma da Cunha (ed.) *Film India: The New Generation, 1960-1980*. New Delhi: The Directorate of Film Festivals, 1981.

Unterburger, Amy L., *The St. James Women Filmmakers Encyclopedia: Women on the Other Side of the Camera*. Visible Ink Press, 1999.

Usai, P.C. & Codelli, L. (eds.) *Before Caligari: German Cinema, 1895-1920* Edizioni Biblioteca dell'Immagine 1990.

Vane, E.T. and Gross, L.S. (1994). *Programming for TV, Radio and Cable*, Boston: Focal Press.

Vijay Mishra. *Bollywood Cinema: Temples of Desire*. New York: Routledge, 2002.

Vincent F. Rocchio. *Reel Racism: Confronting Hollywood's Construction of Afro-American Culture*. Boulder, CO: Westview, 2000.

Vito Russo. *The Celluloid Closet*. Revised edition. New York: Harper and Row, 1987.

Vogel, Amos (1974). *Film as a Subversive Art*. New York: Random House. ISBN 0394490789.

W. Barnes Tatum. *Jesus at the Movies: A Guide to the First Hundred Years*. Polebridge Press, 1998.

Wayne Michael Sarf. *God Bless You Buffalo Bill: A Layman's Guide to History and the Western Film*. Rutherford, NJ: Farleigh Dickinson University, 1983.

Wes D. Gehring (ed.) *Handbook of American Film Genres*. Westport, CT: Greenwood, 1988.

Wheeler Winston Dixon (ed.) *Film Genre 2000: New Critical Essays*. Albany: State University of New York Press, 2000.

Wheeler Winston Dixon. *The Exploding Eye: A Re-Visionary History of 1960's American Experimental Cinema*. Albany: State University of New York Press, 1998.

Will Wright. *Sixguns and Society: A Structural Study of the Western*. Berkeley: University of California Press, 1975.

William Alexander. *Film on the Left: American Documentary Film from 1931 to 1942*. Princeton University Press, 1981.

William K. Everson. *American Silent Film*. New York: Oxford University, 1978.

William K. Everson. *The Hollywood Western*. Seacaucus, NJ: Carol, 1992.

William T. Pilkington and Don Graham (eds.) *Western Movies*. Albuquerque: University of New Mexico, 1979.

Wimal Dissanayake (ed.) *Colonialism and Nationalism in Asian Cinema*. Bloomington: Indiana University Press, 1994.

Yves Lavandier (2005). *Writing Drama, A Comprehensive Guide for Playwrights and Scritpwriters*. Le Clown & l'Enfant.

Links

- Dictionary definitions from Wiktionary
- Textbooks from Wikibooks
- Quotations from Wikiquote
- Source texts from Wikisource
- Images and media from Commons
- News stories from Wikinews
- Learning resources from Wikiversity
- View inside an ancient film camera
- Museum of Motion Picture History, Inc.
- History exhibit of filmmaking in Florida, presented by the State Archives of Florida
- American Cinematographer—January, 1930, THE EARLY HISTORY OF WIDE FILMS
- History of Film Formats

- Technicolor History
- What is a Camera Obscura?
- Film Sound History at FilmSound.org
- An Introduction to Early cinema
- Official Web Site of Film Historian/Oral Historian Scott Feinberg
- Reality Film
- Film History by Decade *popup warning*
- Project "Westphalian History in the film"
- Cinema: From 1890 To Now
- A Brief, Early History of Computer Graphics in Film
- http://www.video-film.info/sites/filmhistory.html
- History of Film poster
- Burns, Paul The History of the Discovery of Cinematography An Illustrated Chronology
- Israeli Film, Filmography—Home for Early Israeli Film
- Cinematography.com discussion forums
- Cinematography Mailing List archives
- Retrieved from "http://en.wikipedia.org/wiki/Cinematography"
- Screenplays at the Open Directory Project
- AMPAS screenplay formatting
- BC Radio National Radio Eye
- ABC The Night Air
- CultureWorks
- Feature-Portal (in German)
- Lichtenstein Creative Media
- Sound Portraits
- The Radio Ballads
- Radio Diaries
- Amature stories

Index